CONGRESS AND
CIVIL-MILITARY RELATIONS

CONGRESS AND CIVIL-MILITARY RELATIONS

Colton C. Campbell and David P. Auerswald, Editors

GEORGETOWN UNIVERSITY PRESS / WASHINGTON, DC

©2015 Georgetown University Press. All rights reserved. No part of this book may be reproduced or utilized in any form or by any means, electronic or mechanical, including photocopying and recording, or by any information storage and retrieval system, without permission in writing from the publisher.

Library of Congress Cataloging-in-Publication Data

Congress and civil-military relations / Colton C. Campbell and David P. Auerswald, editors.
    pages   cm
    Includes bibliographical references and index.
    ISBN 978-1-62616-185-6 (hardcover : alk. paper) — ISBN 978-1-62616-180-1 (pbk. : alk. paper) — ISBN 978-1-62616-181-8 (ebook)
    1. Civil-military relations—United States. 2. United States. Congress. I. Campbell, Colton C. 1965– editor II. Auerswald, David P., editor
    JK330.C66 2015
    322'.50973—dc23

                            2014024869

♾ This book is printed on acid-free paper meeting the requirements of the American National Standard for Permanence in Paper for Printed Library Materials.

16 15   9 8 7 6 5 4 3 2   First printing

Printed in the United States of America

Cover design by Beth Schlenoff. Cover image courtesy of the US Senate Historical Office.

For Marilyn and Caden, with all my love
—C. C. C.

For Jen, Robin, and Katie, with all my love
—D. P. A.

Contents

Illustrations

Acknowledgments

We would like to thank the many people who contributed to the production of this book. Don Jacobs at Georgetown University Press deserves special thanks for agreeing that a better understanding of Congress and its relationship with the military was worth publishing. Thanks to Glenn Saltzman and Don McKeon, who shepherded the book through the production process. The chapter authors deserve particular mention for committing to this novel project and for delivering such insightful chapters in an efficient and professional manner. A special thank-you goes to Dr. Dave Dulio of Oakland University and Dr. John Allen (Jay) Williams of Loyola University Chicago, who provided thoughtful and timely reviews. We would also like to thank Heather Moore at the United States Senate Historical Office for assistance with the photographs that appear in the book. Finally, we are indebted to our National War College students, whose service to the US military and our country is limitless. We learn more from them than they learn from us.

1

Introduction

Congress and Civil-Military Relations

DAVID P. AUERSWALD AND COLTON C. CAMPBELL

The Constitution make[s] Congress the link between the American people and the military whose mission it is to protect them. And, thus, it helps ensure that there is public support for the military.

—*Rep. Ike Skelton (D-MO), Naval Postgraduate School, April 19, 1999*

I have always believed that, as painful and frustrating as it can be, that congressional oversight, whether it's over intelligence or over the military, is absolutely essential to keeping us all on the right track.

—*Secretary of Defense Robert M. Gates, Army War College, April 16, 2009*

Congress plays a significant and underappreciated role in American civil-military relations. Over the past few years it has taken significant steps to change cultural and organizational behavior in the military. Congress has overturned the military ban of gays serving openly and has had a say in lifting the combat exclusion for military women. It has imposed significant budget cuts through the sequestration process, forcing the Department of Defense (DOD) to reexamine military strategy, personnel numbers, and weapon purchases. And most recently, lawmakers from both sides of the aisle have proposed legislation to take the decision for prosecuting sexual assault cases out of the hands of commanding officers—a move that military leaders say would hurt their ability to maintain order and discipline. We cannot understand civil-military relations in the United States without an appreciation of

The views expressed in this chapter are those of the authors and not necessarily those of the National Defense University, the Department of Defense, or any other entity of the US government.

Congress. Indeed, doing so neglects an important element in civil-military relations because, as one student of the subject aptly reminds members of the military, "Congress is the 'force planner' of last resort."[1]

Stable civil-military relations in the United States have a long history, dating back to when George Washington symbolically surrendered his sword to the Continental Congress upon resignation of his commission. Yet the relationship between elected officials and the military establishment has gone through significant fluctuations over time and across issues.[2] Attempts by lawmakers to make significant change within the armed forces have historically been met with strong resistance from the individual services, which are, according to one student of civil-military relations, "conservative and evolutionary by nature and who resent outsiders presuming expertise in their profession."[3] This was especially conspicuous with passage of the Goldwater-Nichols Department of Defense Reorganization Act of 1986, broad-sweeping legislation designed to scale back the power, influence, and prerogatives of the separate services and rework the military's command structure.[4]

The ebbs and flows in US civil-military relations depend in part on civilian authorities' use of the four main tools available to provide direction to the military. These are the selection of military officers, determining how much authority is delegated to the military, oversight of the military, and establishing incentives (positive and negative) for appropriate military behavior.

Officer selection is a potentially powerful tool in the civil-military relations toolkit. From a civilian perspective, the goal is to select military leaders who share the same policy preferences as the civilian leader doing the selecting. Such military officers will be more likely to craft war plans or otherwise behave in ways that mirror civilian leaders' priorities and be less likely to try to circumvent civilian authority, thus requiring less oversight than would otherwise be the case. One could select officers based on particular traits, such as an officer's ethical code, preferences for specific military doctrines, or even willingness to follow civilian orders.

If Congress alone were doing the selecting, it might be inclined to choose officers who share congressional preferences (assuming that members could reach agreement on those preferences). The Constitution, however, grants the president the authority to select officers through the nomination process and the Senate the authority to confirm or reject those nominations. The most the Senate can do is weed out officers who have acted inappropriately or officers who seem resistant to implementing congressional initiatives or providing "honest" military advice to Congress (which is shorthand for advice that may conflict with presidential policy). Of course the Senate does not have the staff or the expertise to vet the thousands of military officers nominated each year, especially to the military's junior ranks, but the Senate can and does require that the executive branch itself conduct that vetting and report its results to the Hill. Officers who are flagged for some reason—particularly in the senior ranks—face increased scrutiny by congressional staff, if not outright rejection. And the vetting process itself forces the executive branch to anticipate congressional objections and weed out potentially undesirable officers before they are nominated in the first place. The confirmation process, then, is a useful congressional tool, particularly when applied to senior military officers.

A second tool in the civil-military toolkit is to *delegate authority* to military officers. Congressional delegation to the military can take many forms. It can encompass authorities related to rules of engagement, specifying when hostilities can be initiated. An example would be the rules of engagement given to US pilots during air patrols in northern and southern Iraq during the 1990s. It can take the form of where and under what circumstances the military can act as a lead government agency and when it must play a supporting role. Think here of the 1878 Posse Comitatus Act, which prohibits the active-duty military from engaging in domestic law enforcement activities. Delegation can take the form of fine-tuning the military chain of command to meet particular circumstances. This is illustrated by the recent congressional debate over whether sexual assaults within military units should be investigated and punishments decided within the normal chain of command. Finally, delegation can specify the missions undertaken by the military. In Iraq and Afghanistan, for example, the US military under President George W. Bush's administration was given combat missions as well as reconstruction and foreign assistance duties traditionally under the purview of civilian agencies.

To be sure, delegation of day-to-day authority often comes from the president in his role as commander in chief. That said, Congress can play a significant role determining which military units or officials have authority in specific circumstances. It gets its authority through Article I, Section 8 of the Constitution, which grants the legislative branch the authority to regulate the armed forces and provide for their arming and equipment. And Congress exercises that authority on a regular basis through regulations written into the defense authorization and appropriations bills. Congress, however, must reach a careful balance when delegating authority to the military. Delegating too little authority can paralyze the military during crises and war. Too much authority can lead to unpredictable or undesired behavior.

That balancing act raises a final point with regard to delegating authority, and that is that delegated authority and officer selection are related concepts. It is easier and even tempting to delegate significant authority to an officer who shares your perspective. Indeed, there are few reasons not to give such a trusted agent the needed authority to carry out your policies. Conversely,

Congress might hesitate to delegate significant authority to an officer (or group of officers) who does not share its preferences or who in some other way may be perceived as untrustworthy or working against congressional wishes. It is important to consider officer selection and delegation together.

Officer selection and delegation are largely irrelevant to civil-military relations without effective congressional *oversight*, the third tool in the civil-military relations kit bag. After all, there is no way to know if the authority one has delegated to the officers selected for military service is serving the public good absent some way of monitoring what the military is doing. And oversight of the military is not necessarily easy, given the security surrounding military doctrine, capabilities, and operations and the decreasing level of military expertise possessed by most members of Congress since the 1970s.

Figure 1.1 reinforces that last point. It shows that since a peak in the late 1970s, fewer and fewer members of Congress have any military experience.[5] In 1977, just a few years after the end of the draft and the creation of the all-volunteer professional force, 347 of the 435 members of the House of Representatives had served in the military, or roughly 80 percent. That number was down to eighty-nine members by 2013, representing just 20 percent of the chamber. An identical trend is evident in the hundred-seat Senate, with a peak of seventy-six senators in 1983 having had military service, falling to twenty senators in 2013. Members lacking military experience have to work that much harder to understand military service cultures, know the differences between weapon systems, understand the dislocations of repeated moves from installation to installation every two to three years, and comprehend the toll of combat on members of the military and their families. Despite these difficulties, Congress has come up with formal and informal ways to conduct oversight of the military and gather the information necessary to make relatively informed decisions regarding military policy.

Congress conducts formal oversight of the military through the annual budget cycle. So-called regular order oversight takes place in multiple stages associated with the president's submission and congressional consideration of the defense budget. Before the defense budget is submitted, the secretary of defense normally meets with the chairs and ranking members of the two defense committees and the appropriations committees. Once the budget is submitted, the Armed Services Committees and their subcommittees will hold hearings on the various elements and programs contained in that budget request. In addition to formal hearings, committee staff will be briefed on specific programs by the relevant military services and combatant commands, and individual committee members will be briefed by senior flag officers. Members can submit formal questions for the record during hearings and requests for information during less structured briefings. Committee

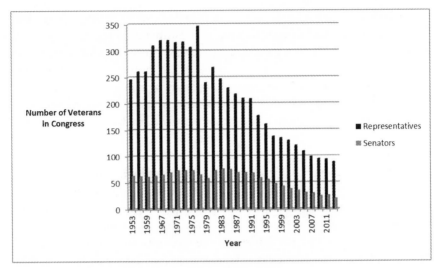

Figure 1.1. Number of Veterans in Congress, 1953–2014

Source: Data derived from Norman J. Ornstein, Thomas E. Mann, Michael J. Malbin, and Andrew Rugg, *Vital Statistics on Congress* (Washington, DC: Brookings Institution, 2013), www.brookings.edu/research/reports/2013/07/vital-statistics-congress-mann-ornstein.

members and staff will ask the Office of the Secretary of Defense for its views on proposed legislative language in the annual defense authorization bill. And the relevant committees may even ask affected industry representatives for their views on the defense budget and specific defense acquisition programs. And all this varied and surprisingly thorough oversight occurs before the authorization bill is actually marked up by the Armed Services Committees or considered by each full congressional chamber.

Congress may also conduct formal oversight through means not associated with the budget cycle. It regularly includes formal reporting requirements in defense-related legislation, which forces the administration to take a new policy position or explain an existing one. The Senate has increasingly linked reporting requirements to the passage of treaty ratification documents.[6] Members of Congress can also ask any of its three support agencies—the Congressional Research Service (CRS), the Government Accountability Office (GAO), and the Congressional Budget Office (CBO)—to engage in oversight on behalf of individual members or committees. The CRS focuses on policy reviews. The GAO conducts audits of existing programs. The CBO examines the likely budgetary impact of proposed initiatives. Together these agencies and mandated executive reports provide Congress with an additional means of conducting formal oversight.

Then there are the informal means of oversight, which are usually sparked by international crises or specific events, constituency complaints, business concerns, or investigative reports in the press. An international crisis can spark intensive consultations between the White House, the DOD, and the relevant congressional committees. Complaints by constituents or business concerns can lead to individual members asking the DOD for information or for help in resolving them. Press exposés can lead to demands for explanations by the DOD, hearing testimony by senior officials, formal questions for the record, and even legislation.

The fourth and final civil-military tool considered here is the manipulation of positive and negative *incentives* aimed at the military. Incentives used by Congress tend to focus on the foreign policy powers granted to the legislature by Article I, Section 8 and Article II, Section 2. The former include the congressional power of the purse and the authority to regulate the armed forces, while the latter specifies the requirement that the Senate confirm military appointments. Consider each of these in turn.

Budget Authority

Article I, Section 8 of the Constitution specifies that Congress "shall provide for the common defense" and have the power "to raise and support Armies" and "to provide and maintain a Navy." These clauses give Congress the authority to use the military budget to nudge the military toward particular types of behavior or away from certain actions. During the Vietnam War, for example, Congress used its budget power to keep the army focused on major ground combat in Europe at the expense of counterinsurgency operations in Vietnam.[7] Congress tailored army acquisition toward main battle tanks and artillery that were ill-suited for the jungles of Southeast Asia. The army responded, keeping its focus on Europe and failing to innovate in Vietnam. More recent examples include Congress providing the funds to prepare an East Coast missile-defense site, despite the military's reluctance to build such a facility, and the recent congressional demands to maintain all eleven aircraft carriers in the US arsenal rather than retiring the USS *George Washington* in 2014. The budget—and specifically defense acquisition and procurement programs—is a powerful incentive.

Regulating the Armed Forces

Article I, Section 8 of the Constitution also provides Congress with the power "to make rules for government and regulation of the land and naval forces," "to call forth the militia," and to "provide for the organizing, arming, and disciplining of the militia, and for governing such parts of them as may be employed in the service of the United States." Setting promotion rates and the requirements for military promotions is an example of this type of incentive. A specific instance is the educational requirements for promotion beyond specific ranks, such as the inability to be considered for flag rank unless one has attended a senior war college or the civilian equivalent. The military services have every incentive to send their promising officers back to school at regular intervals. Individual officers who want to advance up the chain of command have every incentive to demand attendance at approved educational institutions. Another example is the mandated promotion rates for air force unmanned aerial vehicle (UAV) operators, aimed at increasing the positive benefits of choosing that career track instead of becoming a manned aircraft pilot.

Confirmation of Appointees

A final type of incentive involves threatening or placing holds on DOD nominees, often for unrelated issues. Sen. John McCain (R-AZ), for example, placed a hold on all air force nominees—military and civilian—until the air force revisited the contract for tanker aircraft. The longer the holds continued, the greater was the pressure on the air force to settle the issue. More recent examples include the threat of holds on nominees to protect the A-10 aircraft fleet and until the DOD makes the intercontinental ballistic missile fleet immune to base closing and realignment consideration.

In sum, Congress has at least four significant tools at its disposal to affect US civil-military relations, and the legislature has played a vital role in the exercise of each tool. Lawmakers influence the choice of military officers via the Senate confirmation process. They delegate authority to the military through the budget process and regulations in the annual defense authorization bills. Congress conducts both regular and episodic oversight of the military in publicly accessible hearings, closed-door briefings, staff investigations, and special commissions. And finally, Congress has a long track record of using incentives to influence military behavior on everything from acquisition policies to social welfare issues.

The success of such congressional initiatives depends on a variety of factors internal to congressional deliberations. What type of change is desired has a large influence on the chances of a proposal's success. Legislating changes in military regulations requires a two-chamber majority (and a supermajority if opposed by the president), a high hurdle to overcome. Confirming a military officer is easier, requiring the support of a majority of senators present and voting. Conversely, a single senator can deny a military promotion by putting a hold on a nominee. That same senator or a House counterpart may also spur executive branch action by calling a hearing or initiating a staff investigation.

Whether proponents of congressional action reach these milestones depends on the degree to which members prioritize national versus parochial interests for that issue, whether the two political parties hold different philosophies when it comes to national defense, and whether majorities in the two chambers can reach agreement when required. Finally, the success of initiatives can also depend on factors beyond the legislative branch. After all, the US military answers to both ends of Pennsylvania Avenue, and legislative efforts are less effective when lawmakers and the president have different priorities vis-à-vis the military. In such a complex policy environment, the extent of Congress's influence over the US civil-military contract may depend on the sustained attention of key lawmakers who are willing to see the process through, from a staff investigation to a hearing to legislation.

Overview of the Book

The volume is divided into two parts. Part I consists of chapters 2 through 6, with a focus on the tools available to Congress when attempting to alter the civil-military relations contract. Individual chapters discuss the use of officer selection, congressional oversight, delegation of authority to military components, and incentives given to the military.

Chapter 2 begins the discussion with a historical analysis of the military officer selection and promotion process. This chapter, written by Mitchel A. Sollenberger, discusses how political parties and executive-legislative interactions have shaped military appointments over time. Sollenherger addresses how and why military appointments were used as patronage for political parties and the reforms that focused on geographic representation within the officer corps as well as the trend toward a merit-based promotion system. Specifically the chapter reviews how political parties dominated the military appointment process in the early years of the republic, from the Federalists in the 1790s to the Jeffersonian Republicans in the early 1800s. Party dominance continued into the 1850s, with the exception that appointments to the military academies were made by members of Congress, which provided geographic representation to the young officer corps. The Civil War resulted in a major reshuffling of the officer corps based on Republican Party exclusion of Southern officers from the military and the beginnings of a seniority system dominated by promotions among Republican-affiliated officers. The twentieth century saw the rise of a merit-based military promotion system, cemented in the 1947 Officer Personnel Act, though service academy appointments were still dominated by congressional nominations. The chapter concludes with reflections on recent developments in the appointment and promotion process.

Chapters 3 and 4 focus on congressional oversight. Chapter 3, written by Katherine Scott, provides an example of direct congressional oversight in the form of the Truman Committee on wartime spending and procurement. The background for the committee's work was the relatively unrestrained US defense spending patterns in 1940–1941. The then senator Harry Truman (D-MO) engineered the creation of a new defense oversight committee that would simultaneously serve the national interest—in that it aimed to ensure that the country got quality military equipment at a reasonable price—and protect Missouri's business interests against large and potentially unscrupulous defense contractors. The Truman Committee was pathbreaking in a number of senses. It was a bipartisan effort that enfranchised regular citizens into the oversight process and relied on on-the-ground investigations by committee staff and members. The result was a committee that shed unprecedented light on defense procurement corruption and malfeasance during wartime while also acting as an arbiter between executive branch agencies that each possessed different wartime priorities. Scott concludes with thoughts on how Truman's committee experience helped him shape and guide the passage of the 1947 National Security Act, the law that reorganized the US military in the aftermath of the war.

Chapter 4, written by Jordan Tama, considers the role of ad hoc congressional defense commissions. Tama argues that Congress has formed congressional commissions to enhance oversight, push for military reforms and policy change, and in some cases avoid blame by delaying tough decisions. Commissions differ from congressional committees in that commissions are temporary, their members are often selected by Congress *and* the president, and commissions include at least one member who does not serve in government. Ad hoc commissions have been used more frequently since the end of the Cold War, and Tama provides examples of all three commission types. He explores policy change through the Ballistic Missile Threat Commission and the Commission on Roles and Missions of the Armed Forces, both created in the 1990s. He reviews the Commission on Wartime Contracting in Iraq and Afghanistan in 2008 as an example of a commission charged with oversight. Finally, his chapter discusses congressional blame avoidance through the Chemical Warfare Review Commission from the 1980s. Ad hoc congressional commissions show no sign of going away, as demonstrated by the 2013 Military Compensation and Retirement Modernization Commission. Chapter 4 concludes with thoughts on the efficacy of past commissions and sets the stage for assessments of future commission efforts.

Chapter 5 marks a transition from considering officer selection and oversight to the analysis of congressionally delegated authority to the military. Written by John Griswold, it discusses the evolving role of the National Guard and reserves. Lawmakers take a deep and personal interest in the Guard and reserves. Members of the Guard and reserves are constituents. Members of Congress without an active-duty installation in their district consider the Guard and reserves as "their" military, and the Guard and reserves play a crucial role in local disaster response and recovery. Griswold explores the tough balancing act between the domestic and foreign roles of the Guard and reserves by first reviewing the statutory authorities associated with internal and external missions. He then unpacks this tension by examining the chief of the National Guard Bureau's ascension to the Joint Chiefs of Staff in 2011. This is a fascinating case that illustrates the complex relationship that the reserve components have with Congress and the active-duty armed forces and furthers our understanding of officer selection (in chapter 2) and congressional commissions (chapter 4). The chapter concludes by reviewing the challenges facing Congress in legislating Guard and reserves policies under conditions of fiscal austerity in the post-Iraq and -Afghanistan era.

Chapter 6 concludes this part of the book with an examination of defense entitlements—including military compensation, family benefits, and health care—as incentives to encourage reenlistment. The prevailing academic consensus is that Congress does not exercise its full authority on national security matters and usually defers to the president to establish military policy. Alexis Lasselle Ross argues in this chapter, however, that such a conclusion overlooks policymaking on military pay and benefits, a costly and increasingly debated issue. Her chapter argues that Congress does indeed assert its policy agenda when it passes legislation on military compensation and that these "defense entitlements" have important budgetary and policy implications. Using a case study on TRICARE-for-Life, a policy that provides health care to military retirees, the chapter examines how Congress established and later protected this program despite the objections of the executive branch. The chapter fills a void in the literature by reviewing different types of military compensation, the history of their growth, and the profound budgetary, political, and strategic ramifications of congressionally mandated defense entitlements.

Part II focuses on the tension between national interests and parochial concerns that seems to be endemic to congressional debates over military policy and that can affect everything from a congressional hearing to the passage of the national defense authorization act. It includes a chapter on the devolution of the Cold War foreign policy consensus and its implications for the future of Congress and US defense policy, a chapter on the role of

Congress in military innovation, a chapter on the executive-legislative debate over closing the detention facility at the Guantánamo Bay Naval Station in Cuba, and a chapter on congressional attempts to legislate civil-military relations in Latin American countries.

In chapter 7, Chuck Cushman sets out the landscape for part II of the book. He reviews the effort of balancing lawmakers' local, parochial interests with the legislature's national policy responsibilities, an effort that has shaped defense policy in different ways over time. A clear policy consensus during the Cold War helped Congress rein in parochialism and enabled the congressional defense policy committees to concentrate successfully on macro issues. The regular passage of defense authorization and appropriations bills put "Congress squarely in the center of defense policy making." But the end of the Cold War ended that policy consensus, and the costly wars in Iraq and Afghanistan have accelerated the divergence in foreign policy views on the Hill. This has occurred between and even within political parties, as witnessed by debates over defense spending between Tea Party and establishment Republicans. Events since 1991, then, have made it easier for individual members to treat defense policy more like other policy, with all the parochial, partisan, and ideological concerns entailed in such policy. Politics no longer stops at the water's edge, and the "regular order" associated with defense policy is gone.

Charlie Stevenson details in chapter 8 how Congress has responded to new technologies and methods of war. This is a chapter that highlights the congressional use of delegation and incentives to achieve desired military behavior. Specifically Stevenson uses historical examples to review how Congress deals with major innovations in military technology, operations, and strategy. The chapter argues that lawmakers tend to embrace promising technologies, to resist high or unanticipated costs, to empower new organizations to take advantage of new ways of war, and to question innovations that raise significant domestic issues. While Congress usually endorses and sponsors ideas and programs that originate within the military, it sometimes imposes its own proposals on a reluctant Pentagon. Lawmakers have been most active on technology issues, particularly when they offered dramatic improvements in military capability or local economic benefits. On major strategic and doctrinal debates, Congress has sometimes raised questions but has generally been deferential to executive branch policies. The chapter concludes with discussions of recent congressional reactions to cyber operations and UAVs used for lethal attacks, two of the most challenging new ways of war.

Chapter 9, by Louis Fisher, reviews the politics surrounding the detainment and interrogation facility at Guantánamo. Fisher's argument should be read in light of our earlier discussion of congressional oversight and delegation.

The chapter critiques President Barack Obama's promise to close the detention facility and find an alternative facility in the United States without ever reaching out first to members of Congress to see how they would respond. The predictable reaction by both Democrats and Republicans in Congress was to block the closure of the facility. The chapter also reviews the administration's backup plan to secretly bring eight Uighurs from the naval base to facilities in local American communities. The Obama administration's attempt at a swift, secretive operation that would preempt any political outcry and interference by Congress was stymied when leaks of the plan forced the administration to shelve it in the face of congressional opposition. That said, Congress repeatedly conditioned its opposition to changing the status quo on the administration providing a detailed plan for the facility's closure. The Obama administration never provided Congress that plan.

Chapter 10 expands our discussion beyond US shores by exploring congressional efforts to legislate the civil-military relations contract in other nations, specifically in Latin America and the Caribbean. This is a chapter on oversight and incentives tailored toward human rights. The chapter's authors, Frank Mora and Michelle Munroe, argue that the Alliance for Progress and the rise of military rule in Latin America and the Caribbean in the 1960s and 1970s led to an unprecedented congressional focus on the region, contributing to legislation and appropriation bills that sought to address the challenge of democratic breakdown, human rights, and militarism in the region. As the Cold War intensified in the region during the 1970s and 1980s, particularly in Central America, the public's attention to civil wars and human rights violations helped drive congressional action. A significant number of lawmakers and their staffs sought to sanction or cut aid to governments whose militaries were involved in alleged human rights violations. Mora and Munroe document how congressional interest in Latin American civil-military relations faded as democratic regimes emerged throughout the region by the end of the Cold War. A few members of Congress, however, attempted to consolidate democratic gains by funding programs that helped professionalize militaries in the region. Yet congressional interest and corresponding resources continued to decline, especially after 9/11. Mora and Munroe explain this gradual decline in congressional interest and influence toward Latin America and the Caribbean.

We conclude the volume in chapter 11 with general thoughts and observations on the future of US civil-military relations drawn from the preceding chapters. Here we touch on three main debates. The first is on the future of the defense budget in the aftermath of the Iraq and Afghanistan wars and a much-constrained national budget. Debates over the defense budget will no longer be limited to the classic guns-versus-butter trade-off pitting the defense budget against nondefense discretionary programs. Certainly that will be part of the debate, yet future defense budget battles also will focus on the choice between taking care of the people who serve in the military—and prioritizing personnel-related areas of the defense budget, such as pay, pensions, health care, and other benefits—or the equipment they need to fight and prevail in future conflicts—which would prioritize research and development and procurement. Who comes down on which side of these decisions is not necessarily as self-evident as it might once have been, as debates within the Republican Party have already proven. The ultimate choice could depend on how Congress decides to use the tools at its disposal to affect the civil-military relations contract in the United States.

A second and related question is how and to what degree Congress will use the military as a vehicle to advance social, gender, and human rights change. The military has long been an agent of social change, such as when President Truman integrated the armed forces in 1948. As the country works to solve new social issues, the military is likely to be a part of that transformation. Notable examples include sexual assault (e.g., removing the military from the chain of command), gays serving openly and receiving spousal benefits, greater diversity in the military's leadership, women in combat (e.g., the inclusion of women in submarine crews), the recruitment of religious minorities, and geographic- rather than merit-based admissions into the Coast Guard Academy.[8] Our conclusions explore the reasons why Congress might use civil-military tools to advance these changes and which tools would make the most sense to use.

A third and final question we focus on in the concluding chapter is the growing rift between Congress and the military. We have already touched on the decreasing proportion of legislators who have direct military experience. A related trend, however, is the degree to which the active-duty and reserve components of the military have self-selected from a particular slice of the electorate, a slice that remains predominately conservative and believes in its own unique expertise on defense issues. The combination of congressional inexperience and military self-identification raises difficult questions as to how Congress can and should use civil-military relations tools in the future and the efficacy of that use.

Notes

1. Mackubin Thomas Owens, "What Military Officers Need to Know about Civil-Military Relations," *Naval War College Review* 65, no. 2 (2012): 71.
2. See, for instance, Robert S. Benson, "The Military on Capitol Hill: Prospects in the Quest for Funds," *Annals of the American Academy of Political and Social Science* 406 (1973): 48–58;

Harvey M. Sapolsky, Eugene Ghotz, and Caitlin Talmadge, *US Defense Politics: The Origins of Security Policy* (New York: Routledge, 2008).

3. Charles A. Stevenson, *Warriors and Politicians: US Civil-Military Relations under Stress* (New York: Routledge, 2006), 202.

4. See James R. Locher III, *Victory on the Potomac: The Goldwater-Nichols Act Unifies the Pentagon* (College Station: Texas A&M University Press, 2002).

5. See, for example, Tim Hsia, "The Role of the Military and Veterans in Politics," *New York Times*, February 1, 2013, http://atwar.blogs.nytimes.com/2013/02/01/the-role-of-the -military-and-veterans-in-politics/; Ashley Southhall, "A Changing of the Guard among Veterans in Congress," *New York Times*, January 4, 2013, http://thecaucus.blogs.nytimes .com/2013/01/04/a-changing-of-the-guard-among-veterans-in-congress/?_php =true&_type=blogs&_r=0; and Drew Desilver, "Most Members of Congress Have Little Direct Military Experience," Pew Research Center, September 4, 2012, www.pewresearch .org/fact-tank/2013/09/04/members-of-congress-have-little-direct-military-experience/.

6. David P. Auerswald, "Senate Reservations to Security Treaties," *Foreign Policy Analysis* 2, no. 1 (January 2006): 83–100. See also David P. Auerswald and Forrest Maltzman, "Policymaking through Advice and Consent: Treaty Consideration by the United States Senate," *Journal of Politics* 65, no. 4 (November 2003): 1097–1110, and David P. Auerswald, "Advice and Consent: The Forgotten Power," in *Congress and the Politics of Foreign Policy*, ed. Colton C. Campbell, Nicol C. Rae, and John F. Stack Jr. (Upper Saddle River, NJ: Prentice Hall, 2002), 44–69.

7. Deborah D. Avant, *Political Institutions and Military Change: Lessons from Peripheral Wars* (Ithaca, NY: Cornell University Press, 1994).

8. A recent report by a congressionally chartered commission, for example, found that racial and ethnic minorities and women are underrepresented among the military's top ranks as well as its senior noncommissioned officers. See, for example, Military Diversity Leadership Commission, *From Representation to Inclusion: Diversity Leadership for the 21st-Century Military; Final Report* (Washington, DC: Government Printing Office, 2011), and Daniel Sagalyn, "U.S. Military Leadership Lacks Diversity at Top," *PBS Newshour*, March 11, 2011, www.pbs.org/newshour/rundown/military-report/.

Part I

Congressional Tools and Civil-Military Relations

2

Presidential and Congressional Relations

An Evolution of Military Appointments

MITCHEL A. SOLLENBERGER

The subject and title of this book, *Congress and Civil-Military Relations*, offers an interesting and useful framework for studying military appointments. The actual process for making military appointments involves both civil and military actors at several points. However, the two most dominant institutions involved in the military appointment process are the presidency and Congress. They—above all others—have the most influence and control over the personnel who embody the armed forces of the United States. That is not by accident, as the Constitution provides for a system of checks and balances where the president and Congress are given the authority to create and control the armed forces.

The constitutional authority over the armed forces, however, is not clearly delineated. The constitutional system in the United States is based on principles of separation of powers and checks and balances. Powers and duties often overlap. For example, Congress passes a bill, but it takes the president's signature for it to become law. In other regards, the Constitution does not clearly spell out how powers should be exercised or shared. The ability to suspend the writ of habeas corpus is one example. Does the president or Congress have suspension authority and under what conditions can habeas be set aside? The process of making military appointments is no different. That has meant that the president and Congress together have been able to shape the military appointment process through repeated practice, not by the way of some grand design spelled out in the Constitution. Such an understanding fits well with what Supreme Court justice Robert H. Jackson said about constitutional meaning and governing: "While the Constitution diffuses power the better to secure liberty, it also contemplates that practice will integrate the dispersed powers into a workable government. It enjoins upon its branches separateness but interdependence, autonomy but reciprocity."[1]

Much of the way military appointments have been—and are currently—made in the United States reflects that understanding of how the Constitution intended our governing institutions to function. As a result this chapter primarily focuses on the interaction of presidents and Congress in the selection and confirmation of military appointments and promotions. It traces the development of military appointments from the founding period to the present day. More important, it attempts to explain why some of the more significant milestones in the evolution of the military appointment process occurred. The chapter also covers the cadet and midshipmen appointment process in the academies. Finally, it addresses the charge that Senate confirmations serve no purpose in the military appointment process.

Early Development of Military Appointments, 1789–1801

Although the country had experience with a temporary military force in the Continental Army during the Revolution along with the creation of a regular army in 1784, the origins of the current US military appointment system trace back to 1789. The primary reason has to do with the requirement in the Articles of Confederation that the states raise the troops and select officers for the common defense. That meant appointments were controlled at the state, not national, level.[2]

The ratification of the Constitution greatly changed the preexisting process for making military appointments. Article I, Section 8 stipulates that Congress can raise an army and navy along with establishing rules for regulating the land and naval forces. In addition, Article II, Section 2 provides that the president and Senate appoint "officers of the United States" and leaves to Congress the ability to vest the power to appoint "inferior officers" to others than the president, such as department heads.

Despite the clear intent of the framers of the Constitution to move the control of military appointments to the national level, there were a number of details that needed to be worked out either in law or practice. For the most part the customs that George Washington initiated as president would become the basis for handling military appointments going forward. The most important decision Washington made was to delegate his appointment authority to his secretary of war, Henry Knox.[3] Adopting the practice of recruiting new units from the states and regions, Knox ensured that the first regiments were of a balanced geographic makeup.[4] This practice was largely born out of "the prevailing localism of the American social order" and the need to mitigate fears of military power that many citizens possessed.[5]

Initially party patronage did not have an impact on military appointments as the Federalist and Republican parties only took shape in the mid-1790s. As Washington's administration progressed, however, party politics and legislative influence came into play with military appointments as Federalist Party members began to dominate the officer corps. The connection between political party and legislative influence quickly became so strong that a number of relatives of Federalist members of Congress secured officer positions under Washington.[6] Even in the Senate the practice began to emerge that it would not just be a rubber stamp for military appointments. Instead, senators saw their role to be taking some care to understand what kind of men they were confirming. In one case, Anti-Administration senator William Maclay of Pennsylvania rose and objected to "giving my advice and consent to the appointment of men [of] whom I knew nothing." Only after several senators announced their support for their home-state nominees did the Senate move to a vote and confirmed the military appointments.[7] The growing sense that lawmakers would have an important role in making military appointments had the benefit of linking the still fragile national army to elected political leaders who would fight against the still dominant attitude among citizens that a republic should not have a standing army.

The rise of the first party system and the Quasi-War with France, however, would soon threaten any inroads made to alleviate citizens' fears of a national military establishment. In 1798 John Adams was president and led the moderate wing of the Federalist Party. At that time Adams not only faced a pending war with France but also two domestic political opponents in Republican Party leader Thomas Jefferson and High Federalist Alexander Hamilton, who had been battling the president since their time in the Washington administration.

The Federalist Party had deep-seated fears that many Republicans— because of the party's support for France—were domestic traitors seeking to destroy the new national government. Partially because of those fears and the need to confront an international threat in France, the Federalist Congress expanded the ranks of the army and created the positions of one lieutenant general and several major generals. Adams quickly appointed former president Washington to the lieutenant general post. Washington asked Adams to name Hamilton as a major general, which the president eventually did despite his hostility to the High Federalist leader.

Hamilton's appointment, however, created problems for Adams. Because of his age, Washington delegated to Hamilton many of the duties of commander of the army. Normally this would not have been a problem, but Secretary of War James McHenry had handed over his appointment functions to Washington.[8] With Hamilton now in control of the administration of the new army, including appointments, the High Federalist leader had tremendous power to shape the military, which meant that President Adams found himself nearly completely removed from the selection process.[9] When Adams tried to exert some influence over the appointment of military officers, the Senate—controlled by Hamilton supporters—rejected his choice for adjutant general.[10] Only later in his administration did Adams take control of the selection stage by ordering McHenry to present all military appointments to him for "explicit approval of the President."[11]

The internal battle within the Adams administration had the potential to hurt the military as more and more Federalists were given officer corps appointments while Republicans were nearly shut out of the selection process for the new army. Even the few successful Republicans were barred from high-ranking positions.[12] Although it is doubtful that Adams, Hamilton, or Washington could envision in the 1798–99 time period the election of Thomas Jefferson, the implications of creating a one-party army were troubling. Political leaders opposed to the Federalist Party could have viewed the new partisan army as a threat and moved to eliminate it once they took control of the presidency and Congress.

Regardless of the future implications resulting from the officers whom Adams and his generals decided to select, the evidence clearly suggests that lawmakers played a vital role in making military appointments at the initial vetting stage and during the confirmation process.[13] Only having left the presidency in 1797, Washington expressed his dismay at the growing custom of lawmakers possessing a recognized voice in the selection of military officers. For instance, in the fall of 1798 Washington declared that many military "applications are made, chiefly through members of Congress. These oftentimes to get rid of them; oftener still perhaps, for local and Electioneering purposes, and to please and gratify their party."[14] A few months later, Washington again showed his frustration: "Any Member of Congress who had a friend to serve, or a prejudice to endulge [sic], could set [appointments] at naught." In one case, Washington, along with four generals, had recommended a Revolutionary War veteran for promotion, but "the Veto of a Member of Congress (I presume) was more respected, and sufficient to set him aside." The ex-president warned that "if the practice is continued, you will find that serious discontents, and evils will result from it."[15]

Congressional Patronage Takes Hold, 1801–43

The military was in a precarious place at the beginning of 1801 with the election of Thomas Jefferson as president. The army—like the federal judiciary—was a stronghold of Federalism despite Republicans having taken control of Congress and the presidency. Just as Jefferson refused to let Adams pack the judiciary with the last-minute creation of federal judgeships and appointments, so did he turn against the Federalist-dominated military establishment. However, unlike his fellow Republicans, Jefferson did not want to eliminate the standing army, but instead he moved to transform it into a Republican-supporting entity.

Jefferson first secured the passage of the Military Peace Establishment Act of 1802, which required the dismissal of officers to ensure a balance with the reduced authorized size of the army.[16] The officers being discharged naturally were Federalists, and any replacements in the officer corps would be Republicans. Next, the president had his secretary of war, Henry Dearborn, restructure the army to ensure even more removals of Federalist officers. By combining companies, Jefferson succeeded in increasing the number of cuts made to the largely Federalist officer corps.[17] The changes permitted Jefferson to eventually replace three-quarters of the 267 Federalist officers who had held commissions in 1801. By the end of Jefferson's tenure, Republican appointees in the army made up a majority of nearly every officer rank.[18]

The most important step in remaking the army, and a key part of Jefferson's lasting legacy, was the establishment of an academy to train officers for military service. Jefferson himself had earlier opposed such a move, but as president he quickly came to understand that transforming the Federalist army required men who would support republican values and the new Republican administration.[19] But Jefferson faced a problem in that there were few fellow partisans who had the required background and training to become officers. As a result Jefferson understood that he needed to establish a military academy to train young Republicans to become part of an officer corps that would support the new regime. As one scholar explained, "loyal Republican sons—who otherwise might not be prepared for officership— were trained for commissioned service in Mr. Jefferson's army" at the new United States Military Academy at West Point, New York.[20]

At least initially, the appointment of cadets, as one military historian noted, "followed no uniform pattern." Likely this result can be traced to the isolation and obscurity of the Military Academy during its early years.[21] There were, however, clear signs that Secretary of War Dearborn took seriously the Republican affiliation of cadet applicants and appears to have made that the overwhelming criterion in Jefferson's reform efforts.[22] Still, the Military Academy failed to become a stable institution for the purpose of training officers until the 1810s. The reason had to do with Jefferson's political coalition, which included a good number of individuals who continued to distrust a standing army and any institutions created to support it. That opposition resulted in Congress providing inadequate resources in the form of infrastructure and personnel for West Point to carry out its mission of train-ing future officers.[23] The War of 1812 was the primary catalyst for changing the lingering congressional opposition and convincing lawmakers to provide the much-needed support to the fledgling Military Academy.

As with the Quasi-War, the War of 1812 resulted in the strengthening of politics and patronage with military appointments. The military buildup to fight Great Britain meant an expansion of the regular army. Secretary of War Dearborn—likely acting in the same tradition as his predecessors—sent let-ters to Republican lawmakers asking them to recommend qualified men from their states. Connecticut was the only state not to be included, as it was still a Federalist stronghold. In that case, Dearborn wrote to an administration sup-porter asking for similar recommendations based on merit and party politics.[24]

Cadet appointments were eventually regularized in the postwar era. The "unwritten rule" required the selection of cadets "from as many states and districts as possible."[25] In addition, by at least James Monroe's administration, Secretary of War John C. Calhoun relied on the recommendations of law-makers in making cadet appointments.[26] The same devotion to seeking the advice of lawmakers was evident in the actions of Calhoun's successor, James Barbour, who noted, "In making selections, I have received, and treated with great respect, the recommendations of the members of Congress." He also explained that a practice of dividing the cadet class among the states and congressional districts "having been already established," it was his goal "to appoint a cadet from every congressional district and two from each State."[27] That meant each representative and senator was assured of making at least one cadet selection for an incoming class.[28]

In 1843 Congress formalized the established custom of members of Con-gress selecting cadet appointments. Specifically Congress included a provi-sion in its annual army appropriations bill that required individuals selected "be an actual resident" of the state or district "from which the appointment purports to be made" along with ensuring that each district "shall be entitled to have one cadet at" the Military Academy.[29] Despite the imprecise language of the law, the intent of Congress was to ensure the continued practice of lawmakers making the nominating decisions of cadet positions.[30] Only with at-large cadet appointments did the president have discretion to choose nom-inees. Even in those cases, the tradition of reserving at-large appointments to the sons of army officers greatly limited the president's pool of candidates.[31]

The 1843 law had two primary benefits. First, it helped to strengthen the idea that all citizens had a chance to benefit from a military education by ensuring members of Congress made most of the selection decisions. Since the 1830s Republican lawmakers had begun to renew their attacks against the Military Academy, believing it a "school for aristocrats" as well as an institution that promoted a dangerous standing army.[32] After passage of the 1843 law, the attacks against the Military Academy "softened," and the threat of abolishing the institution ended.[33] Second, the law had the ancillary effect of mitigating the fears of an officer corps dominated by Northern or Southern sympathies regarding the issue of slavery.[34]

Two years after the passage of the cadet appointment statute, Congress established the United States Naval Academy in Annapolis, Maryland.[35] Congress immediately adopted statutory language providing members of Congress the authority to make midshipmen appointments.[36] As with cadet appointments, patronage became the driving force for selecting candidates at the Naval Academy. In his annual report of the Navy Department, Secretary of the Navy William E. Chandler noted, "Nearly all the patronage of cadet selection for Annapolis is enjoyed by members of Congress." Moreover, he claimed that even when candidates are "sent away for fraud and other moral delinquencies" by the academy's academic board, some return on the backing of members of Congress. If that occurred, the once rejected candidates were admitted, as the Naval Academy had no authority to refuse them. Chandler declared that "this is an abuse the effects of which cannot fail to be highly injurious."[37]

Although the country had entered the "spoils era" by the 1840s, academy appointments did not evolve in the same way as typical patronage gifts for party members to hand out to their faithful supporters. The early practice of party politics playing a vital role in the selection of cadet appointments had given way to two requirements: a geographic balance in making appointments and the solicitation of lawmakers'—regardless of political party—recommendations. Speaking in 1859, Jefferson Davis, just two years removed from duties as the secretary of war under President Franklin Pierce, defended the congressional recommendation requirement: "We do not have with each change of Administration, a change in the political character of the appointments to the academy; they follow still the political sentiment of the district which each one represents in the academy. They thus carry into the Army every variety of opinion and of feeling which exists in the country."[38] A midshipman from the 1850s had similar thoughts, calling the practice a "strictly democratic method of appointment" that produced candidates "from every section" of the country.[39] As a result, unlike the practice of selecting federal judges, the recommendation of academy candidates did not only come from members of the president's political party. All members of Congress, regardless of partisan affiliation and sectional affinities, were empowered to recommend academy appointments.

The nonpartisan patronage system for the Military Academy and the Naval Academy did not extend to military appointments. As one historian of the army officer corps noted, "in contrast to the bipartisanship intrinsic to cadet appointments, Democratic administrations controlled virtually all direct appointments and tended to favor their own supporters."[40] During the Mexican-American War, President James K. Polk used military appointments to reward Democratic supporters while transforming the army into an entity that would be loyal to him.[41] Polk's primary obstacle, however, was the two senior generals in the army, Winfield Scott and Zachary Taylor, who were both Whig Party members. In order to mitigate the impact of the Whig leadership, Polk appointed thirteen volunteer generals who all had a history of Democratic Party service.[42] Polk even planned on appointing Democratic senator Thomas Hart Benton as the lieutenant general, which would have made him the highest-ranking officer in the army. The House of Representatives approved the plan, but the Senate—led by Whig opposition—rejected it.[43]

Military Appointments: From the Civil War through the Gilded Age

Politics and patronage largely dominated officer appointments through the Civil War. From 1802 to 1861, thirty-seven generals were appointed in the army. None were West Point graduates, and twenty-three had little if any military experience.[44] President Abraham Lincoln followed the tradition of appointing politically connected men who were known at that time as "political generals." During the first year of the Civil War, Lincoln named several generals from civilian life whose "chief recommendation was their prominence as politicians or as leaders of the German American and Irish American ethnic communities."[45] Unlike Polk during the Mexican-American War, Lincoln largely appointed politicians to officer positions to mobilize support for the Union. As one scholar noted, "Democrats, Irish-Americans, many German-Americans, and residents of the watersheds of the Ohio and Missouri rivers had not voted for Lincoln in 1860 and were potential defectors from a war to crush the rebels and coerce the South back into the Union."[46] Handing out military patronage not just for party but also national interests became for Lincoln an effective military strategy and an essential one.

Lincoln could not, however, escape the need to reward military patronage to his fellow Republicans in Congress. The Republican congressional delegation from Illinois not only decided how to divide military patronage in their state but also met specifically to choose brigadier generals.[47] The initial patronage fights over officer appointments became so heated that in 1862 Congress authorized an increase in major general and brigadier positions.[48] Certainly congressional involvement in military appointments resulted in some misguided selections. For example, Benjamin Butler secured his position as major general through political connections and became known as one of the most incompetent political generals during the Civil War. Congressional patronage, however, did have its value, as it helped to advance the military career of Ulysses S. Grant. Early on in the war, Republican senators Orville H. Browning and Lyman Trumbull of Illinois supported Grant's appointment as brigadier general.[49]

During the post–Civil War years, cadet and military appointments generally operated the same way as before the war. However, the number of officer appointments and who could be selected were impacted by changes to the armed forces. First, the size of the authorized army grew to 54,302 officers and men, which was three times its size in 1860.[50] This created greater patronage opportunities for presidents and lawmakers. Second, Congress required that officer candidates show evidence of their service in the war. The restriction meant that for the first time in the nation's history the South would be largely excluded from the officer corps. Congress also wrote into the law a requirement that all officer vacancies be proportioned according to the number of volunteers each state provided during the war. This meant that New York, Pennsylvania, and Ohio would account for 38 percent of all new commissions.[51] The regional dominance stipulated by Congress meant that the officer corps would remain sympathetic to the Republican Party for years to come.

Over time Congress found the appointment restrictions established after the Civil War too constraining, as they had the natural result of limiting the discretion that presidents and members of Congress had in making officer selections. In 1875 Congress repealed those statutory restrictions. In the case of army paymasters, over the next ten years those positions went to various relatives or political allies of lawmakers and presidents.[52] Even during peacetime, military appointments were valued patronage plums for lawmakers. As civil service reforms in the executive branch took hold starting in 1883 with the passage of the Pendleton Act, appointments to the academies and officer corps increased in importance for lawmakers.

Academy and officer appointments were not the only parts of the military patronage system. Members of Congress at times paid close attention to military promotions and occasionally involved themselves in advancing a career of a military officer, especially during periods of war when the army expanded.[53] As a result, lawmakers did take it upon themselves to convince presidents to promote their special favorites.[54] Occasionally, deciding who would receive a promotion became a heated contest among a president, the War Department, and a member of Congress.[55] A late nineteenth-century general complained that congressional influence had "an undue share in these selections."[56] However, congressional involvement in promotion cases was the exception to the general rule. By at least the mid-nineteenth century, the length of service of an officer had become the primary criterion for promotions.[57]

After the Civil War the political strength of the Grand Army of the Republic within Republican Party circles meant that the seniority system remained a heavily entrenched part of military promotions, at least through the end of the century.[58] During this period, however, Congress established physical examination regimes for promotions in the navy and army. Navy examinations for promotion were instituted in 1864 and stipulated that "no officer in the naval service shall be promoted to a higher grade" until a board of naval surgeons pronounces him "physically qualified."[59] Examinations within the army did not occur until 1890 when Congress required the "examination of all officers of the Army below the rank of major" for the purpose of determining their physical fitness for promotion. The law also stipulated that a similar examination would occur for the appointment of officers from civil life.[60] Neither law created a promotion-by-merit system; seniority as the primary factor for promotion consideration still dominated. What the law meant was that physically unfit officers would at least have a difficult time advancing in the ranks.[61]

Although Congress began to instill more professionalism in the military promotion system, the initial appointments to the officer corps continued to face the realities of patronage politics. During the Spanish-American War, President William McKinley largely followed the practice established under Lincoln and used military appointments to build not only a political coalition but also national support for the war. McKinley did that by taking into account geographic diversity when making selections. In particular, he purposively selected former Confederate officers in Joseph Wheeler and Fitzhugh Lee as major generals to build support among Democrats and Southerners.[62] Despite such appointments, McKinley selected fewer political generals than Lincoln, but the officer ranks still included family members and others closely associated with Republican senators and representatives.[63] Sometimes such appointments caused friction in his administration. In one case Sen. Redfield Proctor (R-VT) secured an officer appointment against the wishes of the secretary of navy.[64]

The Military Appointment System in the Twentieth Century and Beyond

Writing in 1953, Joseph P. Harris noted that there had been a great decline in the influence of lawmakers in the military promotion process where "this practice seems to have almost disappeared."[65] Harris was partially correct. The seniority system, not patronage or politics, primarily determined military promotions in the nineteenth century. During the Progressive Era, military reformers began to discuss the possibility that promotion decisions be based on merit, not length of service. President Theodore Roosevelt opposed the seniority system and exercised his authority to assist in John J. Pershing's career by promoting him "from captain to brigadier general, jumping over 257 captains, 364 majors, 131 lieutenant colonels and 110 colonels."[66] He could do that because the seniority system only controlled promotions for the ranks of colonel on down, so Roosevelt was free to place any person in the grade of brigadier general. Even President McKinley used that loophole in the seniority system to promote thirty-nine officers.[67] Also likely aiding in Pershing's promotion was his father-in-law, Republican senator Francis Warren of Wyoming, who was the chair of the Senate's Military Affairs Committee (now the Senate Armed Services Committee).[68]

The Pershing promotion did not mean that the political generals experience during the Civil War continued into the twentieth century. First, Pershing's record of service before and after his promotion demonstrated the merits of his rapid advancement. Second, by the start of the twentieth century, the army and navy had in place examination boards and rules that required "a minimum level of professional competence" to secure a promotion.[69] Still, promotions were based on seniority, not merit. In 1916 Congress implemented a limited promotion-by-selection system in the navy by creating selection boards to consider advancements from captain to rear admiral and from commander to captain.[70] Not until 1947 did a similar merit-based system of promotion take hold in the army when Congress passed the Officer Personnel Act.[71] The law became the foundation for the current merit-promotion system in the army. More important, it did much to limit the patronage opportunities by establishing a merit-based examination system that required a showing of professional competence in the duties required of an officer of higher rank.

Unlike the promotion system, academy appointments did not experience the same transformation to a merit-based selection process. To be sure, at the start of the twentieth century, progressives and military reformers questioned the congressional patronage system for academy appointments to West Point and Annapolis and called for "open competitive examinations."[72] Such criticisms were not new. Lincoln's navy secretary, Gideon Welles, tried to convince Congress to agree to the creation of three-member boards that would examine candidates for the Naval Academy. In addition, Welles asked Congress to give him the authority to create regulations that would guide the examination process of the boards. The proposed changes never made their way into law.[73] In the 1860s Sylvanus Thayer, a former superintendent of the Military Academy, argued for "open competition" in West Point selections that would prevent any consideration of "class or condition, race or color" of a potential candidate.[74] Congress did not act on Thayer's recommendation either. The inability of the reform measures to take hold has meant that approximately 86 percent of cadet appointments are still made by lawmakers.[75]

In 1950 Congress slightly modified the academy appointment process law to indicate that cadets would be "nominated by the Representative in Congress."[76] Before this time the cadet appointments law vaguely referenced congressional districts and states. Only in 1935 did Congress begin to provide more precise language: "There shall be allowed at the United States Military Academy three cadets for each Senator, Representative."[77] Of course, that law did not make clear that senators and representatives controlled cadet appointments. The 1950 change to "nominated by the Representative in Congress" resolved the vagueness issues in the law. Rep. Carl T. Durham (D-NC) confirmed this understanding when he said on the House floor that the change "is a codification of the existing law relating to the source of appointments to the Military Academy."[78] No similar action needed to occur for midshipmen appointments, as Congress had provided more precise language for Naval Academy selections in 1862 when it passed a law providing that "the nomination of candidates for admission into the Naval Academy shall be made . . . upon the recommendation of the member or delegate" of the House of Representatives.[79] In 1954 Congress—in establishing the Air Force Academy—used equally clear language to ensure everyone understood that members of Congress nominated air force cadets.[80]

A more significant mid-twentieth-century change to the academy appointment laws dealt with the problem of the unequal distribution of qualified candidates for the service academies, especially after the standards for admitting cadets and midshipmen had risen significantly since the turn of the century. Many districts and states had more than enough candidates who qualified for an academy appointment. Some districts and states, however, failed to send qualified candidates, which left unfilled vacancies—usually more than a hundred—at West Point and Annapolis.[81] In 1942 Congress found a solution by creating what have come to be known as "qualified alternate" appointments. The change gives the secretary of defense the authority to select additional cadets from a general pool of congressionally endorsed candidates if the number of cadets falls under the authorized total set by law.[82] Specifically the new system still gives preference to the principal cadet nominations if made by members of Congress. However, after the initial selections are made, the remaining congressionally endorsed candidates are placed into a general pool from which the secretary is free to make additional appointments.

Everyone benefited in the creation of qualified alternate appointments. The Military Academy succeeded in filling out its ranks, qualified candidates who under the former system would not have had an additional opportunity of being selected were admitted to West Point, and members of Congress increased their patronage opportunities by getting the chance to see not only their principal nominations selected but their alternates as well. As one scholar noted, it was "an obvious boon to them politically."[83] Initially the law only applied to the Military Academy, but Congress eventually extended the qualified alternate practice to the Naval Academy and Air Force Academy as well.[84]

Does the Senate Confirmation Process Serve a Purpose for Military Appointments?

At present any individual seeking an original appointment or promotion above the rank of captain in the army, air force, and Marine Corps is subject to Senate confirmation.[85] The same is true for all officer appointments in the navy above the rank of lieutenant.[86] That adds up to hundreds of military appointments and promotions that the Senate needs to confirm each Congress. Joseph P. Harris, who wrote *The Advice and Consent of the Senate*, argued that such confirmations serve "little purpose."[87] That judgment hinges on the value one places on the Senate confirmation process in the context of military appointments and promotions.

There are at least three reasons why Senate confirmation is required of military appointments and promotions. First, one could argue that Article II of the Constitution requires it. The relevant provision of Article II stipulates that the president "shall nominate, and by and with the advice and consent of the Senate, shall appoint . . . officers of the United States, whose appointments are not herein otherwise provided for, and which shall be established by law, but the Congress may by law vest the appointment of such inferior officers, as they think proper, in the President alone, in the courts of law, or in the heads of departments." Better known as the Appointments Clause, it provides for two classes of officers: principal and inferior. The answer to whether military appointments and promotions require Senate confirmation hinges on if one considers them to be principal or inferior officers.

This is not the place for extensive analysis of the difference between principal and inferior officers. However, the most recent guidance by the Supreme Court is *Morrison v. Olson*, where the court cited four factors to help determine whether an officer is inferior: The officer is subject to removal by a higher-level executive branch official other than the president, and the scope of the office is limited in duty, jurisdiction, or tenure.[88] Yet in another opinion the court declared that "Morrison did not purpose to set forth a definitive test for whether an office is 'inferior' under the Appointments Clause." The court then suggested the most relevant factor in deterring inferior status of an officer is whether "he has a superior" other than the president who has received Senate confirmation.[89]

Trying to craft and apply a standard based on the Supreme Court's holdings is nearly impossible. Based on historical practice, Congress has retained the Senate confirmation requirement for most officers in the armed services except at the lowest levels. From time to time Congress has validated the understanding that military officers are principal appointments under the Appointments Clause. For example, the Senate Committee on Military Affairs wrote in an 1861 report:

> No one who considers the subject will assume that officers of the army belong to that "inferior" class specified in [the Appointments Clause], whose appointment can vest solely in the President. On the contrary, a uniform interpretation has been given . . . by Congress since the foundation of the Government; and according to that interpretation, all officers of the rank, dignity, and responsibility of officers of the regular army, have been held to belong to that higher grade specified in the [Appointments Clause], whose appointment could only be constitutionally made "by and with the advice and consent of the Senate."[90]

History, combined with congressional practice, provides strong support for the view that officers are to be considered principal appointments. However, the text of the Constitution is ambiguous enough to leave that conclusion somewhat in doubt.

Another reason in support of a Senate confirmation requirement of military appointments and promotions centers on the strong opposition many founding fathers had to a standing military force during peacetime. As one Anti-Federalist wrote, "a standing army is useless and dangerous. It will inevitably sow the seeds of corruption and depravity of manners."[91] The reason, republican theorists contend, that the Constitution even permits a standing army is because of the compromises embodied in it. To be sure, strong executive supporters such as Alexander Hamilton argued and secured the possibility of a standing army in the Constitution, but in turn Republicans such as Elbridge Gerry also won firm controls on that power.[92] For example, the Constitution authorizes Congress to create an army and navy, to provide regulations, to appropriate money in support (but not for longer than two years), and to declare war. Often overlooked in the controls placed on a standing army is the Appointments Clause. From the First Congress on, Senate confirmation has been a required, and lasting, feature of military appointments and promotions.

Finally, there is a strong practical argument in support of the confirmation requirement of military appointments and promotions. Senators have exercised their advice-and-consent responsibilities to not only shape the personnel in the armed forces but also to have real substantive impact on military policy. For example, the Senate Armed Services Committee did not act on the promotion of Timothy W. Dorsey to admiral in 2012 when it was discovered that Dorsey had intentionally shot down an air force jet in the 1980s.[93] A year later Democratic senator Claire McCaskill of Missouri placed a hold—a Senate device used to block action on a bill or nomination—on the promotion of Lt. Gen. Susan Helms of the air force because of the general's decision to overturn a military jury's sexual assault conviction without explanation.[94] In November 2013 Helms requested that President Barack Obama withdraw her name from Senate consideration.[95]

The Helms promotion controversy was one part of a larger battle over sexual assault policies in the armed forces. Sen. Kirsten Gillibrand (D-NY) had been seeking legal changes to limit the power of military commanders to set aside jury convictions in sexual assault cases. At various points it appeared that Gillibrand's reform measure would not move forward and that her efforts and McCaskill's would be for naught.[96] At one point Senator Gillibrand even placed a hold on President Obama's nominee for undersecretary of the navy, Jo Ann Rooney. Gillibrand did that because Rooney opposed the senator's plan to take away the authority of military commanders to set aside jury decisions in sexual assault cases.[97]

Ultimately Senator Gillibrand succeeded in securing most of her reform objectives. In late December 2013, President Obama signed into law the National Defense Authorization Act with Gillibrand's reform measures. The law eliminates the five-year statute of limitations on sexual assault charges, prohibits retaliation against individuals who report an assault, and provides a victim's advocate to service members who report having been assaulted.[98] It is difficult to envision that any of these reforms would have been considered without the ability of senators Gillibrand and McCaskill to use the Senate confirmation process in a way to convince their colleagues and commanding officers in the armed forces to take their concerns seriously. There was also a greater constitutional principle at play: civilian supremacy. The military was not left alone to administer itself. Congress would decide military policy by law, including the review of sentences by courts-martial.

Conclusion

Presidents and members of Congress have a long and complex relationship when dealing with military appointments. Reform efforts have attempted to end the patronage opportunities that lawmakers have long possessed, particularly with academy appointments. However, it is unlikely that the extensive congressional involvement in the selection of cadets or the appointment and promotion of officers will end. Like many laws, practices, and norms that give life to the federal government, the military appointment system has been shaped by the interactions of presidents and lawmakers. Ending or greatly changing the military appointment process, which has been built over centuries and has proven to be useful, will be difficult, if not impossible, to do.

Notes

1. *Youngstown Sheet & Tube Co. v. Sawyer*, 343 U.S. 579, 635 (1952) (concurring opinion).
2. William B. Skelton, *An American Profession of Arms: The Army Officer Corps, 1784–1861* (Lawrence: University Press of Kansas, 1992), 13.
3. Ibid., 16.
4. Edward M. Coffman, *The Old Army: A Portrait of the American Army in Peacetime, 1784–1898* (New York: Oxford University Press, 1986), 6.
5. Skelton, *American Profession of Arms*, 16, 19.
6. Ibid., 18.
7. Edgar S. Maclay, ed., *Journal of William Maclay* (New York: D. Appleton, 1890), 282.
8. Richard H. Kohn, *Eagle and Sword: The Federalist and the Creation of the Military Establishment in American, 1783–1802* (New York: Free Press, 1975), 241.
9. Ibid., 257. See also William J. Murphy Jr., "John Adams: The Politics of the Additional Army, 1798–1800," *New England Quarterly* 52 (June 1979): 242.
10. Page Smith, *John Adams: 1784–1826*, vol. 2 (Garden City, NY: Doubleday, 1962), 978–79.
11. Murphy, "John Adams," 246–48.
12. Skelton, *American Profession of Arms*, 18.
13. Murphy, "John Adams," 244–45.
14. George Washington to James McHenry, October 21, 1798, in *Writings of George Washington*, ed. Fitzpatrick, vol. 36, 504–5 (emphasis in original).
15. George Washington to Henry Knox, March 25, 1799, in ibid., vol. 37, 160–61 (emphasis in original).
16. Theodore J. Crackel, *Mr. Jefferson's Army: Political and Social Reform of the Military Establishment, 1801–1809* (New York: New York University Press, 1987), 39, 44–45.
17. Ibid., 48.
18. Ibid., 173.
19. Leonard D. White, *The Jeffersonians: A Study in Administrative History, 1801–1829* (New York: Macmillan, 1951), 252.
20. Crackel, *Mr. Jefferson's Army*, 181. See also ibid., 13, and John C. Pinheiro, *Manifest Ambition: James K. Polk and Civil-Military Relations during the Mexican War* (Westport, CT: Praeger, 2007), 13.
21. Skelton, *American Profession of Arms*, 26.
22. Crackel, *Mr. Jefferson's Army*, 71.
23. White, *Jeffersonians*, 253.
24. Skelton, *American Profession of Arms*, 29.

25. George S. Pappas, *To the Point: The United States Military Academy, 1802–1902* (Westport, CT: Praeger, 1993), 191–92.

26. Skelton, *American Profession of Arms*, 139; Coffman, *Old Army*, 46.

27. James Barbour, "List of Cadets at West Point in 1828, and the Rule in Making Appointments and Filling Vacancies," in *American States Papers*, vol. 3 (Washington, DC: Gales & Seaton, 1860), 794. See also White, *Jeffersonians*, 256.

28. Skelton, *American Profession of Arms*, 139.

29. 5 Stat. 606 (March 1, 1843).

30. Sidney Forman, *West Point: A History of the United States Military Academy* (New York: Columbia University Press, 1951), 68.

31. James L. Morrison Jr., *"The Best School in the World": West Point, the Pre-Civil War Years, 1833–1866* (Kent, OH: Kent State University Press, 1986), 63.

32. Pappas, *To the Point*, 193. See also Leonard D. White, *The Jacksonians: A Study in Administrative History, 1829–1861* (New York: Macmillan, 1954), 210.

33. Forman, *West Point*, 69.

34. Russell F. Weigley, *History of the United States Army* (New York: Macmillan, 1967), 189.

35. Nathan Miller, *The U.S. Navy: A History* (Annapolis, MD: Naval Institute Press, 1997), 102–3.

36. 5 Stat. 794 (March 3, 1845).

37. *Annual Report of the Secretary of the Navy for the Year 1884*, vol. 1 (Washington, DC: Government Printing Office, 1884), 68.

38. Jefferson Davis, *Jefferson Davis, Constitutionalist: His Letters, Papers, and Speeches*, vol. 3, ed. Dunbar Rowland (Jackson, MS: Mississippi Department of Archives and History, 1923), 560. See also White, *Jacksonians*, 208.

39. Alfred Thayer Mahan, *From Sail to Steam* (New York: Harper & Brothers, 1907), 71.

40. Skelton, *American Profession of Arms*, 147.

41. Richard Bruce Winders, *Mr. Polk's Army: The American Military Experience in the Mexican War* (College Station: Texas A&M Press, 1997), 12–13, 64.

42. Ibid., 37.

43. Ibid., 48.

44. Samuel P. Huntington, *The Soldier and the State: The Theory and Politics of Civil-Military Relations* (Cambridge, MA: Harvard University Press, 1964), 206.

45. James M. McPherson, *Tried by War: Abraham Lincoln as Commander in Chief* (New York: Penguin, 2008), 42.

46. James M. McPherson, "Lincoln and the Strategy of Unconditional Surrender," in *Lincoln: The War President*, ed. Gabor S. Borit (New York: Oxford University Press, 1992), 37.

47. John Y. Simon, "From Galena to Appomattox: Grant and Washburne," *Journal of the Illinois State Historical Society* 58 (Summer 1965): 171.

48. Donald B. Connelly, *John M. Schofield and the Politics of Generalship* (Chapel Hill: University of North Carolina Press, 2006), 59–60.

49. Theodore Calvin Pease and James G. Randall, eds., *The Diary of Orville Hickman Browning*, vol. 1 (Springfield: Illinois State Historical Library, 1925), 487–88, 490. See also McPherson, "Lincoln and the Strategy," 37–38.

50. Coffman, *Old Army*, 218.

51. Ibid., 219.

52. Fred Perry Powers, "The Reform of Federal Service," *Political Science Quarterly* 3 (June 1888): 250.

53. Charles A. Byler, *Civil-Military Relations on the Frontier and Beyond, 1865–1917* (Westport, CT: Praeger, 2006), 54.

54. Walter H. Hebert, *Fighting Joe Hooker* (Lincoln: University of Nebraska Press, 1999), 182.

55. Connelly, *John M. Schofield*, 59.

56. Byler, *Civil-Military Relations*, 54.

57. Peter M. Karsten, *Military in America* (New York: Free Press, 1986), 119.

58. Matthew M. Oyos, "Theodore Roosevelt, Congress and the Military: US Civil-Military Relations in the Early Twentieth Century," *Presidential Studies Quarterly* 30 (June 2000): 321.

59. 13 Stat. 53 (April 21, 1864).

60. 26 Stat. 562 (October 1, 1890).

61. In 1855 Congress authorized a "selection out" retirement system in the navy whereby an efficiency board would place officers it deemed unfit for service on a "reserved list," making them ineligible for promotion. Incompetent officers would be discharged, and those found incapable of performing the duties required of their rank were retired. See Donald Chisholm, *Waiting for Dead Man's Shoes: Origins and Development of the U.S. Navy's Officer Personnel System, 1793–1941* (Stanford, CA: Stanford University Press, 2001), 286, and James H. Hayes, *The Evolution of Military Officer Personnel Management Policies* (Santa Monica, CA: Rand Corp., 1978), 39.

62. Graham A. Cosmas, *An Army for Empire: The United States Army in the Spanish-American War* (College Park: Texas A&M Press, 2003), 142. See also Kevin Phillips, *William McKinley* (New York: Times Books, 2003), 117, and Byler, *Civil-Military Relations*, 56.

63. Howard Wayne Morgan, *William McKinley and His America* (Kent, OH: Kent State University Press, 2003), 290–91; Cosmas, *Army for Empire*, 143.

64. Huntington, *Soldier and the State*, 183.

65. Joseph P. Harris, *The Advice and Consent of the Senate* (Berkeley: University of California Press, 1953), 331.

66. Richard D. White Jr., *Roosevelt the Reformer: Theodore Roosevelt as Civil Service Commissioner, 1889–1895* (Tuscaloosa: University of Alabama Press, 2003), 171.

67. Oyos, "Theodore Roosevelt," 322.

68. John Eisenhower, *Yanks: The Epic Story of the American Army in World War I* (New York: Free Press, 2001), 28.

69. Huntington, *Soldier and the State*, 245.

70. 39 Stat. 578 (August 29, 1916).

71. 61 Stat. 795 (August 7, 1947). For a detailed analysis of the impact of the Officer Personnel Act, see Timothy Robert Hentschel, "United States Army Organizational Transformation during the Truman and Eisenhower Administrations and Its Impact on the Army Officer Corps," PhD diss., Syracuse University, 2008, 209–27.

72. Forman, *West Point*, 169.

73. Chisholm, *Waiting for Dead Man's Shoes*, 286.

74. Forman, *West Point*, 69.

75. Stephen E. Ambrose, *Duty, Honor, Country: A History of West Point* (Baltimore: Johns Hopkins University Press, 1999), 328.

76. 64 Stat. 303 (June 30, 1950); 10 USC 1092a (1952).

77. 49 Stat. 332 (June 7, 1935).

78. *96 Congressional Record* 7036 (1950).

79. 12 Stat. 585 (July 16, 1862).

80. 68 Stat. 48 (April 1, 1954).

81. S. Rep. No. 1656, 81st Cong., 2nd sess., 2.

82. 56 Stat. 306 (June 3, 1942).

83. Todd A. Forney, *The Midshipman Culture and Educational Reform: The U.S. Naval Academy, 1946–76* (Newark: University of Delaware Press, 2004), 92.

84. 64 Stat. 303 (June 30, 1950); 68 Stat. 48 (April 1, 1954).

85. A promotion is considered a separate appointment to office and is therefore subject to Senate confirmation.

86. 10 U.S.C 531 (2012); 10 U.S.C. 624 (2012).

87. Harris, *Advice and Consent*, 331.

88. 487 U.S. 654, 671–72 (1988).

89. *Edmond v. United States*, 520 U.S. 651, 661–62, 662–63 (1997).

90. Senate Committee on Military Affairs, Report No. 2, 37th Cong., 2nd sess., December 17, 1861, 3.

91. A Federal Republican, "A Review of the Constitution Proposed by the Late Convention," in *The Complete Anti-Federalist*, vol. 3, ed. Herbert J. Storing (Chicago: University of Chicago Press, 1981), 76.

92. It is worth noting, as Samuel P. Huntington explained, that "few provisions in the Constitution were agreed to with more reluctance" than the standing army provision. Huntington, *Soldier and the State*, 167.

93. Rowan Scarborough, "Navy Officer Who Shot Down Air Force Jet Won't Be Promoted after All," *Washington Times*, January 3, 2013, A2.

94. Craig Whitlock, "Senator to Put Permanent Hold on Promotion of Air Force General," *Washington Post*, June 7, 2013, A7.

95. Chris Carroll, "Helms Nomination for Space Command Withdrawn," *Stars and Stripes*, November 8, 2013, www.stripes.com/news/helms-nomination-for-space-command-withdrawn-1.251789.

96. Jennifer Steinhauer, "Sexual-Assault Measure to Be Cut from Military Bill," *New York Times*, June 12, 2013, A19; and Anna Mulrine, "Is Pentagon Response to Sexual Assault Broken? Clash over New Bill," *Christian Science Monitor*, November 7, 2013, 9.

97. Donna Cassata, "Navy Nominee Ensnared in Senate Fight over Military Policy Changes," *St. Louis Post-Dispatch*, November 7, 2013, A7.

98. P.L. 113-66, National Defense Authorization Act for Fiscal Year 2014 (December 27, 2013); Ashley Parker, "Senate Passes Pentagon Bill after Compromise on Obama Nominees," *New York Times*, December 19, 2013, A21.

3

A Safety Valve

The Truman Committee's Oversight during World War II

KATHERINE SCOTT

Since the first congressional investigation in 1792 when the House of Representatives inquired into the failed military campaign of Gen. Arthur St. Clair, members of Congress have understood wartime oversight to be a constitutional prerogative of the legislative branch. Yet congressional investigations of civil-military relations during times of war have at times been criticized as partisan efforts to dictate war policy to the commander in chief. The Senate's Special Committee to Investigate the National Defense Program, led by Democratic senator Harry Truman of Missouri during World War II, remains the most successful wartime congressional investigation. Truman and his colleagues firmly believed that Congress had a role—and a responsibility—to oversee wartime defense spending and procurement. The committee also played a less publicized but equally important role as a "safety valve," providing an outlet for the responsible expression of civilian complaints and concerns about the war effort. By exercising careful and responsible oversight, the committee exemplified effective civil-military relations during wartime. At the end of the war, the chairman would boast that the committee's careful oversight and investigation of a broad range of war-related activities had saved the nation billions of dollars in potential waste, fraud, and corruption and offered a model for future congressional investigations.

The Man from Independence

On February 10, 1941, a neatly coiffed and bespectacled senator in a well-tailored suit rose on the Senate floor to deliver a speech. This second-term senator, then fifty-seven years old, was unknown to most Americans outside the Senate and his home state. On the Senate floor that day, Harry Truman expressed his concerns about the government's national mobilization program. Truman, like many of his colleagues in Congress, was appalled by the lack of organization and coordination exhibited by the War and Navy Departments as they mobilized manpower and matériel. Congress was partly to blame for this overall lack of preparedness. It had approved a series of neutrality laws in the 1930s, discouraged military expansion, and reduced War Department appropriations.[1]

By 1940 Germany's occupation of France and the Netherlands forced the US government to respond. Upon receiving President Franklin Roosevelt's urgent request to increase defense spending, Congress appropriated more than $10.5 billion—"a sum greater than the entire budget of the United States for any of the Depression years of the 1930s"—for defense mobilization.[2] Ill-prepared to efficiently and effectively manage the defense mobilization effort, the Roosevelt administration hastily created new civilian agencies charged with distributing defense contracts. The money flowed rapidly with little planning and no oversight. Citizens observed the wastefulness of the programs in their communities and alerted elected officials. Through constituents' letters, Truman grew concerned about the government's handling and oversight of defense spending.

As a former small-business owner, Senator Truman was troubled by rumors that the government favored large manufacturers in its contract-awarding process. Intentionally or not, these policies hurt small businesses in Missouri and across the nation. Determined to examine firsthand how government dollars were being spent, Truman embarked on a road trip, traveling south from Washington, DC, to Florida, west to Texas and Oklahoma, north through Nebraska, and returning to the nation's capital via Wisconsin and Michigan. His travels took him on tours of cantonment construction sites and through plants manufacturing war matériel. Truman—who never announced himself as a member of the US Senate—saw evidence of waste everywhere. At one cantonment construction site, he was appalled by the sight of "squandered material, idle workers, and exorbitant costs that seemed typical of camp construction around the nation."[3]

The trip served as an "eye opener." He called for a Senate "investigation of the national defense program and the handling of contracts." The government distributed contracts, Truman charged, in a way that "make[s] the big men bigger and let[s] the little men go out of business or starve to death." To curtail wasteful defense spending, Congress must exercise sustained oversight. "I have had considerable experience in letting public contracts," Truman explained, recalling his service as a county judge in Missouri, "and I have never yet found a contractor who, if not watched, would not leave the Government holding the bag." It was imperative, Truman further said, that "the location of these national-defense plants and the profits that are supposed to be made on tanks, planes, and small arms, should be a matter of public record, unless we are to have the same old profiteering situation that we had in the last war."[4]

Formation of the Committee

On March 1, 1941, the Senate unanimously approved Truman's Senate Resolution 71, creating the Special Committee to Investigate the National Defense Program, commonly known as the Truman Committee. It originally comprised seven members (later increased to ten), and the resolution provided Truman with $15,000 to hire staff and conduct the investigation. Even by 1941 standards it was a small allocation for a wide-ranging inquiry, but Truman was determined to make the best of it. The legislative branch's constitutional "power to investigate," he later wrote, was even more significant during wartime, "when the Congress must delegate many of its powers."[5] Truman hired a crack team to assist the committee, including Hugh Fulton, a young prosecutor with a track record of sending corrupt officials to jail. Truman's staff selections lent the committee instant credibility. This would not be a "headline grabbing" effort but a real investigation driven by proven performers.

Truman haggled with leadership over committee membership, settling for relatively young and inexperienced members of the Senate. A few, however, had well-earned reputations as no-nonsense lawmakers—particularly Republicans Ralph Owen Brewster of Maine and Homer Ferguson of Michigan—bolstering the committee's nonpartisan reputation. For his part, Truman pledged that the investigations would not be partisan affairs; all committee decisions would be unanimously approved. Known for his amiable character and well-liked by colleagues on both sides of the aisle, Truman easily cultivated bipartisan cooperation among committee members.

An astute politician, Truman understood the potential risks of leading such an investigation. At a private meeting with the president, he assured Roosevelt that the committee would not attempt to manage the military or publicly critique Roosevelt's performance as commander in chief. Truman carefully studied the reports of the controversial Civil War–era Joint Committee on the Conduct of the War and concluded that the committee had led a "misdirected investigation," overstepping its constitutional prerogatives by attempting to "direct military operations in the field."[6] A veteran of World War I, Truman took heed from congressional investigations of that war. American isolationism during the interwar period had been driven, in part, by revelations of graft, greed, and corruption among defense contractors that emerged after the Great War. The Truman Committee sought to uncover mistakes early, "before irretrievable damage was done."[7] The Special Committee to Investigate the National Defense Program would avoid committing the same mistakes, serving as a "benevolent policeman" by promoting transparency and cost-effectiveness of defense planning and programs for the American taxpayers.

As a "benevolent policeman," the committee would rely heavily on tips supplied by civilians about issues in their communities deserving of investigation. Shortly after the committee's formation, Truman delivered a radio address describing rumors of profiteering and favoritism in the awarding of defense contracts. "When people create delays for profit, when they sell poor products for defense use, when they cheat on price and quality," he declared, "they aren't any different from a draft dodger and the public at large feels just the same way about it." Truman encouraged Americans to report to the committee "information of irregularities, based on facts, where the Government's interests have been violated." Truman and his colleagues believed that a wartime congressional investigation should provide "a safety valve for the vast volumes of complaints that pour in from all sources as to irregularities or inefficiencies in the war effort." To maintain a "united front," this reporting function was vital to the democratic process. Thousands of Americans from across the country responded, flooding Truman's Senate office with complaints. The committee's task would be "winnowing the wheat from the chaff" and working in a collaborative way with executive departments to correct mistakes where they were being made, while keeping "at a minimum the distraction" to those who managed the war effort.[8] The latter would be the Truman Committee's greatest wartime challenge.

While committee staff followed up on civilian leads, the committee called its first hearings. Secretary of War Henry Stimson offered a bleak assessment of the country's defense preparedness. For years the War Department had asked Congress for appropriations to strengthen the national defense. Isolationist sentiment among the public and members of Congress, however, delayed and sometimes reduced those appropriations. Now the government faced a seemingly impossible challenge: How to triple the size of the US military force in six months? The country desperately needed grounds and quarters to train and lodge soldiers, airmen, marines, and seamen. Existing cantonments were wholly inadequate for the vast expansion of the armed forces that Stimson anticipated in the coming months. The military urgently needed new training facilities to accommodate the needs of modern warfare and "large forces which are fully trained to operation in a war of movement." Tanks, aircraft, warships, and other modern specialized weapons were vital to the national war effort, complicated to design, and slow to build. Knowing that American manufacturers were woefully unprepared to manufacture these weapons, Stimson conceded that the War Department had at times sacrificed cost-effectiveness to meet the immediate demands of military preparedness.[9]

Investigating Military Construction

The scramble to meet the nation's defense needs created ample opportunity, Truman and his colleagues knew, for waste, graft, fraud, and corruption in the contracting process. The committee selected for its first investigation cantonment construction sites and training camps. Truman had witnessed waste and inefficiencies at these sites on his cross-country road trip. Members of Congress knew too that the War Department had requested deficiency appropriations totaling more than $338 million for the construction of camp, training, and cantonment facilities. Why was so much more needed than originally planned?

Determined to answer that question, the committee took to the road, visiting nine construction sites around the nation. After hearing witnesses and examining contracts, the committee identified three distinct, though related, problems. The construction sites were plagued by waste and inefficiency. But waste only partly explained extreme cost overruns. The committee uncovered a second problem, the cost of add-ons—projects not included in the original estimate but vital to the completion of these construction projects. Add-ons included necessities such as sewage plants, recreational facilities, parking for motorized equipment, and gasoline-storage facilities and could only be explained as a consequence of poor War Department planning.[10]

The committee learned that the War Department at times ignored its own evaluation process for locating camps. One location in Texas was not recommended as a site because the terrain was found not to meet basic requirements, yet the army invested money to expand Camp Hulen anyway. Other sites were selected, despite their obvious challenges. Camp Davis in North Carolina was constructed on a swamp, requiring extra paving for parking of vehicles. The military leased a site from the state of California near San Luis Obispo though it lacked an adequate water supply. The army developed the camp anyway, with final construction costs including temporary and permanent dams and a tunnel through a mountain to bring water to camp. All of these added costs were borne by American taxpayers, at a price of more than $2.5 million. The army planned to develop one Iowa facility at a cost of $8 million, but after work began plans were scrapped, and the facility was relocated to Missouri. The final cost to American taxpayers for poor planning? Nearly $24 million for the same type of facility. The War Department defended these expenses, citing lack of manpower and funds to provide effective oversight. But the committee reported that the army "could and should have done a much better job than it did" to anticipate problems and plan adequately for them. The committee charged planners with "running the Army along Civil War lines"—in other words, not considering the "requirements of a mechanized Army."[11]

The War Department's contract process was partly to blame for cost overruns, the committee found. Fixed-fee contracts "contained no provision to encourage the contractor to keep costs to a minimum." Investigations and hearings raised questions about "insiders" who gamed the system. In one case, a former brigadier general responsible for overseeing the army's construction division during the Great War, later a lobbyist for the building industry, had negotiated contracts for the War Department. One contract in particular caught the attention of investigators, who found he was to be paid more than $200,000 as an adviser of construction at Fort Meade, Maryland. The cost overruns, whether due to poor planning, waste and inefficiency, or exorbitant contracting fees, troubled Truman: "[We] are going to have to pay for the cost, the waste and the inefficiency in the form of increased taxation for years to come." Editorials praised the committee's work and called for the investigation to continue. The American public surely agreed with one *Washington Post* editorial: "The best way to discourage recklessness on the part of administrative officials is to keep the record of their spending before the public."[12]

It was not enough to identify the problems. The committee endeavored to solve them legislatively, if possible. In a carefully crafted report, it recommended that the War Department implement a "form of substantial contract review" to prevent waste and fraud by defense contractors in the future. These recommendations formed the basis for legislation to provide the executive branch with the tools to renegotiate defense contracts. After the law became effective in April 1942, the committee continued to review its application and later concluded that it had worked sufficiently to cut excessive profits, reduce "cost-plus" contracts, and encourage economical production and distribution among manufacturers with government contracts. The Truman Committee's reports of defense spending forced the executive branch to respond. The president created the civilian War Production Board in 1942 to centralize planning, improve efficiency, and decrease wasteful spending. For his part, Chairman Truman continued to support small business interests in the contract awarding process but, as one historian has noted, "the concept of bringing maximum efficiency to the war effort by involving tens of thousands of small enterprises was never feasible. Inexorably, the war made big manufacturing bigger."[13]

The Japanese attack on Pearl Harbor on December 7, 1941, which prompted Congress to declare war, caused some critics of the committee to call for its dissolution. The White House insisted that the committee's work was no longer necessary. Truman and his colleagues had the support of newspapers, the public, and many members of Congress, however, and stood its ground. With the nation at war, Truman predicted that the committee's work would be more vital than ever. "During the 8 months in which the special committee has operated," Truman observed, "it has noted and called attention to many things which have adversely affected production." Members pledged that the committee would "continue a constant watch for the purpose of assuring that such problems are met head-on and solved."[14]

Able leadership, thoughtful and thorough investigative work, and well-timed press releases won the committee the admiration of the public as well as the media. Though Harry Truman served as chairman for only three of the seven years of the committee, he came to symbolize to the American public and the media the very best in congressional oversight and constitutional checks and balances. Truman's likeability endeared him to the newspapermen who covered his committee's work. Allen Drury, a longtime Washington observer, called him a "fine fellow" and an "excellent man, a fine Senator and sound American." The public, Drury observed, owed a great debt to him for his fine work on the committee. Truman, for his part, enjoyed the attention, writing to his wife Bess, "I'm on the front pages of the *Kansas City Star, St. Louis Star-Times*, and the *Kansas City Journal* . . . and mentioned in about three or four other places."[15]

Investigating Curtiss-Wright

Americans heeded Truman's call to report improper, suspicious, or illegal acts related to the war effort that they witnessed in their communities, and letters continued to flow to Truman's Senate office. In 1943 the committee focused its resources on manufacturing and parts-production facilities. None proved more vital to the war effort than those of the aircraft contractors, as one Truman report concluded, because "the present conflict is largely an air war and requires swarms of airplanes."[16]

Whistleblower accounts suggested a distressingly insufficient, and at times dysfunctional, parts and assembly inspection process at key production plants. One account from an army air forces inspector based at a Curtiss-Wright manufacturing and assembly plant in Lockland, Ohio, caught the eye of committee staff. William Stout complained of the deplorable inspection process that he witnessed at the plant, which produced aircraft parts and engines. The committee organized a special subcommittee to travel to Cleveland to hear testimony.

The committee selected Stout as its key witness. With more than sixteen years' experience inspecting engines, he had been hired by the army air forces in 1942 as a teardown inspector. One of the nation's largest contractors, the Wright Aeronautical Corporation and its subsidiaries such as Curtiss-Wright produced aircraft engines and components. Their components could be found in thousands of the nation's military and transport aircraft such as the Boeing B-17 Flying Fortress, the Douglas A-20 Havoc, and the Douglas Dauntless dive-bomber. Government defense contracts had helped the company to triple in size to more than 180,000 employees. When he started at Lockland, Stout found something "radically wrong" with various vital engine components. For example, company inspectors, to Stout's dismay, repeatedly approved cracked master rod bearings as "O.K." Stout thought this created a "dangerous situation," because, as he explained to the committee, the "disintegration of the master rod bearings [would] immediately render the engine useless." He claimed that company supervisors instructed their inspectors to return bad parts to the table during the teardown process, in hopes that army inspectors "wouldn't see" the faulty parts. Those bad parts, he explained, would later be reinstalled in a final engine. When Stout protested to company inspectors, they dismissed his concerns, he explained, "because [the parts] are inspected again in the packing room." But Stout and the inspectors knew too well that in the packing room company supervisors approved the same bad parts, insisting that "they are good because they were previously inspected in the teardown assembly."[17] A classic Catch-22.

Curtiss-Wright supervisors did not emphasize "safety of operation," Stout complained, but seemed only interested in passing through as many parts and engines as they could. To that end, they worked to silence inspectors such as Stout who refused to approve bad parts and faulty engines, labeling them "troublemakers." Stout's repeated objections to lax inspection policies drew the ire of company supervisors. He recalled, "When I protested about the roughness of these bearings I was told that during war time we couldn't be too choosey." Eventually supervisors tired of Stout and transferred him to another unit with significantly reduced responsibilities. His daily activities, in his words, included "looking after loose nuts and washers in engines." Other witnesses reported similar inspection problems at the plant. Unfortunately, the committee found that some army officials had discouraged employees from exposing wrongdoing at these plants, labeling acts of "whistleblowing" as "insubordination."[18]

Based in part on testimony collected during the executive sessions in Cleveland, the committee issued a scathing report of Wright Aeronautical. The manufacturer, it concluded, was "guilty of gross negligence" in its inspection practices. G. W. Vaughan, company president, publicly challenged the committee's findings. "The only way to judge the merit of a military airplane, engine or propeller is the way that it performs in actual combat," explained Vaughan in a public statement. "By that yardstick," he concluded, "they are making an outstanding contribution to the winning of the war." Vaughan closed his statement by inviting further investigation: "Curtiss-Wright welcomes at all times official investigation of its activities."[19]

One *New York Times* editorial struck a cautious note about the Truman Committee's conclusions. For any company fulfilling thousands of government contracts, "errors almost inevitably must creep in" to the production process. Though the problems uncovered by the committee deserved attention, the *Times* urged a thoughtful approach so as not to harm the morale of thousands of valuable and skilled workers vital to the war effort. The company's record, with propellers and engines in some of the nation's most effective airplanes, deserved greater respect. "It would be extremely harmful . . . to the morale of the flyers using [Curtiss-Wright] engines, propellers, and planes," the *New York Times* cautioned, "if we allowed detailed errors, however serious they might prove to be, to be given an exaggerated prominence in the over-all record of production both as to quantity and quality."[20]

The Truman Committee's wartime oversight of manufacturers such as Wright Aeronautical provided a valuable service to the War Department. The military did not have the manpower, the expertise, or the resources (or perhaps in some cases the will) to exercise effective oversight of its key manufacturers. The demand for essential war matériel in the form of airplane parts and precious metals such as aluminum meant that there was more than a little truth in the Curtiss-Wright supervisor's claim that the nation's military "couldn't be choosey." Surely the committee recognized that the military's demands for equipment and supplies vital to the war effort outweighed all other concerns, though its members believed they had a vital role to play in providing necessary oversight of the process. Sunlight, they reasoned, would prove the best disinfectant. In most cases, open hearings and published reports raised the public's awareness of issues and therefore brought pressure to bear on the nation's manufacturers and the War Department.

The committee's much-publicized report prompted a quick response from the War Department. Undersecretary Robert Patterson explained that the committee's revelations and charges of gross negligence prompted him to take "vigorous action" at the Lockland plant. The army insisted on personnel changes and the implementation of more rigorous testing and inspection procedures and processes there. The army also "substantial[ly] increased" the number of inspectors it employed at the plant. The Justice Department's War Frauds Unit, prompted in part by the committee's investigation, later

The Senate's Truman Committee provided oversight of defense spending and procurement during World War II, traveling thousands of miles and crisscrossing the country to hear witness testimony and perform on-site inspections. Here members of the committee visit a Ford Motor Company plant in 1942. From left to right: Sen. Joseph Ball, Hugh Fulton (counsel), Sen. Prentiss Brown, Sen. Harry Truman, Paul Brown (child), Sen. Ralph Owen Brewster, Sen. James Mead, an unidentified Ford representative, Sen. Monrad Wallgren, Sen. Harold Burton, and Sen. Harley Kilgore. *Library of Congress*

brought charges against Curtiss-Wright. Civilians cheered the committee's efforts, and newspaper headlines reflected the high esteem in which the nation held the committee's work. A *Boston Globe* headline praising the committee's work was typical: "Truman Committee Report Is Masterpiece."[21]

The Canol Project: Arbitration across Federal Departments

In addition to its investigative responsibilities, the committee also served as an arbiter of disputes between civilian and military agencies during wartime. In 1942 Secretary of the Interior Harold Ickes, who served as the petroleum administrator for the war, heard rumors of a War Department plan to extract Canadian oil and transport it to Alaska. When Ickes heard of the price tag for this effort—$135 million—he sought answers from the War Department.

The Canol project, as it came to be called, was first conceived in early 1941 when an explorer brought the existence of oil wells in the Canadian arctic to the attention of the War Department. An engineering professor at the University of Kentucky, James Graham, who served as a War Department adviser on transport issues, recommended the project to Lt. Gen. Brehon Somervell. Somervell instructed Graham to investigate the possibility of obtaining oil at the site, known as Norman Wells. After conferring with a number of oil executives, many of whom were doubtful about the estimates of oil that could be obtained from the region, Graham recommended that the War Department move quickly to implement the project.[22]

The plan might have remained secret, but when Secretary Ickes heard rumors of Canol, he demanded that the War Department make details of the plan public. The Truman Committee called hearings to examine the project. Undersecretary of War Patterson defended the deal, testifying that "Canol represented an effort to develop oil resources close to Alaskan operations when other methods of speeding oil to Alaska seemed largely unavailable." Recent reports of oil reserves estimated that some fifty million barrels of oil would provide the military with a valuable reserve.[23]

Despite Patterson's strong defense of the military necessity of the project, the Truman Committee's investigation found that the project had been plagued by guesswork and uncertainty from the outset. Army air forces major general St. Clair Streett's testimony proved particularly damning. Streett, a member of the general staff, concluded that the entire project had been quickly approved after one informal meeting in late April 1942. In the aftermath of the attack on Pearl Harbor, military planners sought to develop local sources of fuel oil to supply coastal army and navy units. At the time of Graham's enthusiastic recommendation to Somervell, no formal survey of Norman Wells had been completed. No one representing the United States had surveyed the terrain to document the adverse conditions found in this far northern land—including mountains and subzero winter conditions that would make drilling and transporting the oil difficult. Testimony suggested that War Department officials had asked surprisingly few practical questions about the project, including details about transporting the extracted oil from Norman Wells to Whitehorse, Canada, where a refinery was to be erected, a distance of approximately fifteen hundred miles. In part because the plans lacked these crucial specifics, Streett recalled that oil company representatives at the meeting remained "pessimistic" about the cost-effectiveness of developing the oil fields at Norman Wells. A member of the Truman Committee asked Streett, "Were you given enough information for you to be able to form any judgment on the project, whatsoever?" Streett responded, "None except, was there a requirement [for oil]? Would it be a good thing to have it, and locally?"[24]

Testimony revealed that civilian agencies had not been invited to the informational meeting in April, nor had they been advised at any time of the project. Though the army urged development of oil to support navy coastal bases and transports, the War Department did not consult with navy representatives about the project.[25] When questioned about the total cost of the Canol project, Graham defended his initial recommendation saying, "This is war, gentleman. I do not stop to consider the cost of things in time of war."[26] Other civilian organizations with an interest in such projects also demanded answers about Canol, including the petroleum administrator, the War Production Board, the War Shipping Administration, the State Department, and the Lend-Lease Administration. Even the oil contract negotiated on the army's behalf by the State Department drew sharp criticism from members of Congress and civilian agencies. The United States retained no postwar rights to the oil fields developed with US taxpayer money. All costs associated with prospecting for oil and developing any wells would be borne by the US government, not the oil companies hired to do the work. At the end of the war, it was agreed, the United States would sell the oil fields to Canada at cost.[27]

Based upon the testimony of those involved in the early development of the project, as well as an on-the-ground assessment conducted by committee staff, the Truman Committee submitted a highly critical report of the Canol project. When the project was first envisioned in the spring of 1942, the nation "had many needs for transportation, materials, and manpower on military and naval projects vital to the prosecution of the war." The nation's limited resources, the committee argued, should have been invested in projects with the greatest potential return on investment. The Canol project, it concluded, was not one worthy of development.[28] The decision to pursue the project was made by military leadership "without adequate consideration or study." General Somervell, according to the committee's assessment, bore full responsibility. He "acted quickly, but he acted on the basis of faulty and unnecessarily incomplete consideration of the project by himself and his subordinates and without consulting other governmental agencies and private concerns with oil experience." Somervell did not heed warnings from experts that the timeline was unrealistic or concerns about the project's "unsoundness" and "excessive costs." The general's "insistence on the project in the face of these repeated warnings was inexcusable," the committee concluded. The committee urged the War Department to consider discontinuing the project. Patterson launched a media blitz, arguing that the project was deemed a "military necessity" in 1942 and that the project was only being criticized in "light of our good fortune" in 1943. "Wars are not won in retrospect," Patterson asserted.[29]

In a rare public display, two Democratic members of the committee openly disagreed with the committee's final recommendations, declaring their support for continuing the Canol project. In this unusual case, the committee's careful research and the testimony it collected from critics of the project, including high-ranking civilian officials, failed to sway a congressional majority to support its conclusions. Congress continued to fund the project. The War Department insisted that Canadian oil might be needed for an offensive against Japan and therefore was still vital to the war effort. The project was finally completed near war's end, nearly two years beyond its projected completion and too late to have a substantive impact on the US war effort.[30]

As the Canol case suggests, despite its many triumphs the Truman Committee did not succeed in every case to convince the War Department to follow its recommendations. The committee was limited in its efforts to influence certain aspects of defense planning, particularly those handled by strong War Department administrators who had the confidence of the public and members of Congress. It was a lesson that Truman would remember later when, as president of the United States, he pushed to reform the nation's military establishment.

International Oversight

In its first two years, the Truman Committee investigated a broad range of concerns, including high-profile issues such as labor strikes and national oil policy and more mundane matters such as food waste and shortages in cigarette supplies. It proved remarkably successful acting as an intermediary between military and civilian programs and interests during a time of national crisis. The release of its reports, coordinated to achieve maximum publicity with carefully timed press releases, reassured the public that Congress maintained careful oversight over war-related issues. Its relative success on these issues led senators to expand its oversight mission overseas. On July 25, 1943, five senators—two from the Truman Committee and three from the Senate Committee on Military Affairs—set out on a fact-finding mission abroad. Inspired by the work of the Truman Committee, this ad hoc committee, chaired by Georgia Democrat Richard Russell, would "examine every phase of the entire war program."[31]

Owen Brewster and Democrat James Mead of New York served as the Truman Committee's eyes and ears, gathering information about how military and civilian agencies spent "the billions of dollars appropriated for the war effort." How were congressionally appropriated funds being used abroad? Did the matériel it purchased reach the fighting front "quickly and in good condition?" Truman directed Brewster and Mead to provide assessment of six issues: transportation and supply to the front; the condition of landing facilities abroad and US rights to those facilities after the war; administration of the war effort; the distribution of American supplies to foreign civilian populations; the quality of engines, their repair, and replacement parts on the front lines; and the "function of the Office of War Information." Committee representatives would observe the relationships that the US government maintained with civilian organizations abroad that were "authorized to expend funds and to distribute American property." The committee asserted that "the time to correct mistakes" and the "time to gain equitable settlements to our post-war rights" is now.[32]

The fact-finding committee traveled some forty-five thousand miles over sixty-five days, to Great Britain, Italy, North Africa, the Middle East, India, China, and Australia. Its members spoke to military commanders and interviewed soldiers, airmen, marines, and seamen. They met with civilian contractors supplying military bases and inspected their arrangements. Upon their return, Brewster and Mead provided detailed observations of their travel in executive session and in public statements, encouraging members to consider formulating postwar policies before the war concluded. Clearly the Truman Committee's desire to identify and solve problems before "irretrievable damage was done" had influenced their reporting. Of particular concern to participants in the overseas tour was determining US access to airfields and landing strips around the world when the hostilities ceased. The US government had designed, constructed, and paid for these projects, but current arrangements provided that the United States would turn these properties over to the host countries at the conclusion of the war. The overseas fact-finding committee members also emphasized the need for the United States to assume a leadership role in the postwar settlement. Overall, members marveled at the excellent work being performed around the world by civilian organizations such as the Red Cross and praised American troops. In contrast to the typically critical reports generated by the Truman Committee, Brewster and Mead's public observations glowed with admiration for the allied war effort.[33]

Conclusion

The Truman Committee's work as "benevolent policeman" during World War II serves as an exemplar of effective civil-military oversight. The committee's investigations uncovered cases of wasteful spending, fraud, and corruption in the manufacturing and procurement of war matériel.

But it served another purpose, one that scholars have often overlooked. Truman's call for citizens to "police" the war effort was a stroke of genius— politically and socially uniting the civilian and military war effort in significant ways. The committee provided a dedicated outlet for civilians to express their concerns and frustrations about the war effort. More important, the constant and well-publicized investigations suggested to the public that their sacrifices on the home front were not in vain. Defense contractors have always profited from war-related defense spending. The Truman Committee's efforts to assiduously document that spending and to encourage corrective measures when appropriate provided a "safety valve" in civil-military relations, an effective tool for maintaining a united front during war. In recognition of its successful oversight, the Senate made the Truman Committee permanent in 1948, renaming it the Permanent Subcommittee on Investigations of the Governmental Affairs Committee and tasking it with investigating issues of waste and fraud throughout the executive branch.

As first chairman of the Senate Special Committee to Investigate the National Defense Program, Truman earned a reputation as one of the nation's "most valuable" public officials. His political fortune rose with his national reputation, culminating with his nomination as Franklin Roosevelt's vice president in 1944. Truman made his committee service a centerpiece of the campaign. "Proof that a divine Providence watches over the United States," wrote Senator Truman in 1944, "is furnished by the fact that we have managed to escape disaster even though our scrambled professional military set-up has been an open invitation to catastrophe."[34] As committee chairman Truman, perhaps more than another other elected official, understood the numerous challenges faced by the US military during wartime. As an expert at identifying waste, duplication, and inefficiency, he came to believe that one of the greatest problems of the US war effort had been the lack of co-ordination between American military forces. When he became president in 1945 after Roosevelt's unexpected death, he patiently shepherded through Congress legislation to unify the nation's military. The National Security Act, which became law on July 26, 1947, reorganized the army, navy, and newly created air force under one cabinet-level secretary of defense. Thus the Truman Committee investigation had an immeasurable impact on the US war effort during World War II and helped to shape the nation's postwar defense establishment.

Notes

1. Theodore Wilson, "The Truman Committee on War Mobilization, 1941–44," in *Congress Investigates: A Critical and Documentary History*, ed. Roger Bruns, David Hostetter, and Raymond Smock (New York: Facts on File, 2011), 639.

2. Alonzo Hamby, *Man of the People* (New York: Oxford University Press, 1995), 248; "Special Committee to Investigate the National Defense Program," Notable Senate Investigations, US Senate Historical Office, www.senate.gov/artandhistory/history/common/investigations/pdf/TrumanCommittee_fullcitations.pdf.

3. Hamby, *Man of the People,* 249.

4. Harry Truman, *Memoirs, Volume 1: Year of Decisions* (Garden City, NY: Doubleday, 1955), 164–65; US Congress, Senate, 77th Cong., 1st sess., *Congressional Record*, February 10, 1941, 830–38.

5. Truman, *Memoirs*, 168.

6. Ibid., 188–89.

7. Paul W. Ward, "Truman Group Would Avoid the 160 Probes of Last War: Seeks to Prevent Waste, Inefficiency and Fraud and Nip Scandals in the Bud," *Baltimore Sun*, July 13, 1943, 15; Truman, *Memoirs*, 167. For congressional investigations of World War I, see John Edward Wiltz, "The Nye Committee on the Munitions Industry, 1934–1936," in *Congress Investigates: A Critical Documentary*, ed. Roger A. Bruns, David L. Hostetter, and Raymond W. Smock (New York: Facts on File, 2011), 540–84.

8. US Congress, Senate, Special Committee to Investigate the National Defense Program, *Visit to the Various War Fronts by Several Members of the United States Senate*, 78th Cong., 1st sess. (Washington, DC: Government Printing Office, 1943), 22.

9. US Congress, Senate, Senate Special Committee to Investigate the National Defense Program, *Hearings before a Special Committee Investigating the National Defense Program*, Part 1, 76th Cong., 2nd sess. (Washington, DC: Government Printing Office, 1941), 3.

10. US Congress, Senate, Special Committee to Investigate the National Defense Program, *Camp and Cantonment Investigations*, 76th Cong., 2nd sess. (Washington, DC: Government Printing Office, 1941), 1–7.

11. Ibid., 1–9; Paul W. Ward, "4 Firms Named by Marshall as Fee Source," *Baltimore Sun*, May 7, 1941, 28.

12. US Congress, Senate, Special Committee to Investigate the National Defense Program, *Investigation of the National Defense Program*, 76th Cong., 2nd sess. (Washington, DC: Government Printing Office, 1941), 14, 18–19; and "Those Extra Costs," *Washington Post*, May 2, 1941, 10.

13. US Congress, Senate, Special Committee to Investigate the National Defense Program, *Investigation of the National Defense Program: Renegotiation of War Contracts,* 78th Cong., 2nd sess. (Washington, DC: Government Printing Office, 1944), 40; Hamby, *Man of the People*, 258.

14. US Congress, Senate, *Congressional Record*, August 14, 1941, 7118; Paul W. Ward, "Probers Declare Defense Lacking," *Baltimore Sun*, August 15, 1941, 6; and "Special Committee to Investigate the National Defense Program."

15. Allen Drury, *A Senate Journal, 1943–1945* (New York: McGraw-Hill, 1963), 106; "Special Committee to Investigate the National Defense Program."

16. US Congress, Senate, Special Committee to Investigate the National Defense Program, *Investigation of the National Defense Program: Appendix III*, 77th Cong., 1st sess. (Washington, DC: Government Printing Office, 1941), 200.

17. Executive session transcripts, Records of the Special Committee of the Senate to Investigate the National Defense Program, RG 46 SEN 79A-F30, HE 5, Hearings about Wright Aeronautical Corp., Box 1303, 2–12, National Archives and Records Administration, Washington, DC.

18. Ibid., 8–9; "Says Public Should Know Test Results," *Hartford Courant*, October 1, 1943, 7.

19. "Curtiss-Wright President Answers Truman Committee," *Baltimore Sun*, July 11, 1943, 14.

20. "Truman Committee Charges," *New York Times*, July 12, 1943, 14.

21. "Army Verifies Most of Truman Data on Wright: Acted to Remedy Facts, Patterson Says," *Chicago Daily Tribune*, July 13 1943, 10; Ward, "Truman Group Would Avoid"; and Fletcher Pratt, "Truman Committee Report Is Masterpiece," *Boston Globe*, April 24, 1943, 5.

22. US Congress, Senate, Special Committee to Investigate the National Defense Program, *Additional Report of the Special Committee Investigating the National Defense Program: The Canol Project*, 78th Cong., 1st sess. (Washington, DC: Government Printing Office, 1944), 1–5.

23. William H. Stringer, "Canol Project Is Defended as Vital War Need," *Christian Science Monitor*, November 23, 1943, 9.

24. Senate Special Committee to Investigate the National Defense Program, *Additional Report of the Special Committee Investigating the National Defense Program: The Canol Project*, 22–24.

25. Ibid., 9–10.

26. Stringer, "Canol Project Is Defended."

27. Senate Special Committee to Investigate the National Defense Program, *Additional Report of the Special Committee Investigating the National Defense Program: The Canol Project*, 3–5.

28. Ibid., 2.

29. Ibid., 7; John MacCormac, "Canol Condemned by Truman Board," *New York Times*, January 9, 1944, 17.

30. "Canol Report Hit by Truman Group," *Washington Post*, January 9, 1944, M1; "Senate Votes Funds to Continue Operation of Canol Oil Project," *Wall Street Journal*, June 22, 1944, 4; and "Army Insists on Finishing Canol Project Despite Cost: Oil May Be Needed for Offensive against Japan," *Wall Street Journal*, November 24, 1943, 12.

31. US Congress, Senate, Special Committee to Investigate the National Defense, *Investigation of the National Defense Program: Report of Subcommittee concerning Investigations Overseas*, 78th Cong., 2nd sess. (Washington DC: Government Printing Office, 1944), 2.

32. Ibid.

33. US Congress, Senate, Special Committee to Investigate the National Defense, *Visit to the Various War Fronts*.

34. US Congress, Senate, 80th Cong., 1st sess., *Congressional Record*, March 14, 1947, 2064–65.

4

The Political, Policy, and Oversight Roles of Congressional Defense Commissions

JORDAN TAMA

One of the most unappreciated ways in which members of Congress have sought to influence military policy in recent decades is through the creation of ad hoc advisory commissions.[1] From the beginning of the Ronald Reagan administration in January 1981 to the end of the George W. Bush administration in January 2009, Congress established at least twenty-three temporary, independent commissions in the area of defense policy or military affairs.[2] The mandates of these commissions spanned a wide array of defense issues, from broad examinations of military roles and missions to more tailored probes of specific issues, including nuclear weapons policy, defense contracting, military basing arrangements, the roles of the National Guard and reserves, policies concerning women and minorities, the nature of certain security threats, and the value of particular weapon systems. (For a list of these commissions, see table 4.1.) The stories of these commissions provide an important window on many defense policy debates of recent years and reveal important dimensions of the politics of US defense policymaking.

In this chapter, I provide an overview of the role of ad hoc congressional commissions in US defense policymaking and briefly analyze the creation and impact of a few of these commissions. My analysis—which draws on interviews and primary source research—shows that lawmakers have created defense commissions for a variety of reasons, including to advance an agenda of defense reform or policy change, facilitate oversight of the Department of Defense (DOD), and avoid blame or kick the can down the road on a contentious issue. I further show that while the impact of defense commissions has varied widely, some of these commissions have exerted significant influence on legislative debates or policy changes. Overall my analysis demonstrates that commissions are an important tool of congressional defense politics, policymaking, and oversight.

Table 4.1

Ad Hoc Defense Commissions Mandated by Congress, 1981–2008

Name	Chair(s)	Year Authorized
Chemical Warfare Review Commission	Walter Stoessel	1984
Commission on Merchant Marine and Defense	Jeremiah Denton	1984
President's Blue Ribbon Task Group on Nuclear Weapons Program Management	William Clark	1984
Defense Base Closure and Realignment Commission[a]	Jack Edwards and Abraham Ribicoff	1988
National Commission on Defense and National Security[b]	NA	1990
Commission on the Assignment of Women in the Armed Forces	Robert Herres	1991
National Commission on the Future Role of the United States Nuclear Weapons[b]	NA	1991
President's Advisory Board on Arms Proliferation Policy	Janne Nolan	1993
Commission on Roles and Missions of the Armed Forces	John White	1993
Commission on Maintaining United States Nuclear Weapons Expertise	Henry Chiles	1996
Commission to Assess the Ballistic Missile Threat to the United States	Donald Rumsfeld	1996
National Defense Panel[c]	Philip Odeen	1996
Congressional Commission on Military Training and Gender-Related Issues	Anita Blair	1997
Long-Range Air Power Review Panel	Larry Welch	1997
Commission to Assess United States National Security Space Management and Organization	Donald Rumsfeld	1999
Commission on the Future of the United States Aerospace Industry	Robert Walker	2000
Commission to Assess the Threat to the United States from Electromagnetic Pulse Attack	William Graham	2000
Commission on Review of Overseas Military Facility Structure of the United States	Al Cornella	2003
Commission on the National Guard and Reserves	Arnold Punaro	2004
Independent Commission on the Security Forces of Iraq	James Jones	2007
Commission on the Strategic Posture of the United States	William Perry	2008
Commission on Wartime Contracting in Iraq and Afghanistan	Michael Thibault and Christopher Shays	2008
Military Leadership Diversity Commission	Lester Lyles	2008

[a] In 1990 and 2001 Congress authorized additional base closure and realignment commissions.

[b] I found no record that these commissions were appointed or operated.

[c] Congress created the National Defense Panel to provide an independent assessment of the 1997 Quadrennial Defense Review (QDR). In 2007 Congress made permanent the requirement for an independent panel to assess each QDR.

Why Policymakers Create Ad Hoc Commissions

While definitions of them vary, ad hoc commissions have three key characteristics: They are established by an official act of Congress or the executive branch, their mandate is temporary, and their membership includes at least one member who does not serve in government.[3] Scholars have identified a number of reasons why policymakers create such commissions. Amy Zegart has concluded that most commissions are created to build support for an agenda, provide information to government officials, or foster consensus and compromise.[4] Focusing particularly on commissions established by the executive branch, David Filtner, Kenneth Kitts, and Thomas Wolanin have found that presidents also create commissions to provide symbolic reassurance, buy time, deflect criticism, or maintain the initiative in policymaking.[5]

Colton Campbell has conducted the most comprehensive analysis of commissions established by Congress. Through case studies and numerous interviews of congressional policymakers, Campbell finds that Congress usually creates commissions to obtain expertise, reduce the congressional workload, or avoid blame, with other motivations including building consensus around legislative proposals and sidestepping legislative gridlock.[6] Kent Weaver has also highlighted the blame-avoidance motivation for congressional commissions, noting that lawmakers sometimes delay incurring political costs by instructing a commission to report on a sensitive issue after an election.[7]

My analysis of congressional defense commissions builds on the work of these scholars and on my own previous work on the impact of presidential and congressional commissions that have examined national security issues.[8] In this chapter, I extend that scholarship by offering original accounts of several congressional commissions that examined defense issues.

Before proceeding with those accounts, it is worth noting a couple of basic patterns concerning congressional defense commissions. First, Congress has created commissions on defense matters more frequently since the end of the Cold War. Of the twenty-three commissions established between 1981 and 2009, nineteen were created after 1990. This growing use of defense commissions by Congress is one reason why they are worth studying. Second, the annual enactment of national defense authorization acts (NDAAs) provides a useful vehicle for establishing defense commissions. Seventeen of the twenty-three commissions were established through an NDAA, with the remainder established as part of defense appropriation laws or as a stand-alone measure. (Congress's frequent failure in recent years to enact annual authorization laws in some other policy areas—including diplomatic affairs and foreign aid—generally makes it harder for Congress to create commissions in those areas.)

I analyzed each of these commissions using a variety of sources, including legislative text, congressional committee reports, transcripts of congressional hearings and statements, interviews of congressional officials and commission participants, contemporaneous newspaper coverage, and secondary sources. Based on this research, I determined that lawmakers have generally sought to create defense commissions in order to advance a defense policy or reform agenda, aid oversight of the DOD, or shift blame or delay a decision on a controversial issue.

Commissions as Vehicles for Policy Change or Reform

One of the most common congressional motivations for creating defense commissions has been to advance a defense policy or reform agenda, which can be as narrow as developing a specific weapon system or as broad as changing the military's overall roles and missions. Typically in these cases, one or more lawmakers favors adopting a policy or set of reforms that is opposed by the DOD and/or other lawmakers and sees a commission as a useful tool for building support for their policy preference or placing pressure on the Pentagon to make changes.

The Ballistic Missile Threat Commission

In September 1996 Congress established the Commission to Assess the Ballistic Missile Threat to the United States, as part of that year's NDAA.[9] The commission's mandate was to "assess the nature and magnitude of the existing and emerging ballistic missile threat to the United States."

The congressional motivation in creating the commission was to advance a largely Republican agenda of deploying a national anti-ballistic-missile defense system. The commission was created during divided government, with President Bill Clinton in the White House and Republicans controlling the House and Senate. While the Clinton administration prioritized the development of theater missile-defense capabilities and argued that the 1972 Anti-Ballistic Missile (ABM) Treaty prohibited the deployment of a national missile-defense system, Republican congressional leaders sought to require the administration to move forward aggressively with the development and deployment of a national system, despite the ABM Treaty.[10]

In 1995 Congress initially included provisions in the NDAA that required the rapid development and deployment of a national missile-defense system, stipulated that development of such a system did not conflict with the ABM Treaty, and authorized about $300 million more in missile-defense spending than Clinton requested.[11] However, congressional Republicans removed these provisions after Clinton vetoed the legislation in December. Around the same time, the US intelligence community assessed in a national intelligence estimate (NIE) that no country, other than the declared nuclear powers, would develop or acquire a ballistic missile that could threaten the continental United States for at least fifteen years. Republicans argued that this NIE underestimated the ballistic missile threat from so-called rogue nations.[12]

In 1996 Republicans introduced a new stand-alone bill mandating the deployment of a "highly effective" national missile-defense system by 2003 and sought to make their disagreement with the administration on missile defense an issue in that year's presidential campaign.[13] But in the face of another likely presidential veto, Republican congressional leaders chose not to include that legislative language in the 1996 NDAA, opting instead to use the NDAA to take the less controversial step of establishing a commission in the hope that the commission would aid their missile-defense agenda while enabling them to score political points against the administration. As a former DOD official who was involved in the issue commented, "some of the congressional Republicans were true believers [in missile defense], and some of them wanted to take political advantage of this."[14]

The commission's partisan context was reflected in the commission's design, which allowed six of the nine commission members to be chosen by Republican congressional leaders, while the other three members were chosen by Democratic congressional leaders.[15] The then speaker of the House, Newt Gingrich (R-GA), chose former (and future) secretary of defense Donald Rumsfeld to serve as the commission's chairman. The other commissioners included national security experts, former defense officials, and retired military officers.

The commission's full report, issued in July 1998, was classified, but the commission issued an unclassified executive summary. In it, the commission stated unanimously that North Korea and Iran "would be able to inflict major destruction on the US within about five years of a decision to acquire" ballistic missiles with biological or nuclear payloads, while stating that Iraq could do the same within ten years of such a decision.[16] This conclusion clearly contradicted the intelligence community's estimate that these countries would not have such capability until at least 2010. However, the commission did not make any specific policy recommendations regarding the development or deployment of a national missile-defense system. William Schneider, a commission member, recalled: "Rumsfeld made a determination that with its heterogeneous membership the commission had a better chance of producing a unanimous report if it focused on the ballistic missile threat to the US [rather than also considering missile-defense options]. That turned out to be a good move because the Democratic appointees were pretty negative on missile defense but could agree on a narrow assessment of the threat."[17]

Congressional Republicans argued nevertheless that the report's conclusion regarding the threat demonstrated the need to move forward quickly with a national missile-defense system. Rep. Floyd Spence (R-SC), chair of the House National Security Committee, commented after the report was issued, "The American people have been lulled into a false sense of security since the end of the Cold War, and I hope that the commission's report will send out a wake-up call."[18] But Republicans remained unable in 1998 to enact into law a requirement for the deployment of a national missile-defense system. In September 1998—two months after the commission reported—Senate Republicans brought to the floor legislation that would require such deployment as soon as the technology for a system was available, but they fell one vote short of overcoming a Democratic filibuster on the bill.[19] This outcome was the same as an earlier vote on the same legislation in May 1998—two months before the commission reported—suggesting that the commission had not immediately shifted the debate on Capitol Hill.[20]

In July 1999 Congress did enact legislation stating that it is US policy to deploy a national missile-defense system as soon as technologically possible—but only after missile-defense supporters in Congress modified the legislation in order to obtain more Democratic support.[21] These changes included the removal of language criticizing US intelligence assessments and preparedness with regard to the missile threat, the addition of a provision indicating that the legislation did not in itself imply a change in funding levels for missile-defense programs, and the addition of language stating that it was the policy of the United States to seek negotiated reductions in Russian nuclear forces. In a detailed analysis of the debate over this legislation, David Auerswald has explained that these largely symbolic changes—which did not compel any particular action—weakened Democratic resistance to the legislation by allowing President Clinton and congressional Democrats to claim that the legislation emphasized arms control as much as missile-defense deployment.[22] While the commission's trumpeting of the missile threat appears to have contributed at the margins to the legislation's enactment, the willingness of missile-defense advocates in Congress to give Democrats a face-saving way to support the legislation was at least as important to this outcome as the commission itself.

The Commission on Roles and Missions of the Armed Forces

Three years before Congress created the Ballistic Missile Threat Commission to advance a missile-defense agenda, it established the Commission on Roles and Missions of the Armed Forces to advance an agenda of broad defense re-form. This commission's creation in 1993 was driven principally by Sen. Sam Nunn of Georgia, the Democratic chair of the Armed Services Committee. Nunn believed that, with the end of the Cold War, the United States should pursue a major realignment and consolidation of the roles and missions of the military services in order to reduce overlapping functions and adapt the military to the new global environment.[23]

When a February 1993 report on roles and missions by Joint Chiefs of Staff chairman Colin Powell disappointed Nunn by largely maintaining the status quo, Nunn sought to establish an independent commission on the subject through the NDAA.[24] The legislation, enacted in November 1993, mandated that the commission "review the efficacy and appropriateness for the post–Cold War era of the current allocations among the Armed Forces of roles, missions, and functions" and stated, in a reflection of Nunn's frustration with the Pentagon, that "it is difficult for any organization, and may be particularly difficult for the Department of Defense (DOD), to reform itself without the benefit and authority provided by external perspectives and analysis."[25]

The commission's eleven members, who were all appointed by the secretary of defense, included former government national security officials and retired flag officers who had served, respectively, in the air force, army, Marine Corps, navy, and Air National Guard. The commission was chaired by John White, a former Carter administration defense official who was nominated by the Clinton administration to be deputy secretary of defense soon before the commission issued its final report in 1995.

Given the congressional motivation for the commission, the DOD was unsurprisingly unenthusiastic about it. The then deputy secretary of defense, John Deutch, even tried to limit the commission's budget and restrict its ability to hire DOD personnel as staff.[26] The commission also faced resistance from the military services. As Randy Jayne, a senior consultant to the commission, recalled, "The services were frightened to death that we'd raise roles and missions questions that would hurt their budget and force structure."[27] In an effort to prevent that outcome, the services lobbied the commission heavily to protect their priorities.[28]

The commission's inclusion among its members of a retired flag officer from each of the services also presented a substantial obstacle to a major rethinking of roles and missions. Although these officers were retired, they generally maintained a high degree of loyalty to their services and tended—though with varying degrees—to support their service's preferences. Commission deputy executive director Gene Porter commented, "The retired four-star members of the commission didn't want to do anything that would threaten service equities."[29]

This dynamic was particularly evident when the commission considered major force structure changes. For instance, some advocates of major change called for consolidating the air forces of the different services or even consolidating the entire army and Marine Corps—while others questioned the need for all four services to have "deep attack" capabilities for striking enemy forces at a very long distance. But the retired flag officers on the commission generally resisted these ideas.[30] As a result, the commission did not recommend any major roles and missions changes in its May 1995 report. Commissioner Jeffrey Smith said, "What we did was pretty minor considering what Congress was hoping we would do."[31] Indeed, a journalist noted that reaction to the report on Capitol Hill was "decidedly tepid."[32]

The commission's impact was not negligible, however. It did propose a wide range of changes designed to make the DOD operate more coherently, effectively, and efficiently, and many of these proposals were at least partially adopted. The commission's most important recommendations included proposals to create a new military command responsible for joint training and integration of forces based in the United States, consolidate uniformed and civilian staffs within each military department, outsource or privatize many noncombat support functions, and establish a White House–directed interagency quadrennial strategy review that would shape the DOD's own planning processes.[33]

The prospects for adopting these and other commission proposals got a boost when White entered the Pentagon as deputy secretary of defense one month after the commission reported. In his new position, he created and oversaw a systematic process designed to track and advance implementation of the commission's proposals. Ted Warner, who ran this process as assistant secretary of defense for strategy and requirements, commented, "White had invested a lot of time in the commission. Unsurprisingly, he wanted to audit the commission's requirements and what we could do about them. It was his baby."[34]

In the end, some of the commission's proposals were fully implemented, while others were abandoned in the face of resistance from parts of the DOD or implemented in ways that departed from the commission's vision. For instance, with congressional authorization, the DOD did create a new Joint Forces Command and privatize some department functions, but service resistance blocked restructuring of military department staffs. As for the proposal to establish an interagency quadrennial strategy review, the then secretary of defense, William Perry, and the congressional Armed Services Committees chose instead to establish a DOD-led Quadrennial Defense Review—in part so that the DOD and its oversight committees could maintain control of the review process.[35]

Commissions as Vehicles for Aiding Oversight

Another common congressional motivation for the creation of defense commissions has been to help lawmakers conduct oversight of the DOD on a certain issue. Usually when lawmakers seek an independent analysis of a technical defense issue, they mandate a study by a standing advisory body, such as by the Government Accountability Office (GAO), the National Academy of Sciences, or the Defense Science Board, or by a federally funded research and development center such as the Rand Corporation or the Institute for Defense Analyses. But in some cases, lawmakers may seek to give a higher political profile to an independent study and may therefore create an ad hoc commission comprising experts and luminaries instead of turning to one of these standing expert groups.

Commission on Wartime Contracting in Iraq and Afghanistan

In July 2007 Democratic senators Claire McCaskill of Missouri and Jim Webb of Virginia—both members of the Armed Services Committee—introduced an amendment to the NDAA that would establish a commission to study contracting by US government agencies for security, reconstruction, and logistical-support functions in the Iraq and Afghanistan wars.[36] The legislative proposal also mandated the commission to assess waste, fraud, abuse, and potential legal violations by contractors in the two military theaters. Webb and McCaskill advanced the measure in the context of numerous reports of fraud and excess spending by contractors in Iraq and Afghanistan. In a press release, the senators and other cosponsors of the proposal said the commission "would significantly increase transparency and accountability and generate important solutions for systematic contracting problems, potentially saving taxpayers billions of dollars."[37]

At the same time, lawmakers surely knew that an investigation of wrongdoing by contractors who had been hired during the George W. Bush administration could be politically damaging to Republicans. This reality was reflected in the political breakdown of support for and opposition to the measure: All seventeen of the amendment's original cosponsors in the Senate were Democrats, and Bush opposed the commission's establishment. When Bush signed the NDAA, which mandated the commission's establishment, in January 2008, he accompanied his signature with a signing statement that cited the commission's creation as one of four NDAA provisions that "could inhibit the President's ability to carry out his constitutional obligations to take care that the laws be faithfully executed, to protect national security, to supervise the executive branch, and to execute his authority as Commander in Chief."[38]

Nevertheless, Bush ultimately allowed the commission to operate and appointed two of its eight members, as required by the law. Two of the other members were appointed by Republican congressional leaders, while the remaining four were appointed by Democratic congressional leaders. The commission's oversight mission was reflected in the commission's membership, as all of the commissioners—including the Republican appointees—had backgrounds in government management, contracting, and/or oversight. The commission was chaired by former Defense Contract Audit Agency deputy director Michael Thibault and former representative Christopher Shays (R-CT), who had served as the ranking member on the House Oversight and Government Reform Subcommittee on National Security and Foreign Affairs.[39] The commission's investigation was extensive, including twenty fact-finding trips to Iraq, Afghanistan, and other overseas locations; twenty-five public hearings; and more than a thousand meetings with government officials, contractors, and experts.[40]

In its final unanimous report, released in August 2011, the commission concluded, "At least $31 billion, and possibly as much as $60 billion, has been lost to contract waste and fraud in America's contingency operations in Iraq and Afghanistan."[41] The commission attributed these losses to a number of factors, including an overreliance on contractors by the DOD, the State Department, and the US Agency for International Development; inadequate legal, policy, and regulatory guidance for the use of contractors; and a failure by agencies to treat contracting as a core function. The commission also proposed a variety of reforms designed to improve government management and oversight of contracting.

The commission's impact has been substantial. In February 2012 McCaskill and Webb introduced a bill based in large part on the commission's proposals.[42] The senators then successfully attached many of the bill's provisions to the NDAA.[43] That legislation, enacted in January 2013, adopted commission recommendations by, among other things, giving chief acquisitions officers in federal agencies expanded responsibilities for overseeing contracts, requiring the recording by agencies of certain data regarding contractor performance, making the chairman of the Joint Chiefs of Staff responsible for determining contract support requirements throughout the military, increasing military training and education regarding contracting, and requiring new DOD annual reporting about its contract support capability.

A 2012 audit by the GAO, which was requested by McCaskill, Webb, and a third senator, found that a number of other commission proposals were adopted by the DOD through its own authority. For instance, in February 2012 the DOD issued a regulation that gives it a new ability to withhold a percentage of a contractor's payments when a contractor's business systems are flawed. But the GAO also found that the DOD had not taken any action on half of the commission's proposals.[44]

Even with the January 2013 NDAA changes, a large number of commission proposals have not been acted on, including proposals to establish a permanent inspector general for contingency operations and to automatically refer individuals alleged to have engaged in criminal action under a contract to a suspension-and-debarment official. Some of these proposals were dropped from the NDAA in the face of opposition from contractors and/or the Barack Obama administration.[45] In January 2013 McCaskill—who had been reelected to the Senate two months earlier—said continued scrutiny would be necessary to ensure effective implementation of the changes that had been enacted, adding, "I'm not going away. I've got six more years to stay on these guys about the way they spend money."[46]

Commissions as Vehicles for Avoiding Blame or Delaying Action

A final common congressional motivation for the creation of defense commissions is to avoid political blame or delay decision making on a controversial issue. In these cases, lawmakers generally see a commission as a useful tool for passing the buck or kicking the can down the road. On the one hand, a commission's establishment can allow lawmakers to delay dealing with a contentious issue by enabling them to say they are awaiting the commission's findings before taking a position on the issue. On the other hand, lawmakers may expect that, when the commission reports, its political credibility will provide valuable political cover for them to take a position that might be unpopular with important constituencies.

The most well-known blame-avoidance commission in US defense policy is the Defense Base Closure and Realignment Commission (BRAC), which was created by Congress in 1988 to generate a list of US military installations that should be closed. As Colton Campbell, Christopher Deering, and Kenneth Mayer have explained, Congress created this commission to insulate lawmakers from politically unpopular decisions to close military bases in their states or districts.[47] Under the law creating the BRAC, the commission's base closure recommendations, once approved by the secretary of defense, would go into effect unless Congress rejected the entire set of recommendations within forty-five days. This "automation of the decision-making process"—in Deering's words—prevented lawmakers from trying to remove individual bases in their districts or states from the list once it had been submitted to Congress and enabled lawmakers to deflect constituents' complaints by blaming the commission for the closures.[48] Douglas Kriner and Andrew Reeves have further shown that lawmakers also created the BRAC to prevent presidents from targeting their partisan opponents in Congress with base closures in their states or districts.[49]

The BRAC differs from the other congressional defense commissions discussed in this chapter in two ways: Congress gave the BRAC unusual power in stipulating that its proposals would be implemented unless Congress explicitly rejected them, and Congress later ordered the BRAC to be recreated several times. But the story of a less familiar Reagan-era commission shows that other congressional defense commissions serve similar purposes.

Chemical Warfare Review Commission

In 1984 one of the Reagan administration's top defense priorities was to move forward with the production of a new kind of chemical weapon. The United States had not produced chemical weapons since 1969, but the Soviet Union had continued to amass an enormous chemical warfare arsenal. The administration sought to counter the Soviet program by producing new nerve gas munitions, known as binary weapons because they contained separate compartments of chemicals that only became lethal after they were mixed. The DOD argued that this binary design would be both safer to handle and transport, and more effective when used, than older US "unitary" chemical weapons.

The administration faced strong political opposition on this issue, however—particularly among liberals who found chemical weapons reprehensible. In May 1984 the Democratic-controlled House of Representatives rejected by a vote of 247 to 179 a measure that would have authorized funding for the production of binary nerve gas weapons.[50] (The measure had previously passed the Republican-controlled Senate.) Democratic lawmakers did not universally vote against the binary weapons, however, as some prodefense Democrats supported them as a means of reducing the Soviet advantage in chemical warfare.

In this context, Republican and Democratic congressional supporters of producing the weapons worked with the administration to create the Chemical Warfare Review Commission, which was established via the NDAA in October 1984 with a mandate to "review the overall adequacy of the chemical warfare posture of the United States, with particular emphasis on the question of whether the United States should produce binary chemical munitions."[51] The administration and its congressional allies on this issue created the commission based on a realization that some lawmakers who voted against producing binary weapons were personally open to them but found it politically difficult to approve them in an election year because many constituents strongly opposed them.[52] The hope among the commission's creators, in other words, was that a commission might help gain the votes of wavering lawmakers for the weapons after the election, while giving those lawmakers political breathing space in the meantime by taking the issue off the table during the election campaign. Donald Mahley, who handled the issue as director of defense policy and arms control on Reagan's National Security Council staff, recalled, "Democrats didn't want to be blamed for funding binaries. They were looking for an independent commission statement they could use to give them cover for voting for binary funding."[53]

The commission's designers boosted the likelihood that the commission would recommend production of binary weapons by giving the president the power to appoint all of the commission's members. While the White House knew that it needed to include Democrats in the eight-member commission in order to give the commission credibility, the White House only selected prodefense Democrats who were likely to support the weapon program. For chairman, Reagan appointed former State Department senior official Walter Stoessel. Mahley commented, "Stoessel was very carefully screened by the White House to make sure he believed the right thing and was an able organizer."[54] The other commission members included former national security adviser Zbigniew Brzezinski, former secretary of state Alexander Haig, two former lawmakers, and a former army general.

In its June 1985 report, the commission unanimously endorsed the administration's proposal to produce binary weapons, while also recommending an accelerated program to destroy obsolete unitary weapons. The latter proposal was generally favored by liberals—while being acceptable to the administration—so the combination of these two proposals represented a package designed to help build congressional support for producing the new weapons.[55]

Two days after the commission reported, Reagan sent a letter to Congress endorsing its proposals and urging Congress "to authorize funding for the binary munitions program as expeditiously as possible."[56] The following week, the House voted 229 to 196 to authorize production of the new weapons.[57] Several months later, Congress approved $21.7 million for the new program and—through a separate measure—ordered destruction of the existing chemical weapons stockpile by 1994.[58] In 1987 the army began producing the nerve gas munitions.[59] The army ceased this production after the end of the Cold War in 1991, as negotiations for a global ban on chemical weapons were beginning.

The commission's report was not solely—or even principally—responsible for legislative approval in 1985 of producing binary chemical weapons. During that year, the DOD also sharply increased its lobbying of lawmakers on the issue, treating the binary program's approval as its top legislative priority.[60]

In addition, Reagan's November 1984 landslide election victory had strength-ened his standing in Congress and added sixteen Republicans to the House through a coattails effect. These changes would have shifted congressional votes on the issue in Reagan's favor regardless of the commission. But the commission was an important additional contributor to congressional ap-proval of the first US production of chemical weapons in nearly two decades.

Conclusion

This chapter's accounts of several congressional defense commissions illus-trate how lawmakers often see ad hoc commissions as useful vehicles for advancing a policy or reform agenda, conducting oversight of the DOD, or avoiding blame or kicking the can down the road on a controversial issue. The commissions I have highlighted in the chapter, moreover, are not un-usual in being established based on these motivations. To give a few more examples, in 1996 lawmakers created the National Defense Panel to promote broad reform in the DOD, in 2000 lawmakers established the Commission to Assess the Threat to the United States from Electromagnetic Pulse Attack to promote stronger defenses against the potential effects of a nuclear explosion in the atmosphere, in 2003 lawmakers created the Commission on Review of Overseas Military Facility Structure of the United States to provide an independent look at global basing changes being planned by the DOD, and in 2008 lawmakers created the Commission on the Strategic Posture of the United States to delay potential decisions regarding the development of new nuclear weapons.[61]

While I focused primarily in this chapter on the motivations of lawmak-ers in creating defense commissions, the chapter's brief case studies also il-lustrate some common realities about the impact of commissions. In other scholarship I have found that commissions tend to have greater influence when they are established in the context of a crisis, such as a disaster, a war, or a major scandal—primarily because a crisis tends to weaken the status quo's hold.[62] Indeed, the Wartime Contracting Commission—created in response to contracting scandals in the Iraq and Afghanistan wars—appears to have had the greatest influence of the commissions analyzed in this chapter, as it shaped numerous changes in contracting management and oversight policies. Yet the Chemical Warfare Review Commission and Ballistic Missile Threat Commission were also successful, from the perspective of their congressio-nal creators, in the sense that Congress subsequently enacted the preferences of those lawmakers into law—though the commissions were only partially responsible for those outcomes. The Commission on Roles and Missions of the Armed Forces was the most disappointing of the four commissions to its congressional originators, as it did not generate any broad role or mission changes among the services—though it did shape some smaller-scale reforms. Its principal lesson is that a commission is unlikely to advocate far-reaching change if many of its members represent the perspective of one of the military services.

On the whole, commissions are useful congressional tools of defense politics, policymaking, and oversight—though their impact on defense policy is usually modest. In his own study of congressional commissions, Colton Campbell concluded, "At their most productive, commissions provide Congress with a flexible option for policymaking."[63] Similarly, my research indicates that commissions can help lawmakers build support for policy agendas on controversial issues, conduct oversight of the DOD on complex matters, and escape political jams—at least temporarily. In the context of broader pressure for policy change—such as that created by a crisis—they can even sometimes shape important reforms. Given the difficulty of changing the status quo in the US political system, that track record is not too bad. Since it is generally far easier for lawmakers to create a commission than to enact major substantive policy changes, defense commissions will surely remain attractive and frequently used congressional devices.

Notes

1. I am grateful to the Lynde and Harry Bradley Foundation, the Woodrow Wilson School of Public and International Affairs, American University, and the School of International Service at American University for their support of the research on which this chapter is based. I also thank Sami Makki and other participants at an International Studies Association conference panel for helpful feedback on an earlier version of the chapter and thank Kate Tennis for excellent research assistance.

2. My identification of these commissions is based principally on a data set I constructed of national security commissions. For more detail on the construction of this data set, see Jordan Tama, *Terrorism and National Security Reform* (New York: Cambridge University Press, 2011), 197–98. In preparing this chapter, I supplemented the data set with a few additional congressional defense commissions identified in Matthew Eric Glassman and Jacob R. Straus, *Congressional Commissions: Overview, Structure, and Legislative Considerations* (Washington, DC: Congressional Research Service, 2013). I only categorize a commission as a defense commission if it was established as part of a defense authorization or appropriations law or if the commission's mandate principally concerns defense issues. This categorization excludes other commissions that dealt in part with defense issues, including a number that focused on intelligence or terrorism matters.

3. Colton C. Campbell, *Discharging Congress: Government by Commission* (Westport, CT: Praeger, 2002), 1; Amy Zegart, "Blue Ribbons, Black Boxes: Toward a Better Understanding of Presidential Commissions," *Presidential Studies Quarterly* 24, no. 2 (2004): 368–69; and Tama, *Terrorism and National Security Reform*, 5.

4. Zegart, "Blue Ribbons, Black Boxes."

5. David Filtner Jr., *The Politics of Presidential Commissions* (Dobbs Ferry, NY: Transaction, 1986); Kenneth Kitts, *Presidential Commissions and National Security: The Politics of Damage Control* (Boulder, CO: Lynne Rienner, 2006); and Thomas R. Wolanin, *Presidential Advisory Commissions: Truman to Nixon* (Madison: University of Wisconsin Press, 1975).

6. Campbell, *Discharging Congress*; and Colton C. Campbell, "Creating an Angel: Congressional Delegation to Ad Hoc Commissions," *Congress and the Presidency* 25, no. 2 (1998): 161–82.

7. R. Kent Weaver, "The Politics of Blame Avoidance," *Journal of Public Policy* 6 (1987): 371–98.

8. Tama, *Terrorism and National Security Reform*; Jordan Tama, "Crises, Commissions, and Reform: The Impact of Blue-Ribbon Panels;" *Political Research Quarterly* 67, no. 1 (2014): 152–64; and Jordan Tama, "The Power and Limitations of Commissions: The Iraq Study Group, Bush, Obama, and Congress," *Presidential Studies Quarterly* 41, no. 1 (2011): 135–55.

9. Pub. L. 104-201, National Defense Authorization Act for Fiscal Year 1997.

10. For an in-depth analysis of the presidential-congressional politics of missile-defense policy, see David P. Auerswald, "The President, the Congress and American Missile Defense Policy," *Defence Studies* 1, no. 2 (2001): 57–82.

11. H.R. 1530, the National Defense Authorization Act for Fiscal Year 1996.

12. See *The National Intelligence Estimate on the Ballistic Missile Threat to the United States*, Hearing before the International Security, Proliferation, and Federal Services Subcommittee of the Committee on Governmental Affairs, United States Senate (Washington DC: Government Printing Office, February 9, 2000), 91–106, www.gpo.gov/fdsys/pkg/CHRG-106shrg63638/html/CHRG-106shrg63638.htm; also Ronald James Stevenson, "Framing National Security Threats: An Analysis of the Arguments in the Missile Defense Controversy," PhD diss., Wayne State University, 2005, 77–80.

13. H.R. 3489, the Ballistic Missile Defense Act of 1996; and Jamie Stiehm, "GOP Plans 'Spring Offensive' to Highlight Need for $50-60B National Missile Defense System," *The Hill*, May 22, 1996.

14. Author interview of former DOD official, April 2008.

15. The commission's legislative charter said six of the commission members were to be appointed by the director of central intelligence (DCI) in consultation with Republican congressional leaders, while the other three were to be appointed by the DCI in consultation with Democratic congressional leaders, but in practice the DCI followed the choices of the respective congressional leaders in making these appointments.

16. Commission to Assess the Ballistic Missile Threat to the United States, *Executive Summary of the Report* (1998), www.fas.org/irp/threat/bm-threat.htm.

17. Author interview of William Schneider, January 16, 2008.

18. Jonathan S. Landay, "New Dispute over Need to Speed Up 'Star Wars,'" *Christian Science Monitor*, July 21, 1998.

19. S. 1873, the American Missile Protection Act of 1998.

20. Eric Schmitt, "Republican Missile Defense Bill Loses by One Vote in the Senate," *New York Times*, September 10, 1998.

21. Pub. L. 106-38, the National Missile Defense Act of 1999.

22. Auerswald, "President, the Congress," 70–76.

23. Sam Nunn, "The Defense Department Must Thoroughly Overhaul the Services' Roles and Missions," *Congressional Record*, July 2, 1992 (daily ed.), S9559–S9565.

24. Author interview of Gene Porter, October 23, 2007; and John Gordon IV, "The Quadrennial Defense Review: Analyzing the Major Defense Review Process," PhD diss., George Mason University, 2005, 28–29.

25. Pub. L. 103-160, National Defense Authorization Act for Fiscal Year 1994.

26. Author interview of commission staff member, September 18, 2007.

27. Author interview of Randy Jayne, October 4, 2007.

28. Author interviews of commission staff members, September–November 2007.

29. Author interview of Gene Porter, October 23, 2007.

30. Author interviews of Antonia Chayes, David Deptula, Randy Jayne, Jim Kurtz, Phil Lacombe, Robert RisCassi, and Larry Welch, July 2007–February 2008; and Gordon, "Quadrennial Defense Review," 28–30.

31. Author interview of Jeffrey Smith, July 27, 2007.

32. Eric Schmitt, "New Report on Long-Sought Goal: Efficiency in Military," New York Times, May 18, 1984.

33. Commission on Roles and Missions of the Armed Forces, Directions for Defense (Washington, DC: Government Printing Office, 1995).

34. Author interview of Ted Warner, October 10, 2007.

35. Author interview of Fred Frostic, October 29, 2007; and author interview of former commission staff member, October 2007. The QDR was mandated by Pub. L. 104-201, the National Defense Authorization Act for Fiscal Year 1997.

36. Senate Amendment 2206 to the National Defense Authorization Act for Fiscal Year 2008.

37. Claire McCaskill et al., "Freshman Senators Call for Commission to Investigate Wartime Contracting," press release, July 18, 2007.

38. George W. Bush, "President Bush Signs H.R. 4986, the National Defense Authorization Act for Fiscal Year 2008 into Law," press release, January 28, 2008.

39. I briefed the commission in May 2011 on research I had conducted on other commissions.

40. Commission on Wartime Contracting in Iraq and Afghanistan, Transforming Wartime Contracting: Controlling Costs, Reducing Risks (Washington, DC: Government Printing Office, 2011), 190–97.

41. Ibid., 1.

42. S. 2139, the Comprehensive Contingency Contracting Reform Act of 2012.

43. Pub. L. 112-239, the National Defense Authorization Act for Fiscal Year 2013.

44. General Accountability Office, GAO-12-854R Contingency Contracting (Washington, DC: Government Printing Office, 2012),

45. Lindsay Wise, "Sen. Claire McCaskill Leaps Hurdles to Overhauling Wartime Contracting," McClatchy Newspapers, January 19, 2013, www.mcclatchydc.com/2013/01/19/180202/sen-claire-mccaskill-leaps-hurdles.html.

46. Ibid.

47. Campbell, Discharging Congress, 113–28; Christopher J. Deering, "Congress, the President, and Automatic Government," in Rivals for Power: Presidential-Congressional Relations, ed. James A. Thurber (Washington, DC: CQ Press, 1996), 153–69; and Kenneth R. Mayer, "Closing Military Bases (Finally): Solving Collective Dilemmas through Delegation," Legislative Studies Quarterly 20, no. 3 (1995): 393–13.

48. Deering, "Congress, the President," 165.

49. Douglas L. Kriner and Andrew Reeves, The Particularistic President (Cambridge University Press, forthcoming).

50. Steven V. Roberts, "House Vote Drops Binary Nerve Gas over Reagan Plea," New York Times, May 18, 1984.

51. Pub. L. 98-525, Department of Defense Authorization Act for Fiscal Year 1985.

52. Author interview of James Bodner, April 23, 2008; and author interview of Donald Mahley, October 5, 2007.

53. Author interview of Donald Mahley, October 5, 2007.

54. Ibid.

55. Author interview of John Kester, October 3, 2007; and author interview of Donald Mahley, October 5, 2007.

56. Ronald Reagan, "Message to the Congress Transmitting the Final Report of the Chemical Warfare Review Commission," June 13, 1985, www.reagan.utexas.edu/archives/speeches /1985/61385c.htm.

57. Steven V. Roberts, "House Votes Funds to Renew Output of Nerve Weapons," *New York Times*, June 20, 1985.

58. Jonathan Fuerbringer, "Conferees Compromise on an '86 Spending Bill," *New York Times*, December 19, 1985; and Pub. L. 99-145, Department of Defense Authorization Act for Fiscal Year 1986.

59. Jeffrey R. Smith, "Army Begins Producing Chemical Weapons, Ending 18-Year Moratorium," *Washington Post*, December 17, 1987.

60. Bill Keller, "U.S. Preparing New Production of Nerve Gases," *New York Times*, August 11, 1985.

61. Author interview of Fred Downey, June 10, 2013; author interviews of former congressional aides, DOD officials, and commission participants, August 2007–July 2013; and Michael Crowley, "The Newt Bomb," *New Republic*, June 3, 2009; Walter Pincus, "Bipartisan Panel Will Review Nuclear Posture," *Washington Post*, May 3, 2007.

62. Tama, *Terrorism and National Security Reform*.

63. Campbell, *Discharging Congress*, 132.

5

Congress and "Its" Military

Delegating to the Reserve Component

JOHN GRISWOLD

The existence of the Guard will necessarily prevent the development of a strong and ready national reserve organization. The Constitution has made the Guard into a powerful political force, and it is not inconceivable that this political strength may make the Guard into an effective military organization.

—*Samuel P. Huntington,* The Soldier and the State

At first glance, the US military's armed services appear monolithic. Most civilians cannot tell whether a soldier, sailor, airman, marine, or coastguardsman is a member of that service's active component or the reserve component by looking at his or her uniform. It may also appear that members of Congress behave the same way. Lawmakers typically take positions that demonstrate their support and respect for service members, veterans, and their families regardless of the component. When Congress is executing its constitutional role—"to raise and support Armies" and "to provide and maintain a Navy"—legislators have come to man, train, and equip the active and reserve component similarly.

For all of these similarities, there are important differences between the active force and reserve component that affect the ways in which members craft legislation regarding the active component and reserve component. Three key reasons for this variation stand out. First, a reservist is a constituent and, potentially, a very influential one. Reserve-component service members—particularly in the Air and Army National Guard—can exert significant political influence both locally and nationally through their affiliated lobbying associations. Second, many members without an active-duty installation in their district consider their local National Guard or reserve unit as "their" military. As such, members have a more personal connection with the reserve component than an active-component unit. When a local National Guard or reserve unit deploys, longstanding members of the community leave for up to a year at a time for combat duty. The effects of war truly hit home. Third, the reserve component provides the states with crucial military capabilities to assist with disaster response and recovery. Members pay close attention to how reserve-component units are trained, equipped, manned, and managed to ensure that their states are not caught short during a disaster or crisis. When it comes to a member's relationship with the reserve component, all politics is local.

This chapter examines the relationship between Congress and the reserve component by exploring a key debate in defense policy: how best to balance the reserve component's efforts between its domestic and foreign roles. It begins by orienting the reader to the key differences between the active component and the reserve component. Next, the chapter unpacks the debate over the reserve component's roles by examining a major policy change: the ascension of the chief of the National Guard Bureau to the Joint Chiefs of Staff (JCS) in 2011. I use this case to illustrate and differentiate the politics of the National Guard and reserves from the military's active forces. Flowing from this debate, the chapter considers the challenges facing Congress in legislating reserve forces policy under conditions of fiscal austerity and in the post-Iraq and -Afghanistan military.

Differentiating the Active Forces and Reserve Component

Contrary to public perception, the US military is not one force but several. The first force is commonly known as the active component, which operates full time as part of the Department of Defense (DOD) and is governed by Title 10 of the United States Code. The different military services report to the president through the secretary of defense via their respective chains of command. These may include either their service chiefs or their appropriate geographic or functional combatant commander. The second major force—the reserve component—is also broken into two distinct groups. The first group is the reserves. Each service—the US Army, the US Navy, the US Air Force, the Marine Corps, and the US Coast Guard—has its own reserves that operate exclusively under federal control (through Title 10) when training at home or deployed overseas to support the active component. Either as individuals or as units, the reserves augment active-component forces as required. Reserve units tend to be composed of support rather than combat organizations, such as logistical, intelligence, and communications units.

The second group of reservists—the National Guard—differs considerably from the first. The National Guard consists of the Army and Air National Guard, both of which fall under the National Guard Bureau (NGB), a federal-level headquarters under the DOD. The NGB does not provide direct command and control over the Guard. Instead, it is a coordinating authority, through which the states' and territories' National Guards are connected to the DOD. Its personnel are drawn from National Guard units across the country. At the state level, the adjutant general, a National Guard general officer, commands both the Army and Air National Guard units in the state. This relationship is analogous to the role that the chairman of the Joint Chiefs of Staff plays. The chairman is not in any service member's chain of command; his staff coordinates policy and advises the president and the secretary of defense on military matters. Just as the chiefs of staff are responsible for running each branch of the service on a daily basis, so too do the fifty-four adjutants general exercise authority over their jurisdiction's guardsmen.

Unlike the federal reserves that operate under Title 10, the Army and Air National Guard typically fall under the command and control of state governors. During peacetime, the Guard falls under Title 32 of the US Code when conducting monthly training, or drill, and during a two-week activation for training. When responding to domestic emergencies, the Guard can respond under either state control—using state funding—or using Title 32 funding during a presidentially declared disaster. When federalized for deployments overseas, the Guard comes under DOD control, reporting to their respective service chief and typically assigned to a combatant commander for employment under Title 10. Also unlike the federal reserves, the National Guard maintains both combat units (e.g., fighter squadrons and infantry brigades) as well as support elements, and they are more likely to deploy as whole units than as individual augmentees. A key limitation imposed by Title 10 is that the National Guard may not engage in law enforcement activities due to the Posse Comitatus Act of 1878. This prohibition does not apply when the Guard is used under Title 32 or when called up to state active duty.[1] Activation under Title 10 also removes state governors from the National Guard's chain of command. The table below illustrates the key statutory and legal differences between the active component and the reserves and National Guard.

The institutional roots of the active component and the reserve component —and the root cause of tension between the two—can be found in the Constitution. In addition to giving Congress the authority to man and equip the military, Article I, Section 8 also contains the militia clauses that gave birth to the reserve component: "to provide for calling forth the Militia to execute the Laws of the Union, suppress Insurrections and repel Invasions" and "to provide for organizing, arming, and disciplining, the Militia, and for governing

Table 5.1. Control and Funding of the National Guard, Reserves, and Active Component

	Air and Army National Guard			Active Component and Service Reserves
	State Active Duty	*Title 32*	*Title 10*	*Title 10*
Controlled by	State Governor	State Governor	Federal Government	Federal Government
Funded by	State Government	Federal Government	Federal Government	Federal Government
Domestic Role	Governed by state military law	Limited by statute to training, counterdrug, and counterterrorism missions	Highly circumscribed; subject to Posse Comitatus	Highly circumscribed; subject to Posse Comitatus
Overseas Role	NA	May partner with foreign militaries through the State Partnership Program	Falls under the Department of Defense	Falls under the Department of Defense

such Part of them as may be employed in the Service of the United States, reserving to the States respectively, the Appointment of the Officers, and the Authority of training the Militia according to the discipline prescribed by Congress." The militia clauses set in place two key distinctions that the National Guard maintains to this day. The first is a system of dual state and federal control over the militia. The division of the military power between the states and the national government provided a unique check on the federal use of military force—a guiding principle among men distrustful of centralized power.[2]

The second distinction that sets the National Guard apart from the rest of the reserve component and the active component is the dual mission of internal and external defense. The active component and the federal reserves focus almost exclusively on the external defense mission. Only under exceptionally rare circumstances can the active component or their reserves deploy within the continental United States to conduct operations beyond training. On the other hand, the National Guard is trained for both internal and external missions. The National Guard can support or even perform law enforcement functions—such as riot control, counterdrug missions, and so forth—while under state control. Guard units must also maintain their readiness for overseas combat deployments as part of their Title 10 mission, for which they are equipped and trained by the federal government.

Given the significant differences and natural tension between these roles and missions, it is unsurprising that the active component and reserve component each possess their own unique organizational cultures that further divide them. Over a decade of service at war has vastly improved interoperability between the active component and reserve component. However, the experience did not close the chasm between their different cultures. Each component faces unique challenges that create these cultures. In the active component, operations focus predominately on implementing the strategic guidance provided by senior army leaders and combatant commanders. Although companies, battalions, and brigades operated in a very fluid, nonlinear battlefield in combat, leaders in the active component operate predominately within a hierarchical, linear structure. These organizations provide structured channels and patterns of authority that insulate most of the army and its leaders from broader political or societal concerns. Active-component assignments, even those for senior leaders, focus nearly exclusively on tactical and operational concerns over a relatively short duration.

The reserve component faces a different reality. A reserve-component service member operates across a broader set of domains, balancing the demands that their personnel face from civilian employers with their military commitments. Reserve-component leaders tend to remain in units and positions longer than their active-component counterparts do. This is particularly useful for building relationships with allies during recurring overseas partnerships. Senior leaders in the reserve component operate in a much different political and social context than their active-component counterparts. Consider the role that National Guard leaders play in domestic governance. More than half of the state adjutants general are dual-hatted as their state's emergency services chief. In most states, that officer is appointed by the governor. In two states—Vermont and South Carolina—the adjutant general is selected through popular election. A state's National Guard headquarters is a joint army–air force organization responsive to governors, state legislatures, as well as the National Guard Bureau, along with the army and air force chiefs of staff. A reservist's work in the business world, in civil service, and other career fields gives unique insights into governance issues outside the traditional military sphere. The demands from these different societal domains, along with their military expertise, give the reserve component a different perspective than active-component leaders.

The Congressional Role in Shaping the Reserve Component

Members of Congress shape reserve component composition, roles, and missions in four principal ways. The first three are similar to how Congress shapes the active component, while the fourth differs substantially. First, Congress provides policy guidance for the reserve component primarily through the annual defense bill, the National Defense Authorization Act (NDAA). Like their active-duty counterparts, reserve components' leaders testify before congressional hearings regarding proposed legislation that would alter statutes that govern the reserve component. Both the active and reserve components maintain an extensive presence on Capitol Hill through each service's legislative liaison—uniformed service members who routinely interface with members and their staffs to respond to constituents' concerns, arrange congressional visits to military bases, and inform members and their staffs regarding the military's position on proposed legislation.

Also like the active component, the reserve component wields considerable influence beyond its senior military leadership. Each of the services is represented by its own professional organization. The reserve component has an even more extensive network of lobbying organizations working diligently to exert influence over the language in the NDAA that affects the reserve component. Like the active component, the National Guard and the reserves are separate entities from their civilian lobbying organizations. There are numerous groups supporting federal reservists, including the Reserve Officers Association, the Fleet Reserve Association, and the Marine Corps Reserve Association. Each service association also advocates on behalf of its active- and reserve-component constituents.

The National Guard Association of the United States (NGAUS) is the oldest of these organizations. Much like any professional advocacy group, NGAUS lobbies Congress on behalf of its membership. Founded in 1878, NGAUS is one of the oldest interest groups in the country—and one of the most influential.[3] NGAUS advocates for the same things as any other professional society: increased pay, better equipment, and improved training. Unlike other advocacy groups, NGAUS has a unique interest in the composition of the armed forces. NGAUS leaders are particularly interested in parity of equipment, pay, and roles between the National Guard and the army and air force. A smaller but even more influential organization, the Adjutants General Association of the United States, represents each state's senior Guard leaders on Capitol Hill. Because of their influence within the states, the National Guard's lobbying organizations wield considerable influence—more so than their active-component or Title 10 reserve counterparts.

Second, the reserve component receives funding through the appropriations process, just as the active component does. The active and reserve components compete for dwindling resources in an effort to achieve their own institutional priorities. The tension that this causes is particularly acute when one considers the procurement and management of weapon systems.

Consider the army's attempt to reallocate aviation assets across the active and reserve components. Seeking cost savings for the fiscal year (FY) 2015 budget, active-component army leaders proposed moving attack aviation—AH-64 Apache gunships—out of the Army National Guard into the active component.[4] At the same time, the active component would send a smaller number of medium utility helicopters out of the active component and into the Guard. The move has met with considerable opposition from National Guard leaders, congressional delegations, and state governors.[5] What is clear from this example is that cost is not the only thing that lawmakers consider when dealing with funding decisions; broader concerns over things such as strategic depth and size of the reserve component, as well as parochialism, come to the forefront thanks to intensive lobbying efforts by the reserve component.

Third, Congress exercises oversight of both the active and reserve components through hearings and investigations.[6] Oversight may be triggered by information gleaned through the media, visits to troops serving abroad, or by meeting with reservists in their home districts. Members of Congress take this responsibility very seriously, particularly as it applies to military readiness for domestic disaster response. The congressional investigation into the military's response to 2005's Hurricane Katrina is one of many examples where Congress used its investigative powers to examine the reserve component's readiness.[7]

The last method for shaping the reserve component differs significantly from how members of Congress shape the active component. Members typically associate more closely with their state's National Guard leadership than their Title 10 (active-duty or reserve) counterparts. This is particularly true of a state's adjutant general, or TAG, who in most cases is appointed by the state governor. The TAG develops closer relationships with his or her congressional delegation than a federal officer because of the political nature of the TAG's position and the longevity TAGs have relative to their Title 10 counterparts.[8] Unlike an active-component senior officer, the TAG has soldiers or airmen distributed across the state rather than a single base in one district. Taken together, the TAG's longevity, political roots, and distribution of troops increase the chances for TAGs to interact with every member of their congressional delegation.

Revising Roles: Congress, the National Guard, and the Joint Chiefs of Staff

The reserve component and the National Guard in particular wield extensive influence in Congress over their organization and roles. Consider the case of the National Guard's seat on the Joint Chiefs of Staff (JCS). The Guard's argument for a seat on the JCS picked up steam in the wake of Hurricane Katrina. The Guard's initial response to Katrina was not successful. Jackson Barracks in New Orleans' lower Ninth Ward, the Louisiana National Guard's command post inside the city, flooded at the onset of the storm. In describing the scene, Christopher Cooper and Robert Block noted that "if there had been any doubt that the state of Louisiana would need federal help to cope with Katrina, the point had just been hammered home."[9] Although most of the city had been evacuated prior to Katrina's landfall, key elements of the city's response had been rendered useless. The National Guard's joint operation center, the nexus for coordinating emergency relief efforts in and around New Orleans, was also flooded.

Following the investigations by the George W. Bush administration and Congress into Hurricane Katrina, the latter mandated a commission to explore the future of the reserve component. Headed by retired Marine Corps major general Arnold Punaro, the commission made ninety-five recommendations to Congress, the DOD, and the Department of Homeland Security regarding the Guard's role in homeland security. The commission considered testimony from well over a hundred witnesses—most of whom were members of the National Guard or the reserves, state governors, or members of Congress sympathetic to the reserve components.[10] This arrangement gave National Guard leaders an influential stage on which to recommend their preferred institutional changes. The commission strongly recommended that the chief of the NGB be promoted from three-star general to four. The recommendation was made in light of the expanded duties that the reserve components, and in particular the National Guard, faced in providing support both at home and overseas. The promotion would also position the chief of the NGB, or CNGB, to better advise senior DOD officials on how best to employ the Guard: "Once given a four-star rank and increased responsibilities as an advisor to the Secretary of Defense on matters related to the National Guard forces in non-federal status, the CNGB should retain the ability to influence decisions regarding such matters and ensure that the needs of states and their governors are addressed in policies formulated by the Secretary of Defense."[11]

The seat on the JCS would not receive a hearing for three years. On the morning of November 10, 2011, the serving chiefs sat in a hearing before the Senate Armed Services Committee. In his opening remarks, Chairman Carl Levin (D-MI) noted the changing roles and responsibilities of the National Guard over the previous decade—and the manner in which Congress had implemented a number of changes to the Guard to complement its expanded responsibilities. The committee and the JCS were assembled to consider another change, this time to the composition of the JCS itself. "The question of whether to include the Chief of the National Guard Bureau as a member of the Joint Chiefs of Staff," Levin stated, "is a complex issue with significant policy implications."[12]

To the chiefs, the answer was a resounding "no." Army general Martin E. Dempsey argued that the National Guard was already well represented by the army and air force chiefs of staff, under which guardsmen are subsumed when called into federal service. General Dempsey told the committee that the service chiefs, as the senior commanders of their branches of service, had command authority over the soldiers, sailors, airmen, and marines who wore their uniform. The CNGB had no such authority. He also noted that the CNGB was already present at meetings of the Joint Chiefs. "I don't find the argument to change the composition of the JCS compelling," stated General Dempsey. "It is unclear to me what problem we are trying to solve."[13]

None of the chiefs testified to the contrary. In their testimony, each cited the improved relationship between the active and reserve components since the terrorist attacks of September 11, 2001. They noted the increasing difficulty in identifying the difference between the performance of guardsmen and active-component soldiers. They stated that both active and reserve components were nearly equal in terms of equipment, a far cry from when hostilities in Iraq and Afghanistan commenced. Though effusive in their praise for the National Guard, none of the chiefs saw compelling reason to change the law.

Air National Guard general Craig R. McKinley, the chief of the NGB and the sole guardsman called to testify, was the last witness to make a statement. General McKinley made an impassioned plea for ascension to the JCS. Despite the increase in rank of the CNGB and an open invitation to meet with the JCS, the general did not believe this was adequate representation: "Only full JCS membership for the Chief of NGB will ensure that the responsibilities and capabilities of the non-Federalized National Guard are considered in a planned and deliberate manner that is not based upon ad hoc or personal relationships but is, instead, firmly rooted in the law and the national strategy."[14]

Although he could not point to a specific instance where the presence or absence of a representative from the Guard on the JCS would have altered a policy, General McKinley expressed that a change was of vital importance. The National Guard, he argued, had changed significantly in the past three years, but it was not enough. In the closing portion of his remarks, General McKinley emphasized his role as the key conduit from the states to the

Secretary of Defense: "I would be remiss without speaking on behalf of the fifty-four adjutants general. . . . The adjutants general have provided their unqualified support for placing the chief of the NGB on the JCS."[15]

The question-and-answer period brought several issues regarding the addition of the CNGB to the JCS to the forefront. Sen. James Inhofe (R-OK) noted that only three years earlier, Congress had authorized a fourth star for the CNGB. Why was there a need for further change? Senate Majority Leader Harry Reid of Nevada asked General McKinley if it would be appropriate for a state governor to appoint a member of the JCS—a consideration that, if the addition were made, would become reality. Sen. Jim Webb (D-VA) stated that the legislation to add the CNGB to the JCS was unnecessary: "There are a number of other jurisdictions in which non–Title 10 obligations of the National Guard are considered, and some of them, to be quite frank, are jealously guarded by the political processes of the Governors," he declared.[16]

Several senators expressed their unabashed support for the measure. Senators Daniel Akaka (D-HI) and Scott Brown (R-MA) argued that the addition of the Marine Corps to the JCS was also made over the objection of the JCS. Sen. Lindsey Graham (R-SC) championed the Guard's cause: "The institution resisted Goldwater-Nichols, the institution resisted having the Commandant of the Marine Corps on the JCS, and I think we should consider the time has come, given post–September 11 duties of the National Guard, to have a seat at the table. It doesn't change command authority, doesn't turn the world upside down."[17] Senator Graham also noted that the addition of the CNGB to the JCS was advocated by President Barack Obama's presidential campaign in 2008. Senator Akaka's statement appealed to both the functional and emotional aspects of adding the CNGB to the JCS: "Now making the Chief of the NGB a full-fledged member will update the JCS to reflect the operational reality in wars overseas, as well as in homeland defense and security missions. . . . I believe that elevating the Chief of the NGB to the JCS is something overdue and will show our Guardsmen and their families that they are a true partner."[18]

In the end, the Senate resolved this spirited debate over the National Guard's seat on the JCS quickly. Sen. Patrick Leahy (D-VT), the head of the Senate National Guard Caucus, sponsored an amendment to the FY 2012 NDAA to create the statutory seat on the JCS that the Guard sought. With seventy cosponsors, the amendment passed by voice vote. On November 28, the bill was passed and sent to conference committee, where the amendment was included in the final version of the legislation on December 13. President Obama signed the bill into law on New Year's Eve, 2011.

The debate over the National Guard's seat on the JCS can be understood from a variety of perspectives. On one level, this is an example of legislative politics. Throughout its history, the National Guard has had a close relationship with Congress. While the Guard had only one formal seat at the table in the Dirksen Senate Office Building on November 10, General McKinley was not alone. Senator Graham, a former guardsman and member of the air force reserves, was also the cochair of the Senate National Guard Caucus. There are ninety-six members of that caucus. Guardsmen are stationed in every state and territory, with nearly half a million guardsmen living and working in nearly every congressional district. To some observers, promoting the chief of the National Guard Bureau to the JCS was a symbolic gesture, demonstrating congressional support for the armed forces at little budgetary cost.

On another level, this episode is a classic case of inside lobbying.[19] NGAUS applied considerable pressure on members of Congress, both directly on the Hill and indirectly through the media. The push for a seat on the JCS represented the culmination of years of lobbying. NGAUS leaders had a detailed plan to gain cosponsors for the change and implemented in the same fashion as a campaign plan. The NGAUS team forged a coalition with other interest groups that would benefit from the CNGB's seat on the JCS. These included the Veterans of Foreign Wars and the National Governor's Association. The Association of the United States Army and the Air Force Association also lobbied on behalf of the Army and Air National Guard, respectively. The state adjutants general have their own lobbying organization, the Adjutants General Association of the United States.

From a lawmaker's perspective, voting for the CNGB makes complete sense. Voting for the Guard's ascension is another example of what David Mayhew called position taking.[20] It is a cost-free way to express support for a well-organized interest group that the public holds in high regard. Although the consequences of such a change were unclear, the potential negative implications for national security policy did not outweigh the perceived reelectoral benefits that would accompany a pro–National Guard vote.

Perhaps the most important aspect of the vote is what it gave the Guard—as much as what it didn't. The seat on the JCS did not come with greater budget authority, an increase in National Guard manpower, or the promise of new or improved equipment. In government circles—and the DOD in particular—money, manning, and equipment are certainly important. But they are not ends in themselves. The National Guard's lobbying efforts, and the NGAUS campaign on the Guard's behalf, were not focused on a bigger budget, more guardsmen, or the latest tank or helicopter. The lobbying effort

Gen. Frank J. Grass, the twenty-seventh chief of the National Guard Bureau (right), takes over from Gen. Craig R. McKinley (center) during a ceremony at the Pentagon on September 7, 2012. The chairman of the Joint Chiefs of Staff, Gen. Martin E. Dempsey, is at left. *Department of Defense*

focused on changes to statute that would give the Guard an enhanced position from which to advocate on its own behalf. Lobbying is one tactic that National Guard leaders used as a part of a broader strategic campaign. Promoting the CNGB to four-star general brought the Guard's chief into a peer relationship with the service chiefs and combatant commanders, but it was not a high priority for the DOD. Nevertheless, the Guard's leadership successfully advocated for a seat on the JCS, further raising its influence above the other members of the reserve component.

Emerging and Enduring Debates: The Reserve Component after Iraq and Afghanistan

The US military faces an uncertain future after Afghanistan, particularly for its land forces. President Obama's Defense Strategic Guidance, issued at the beginning of 2012, articulates a national security strategy intent on avoiding extensive long-term ground operations. His decision to rebalance American diplomatic, political, military, and economic influence toward Asia and away from the Middle East sends another signal to defense leaders and planners.

While the army partners and interacts with its counterparts in the Asia-Pacific region, the tyranny of distance ensures that the Pacific will continue to be primarily a naval and air theater of operations. American ground forces—mainly the army but also the Marine Corps—appear to be the most likely bill payer for the US military's expanded role in the Pacific.

The policy community contributed several notable reports in the late winter and early spring of 2013 that discuss the active / reserve-component force mix vis-à-vis ground forces. In *National Defense in a Time of Change*, retired admiral Gary Roughead and Kori Schake of the Hoover Institution examined the force mix question across services and components. Their central argument is that "fighting manpower-intensive, sustained ground combat or counterinsurgency operations [is] unlikely, and we choose to accept risk in this element of our force design because it is unlikely that political leaders will choose that approach for at least a decade."[21]

Predicated on this assumption, the authors recommend reducing the active army to approximately 290,000 soldiers while increasing the size of the reserve component to approximately 600,000 soldiers. "Putting more of the responsibilities for ground combat into the combat-proven reserve component," suggest the authors, "is both consistent with the new demands of the evolving international order and justified by the superb performance of National Guard and reserve units in our recent wars."[22] It is unclear what the mix of capabilities between the active and reserve components would be in their proposal.

In May 2013 the Center for Strategic and Budgetary Assessment (CSBA) hosted a strategic planning exercise with experts from CSBA, the American Enterprise Institute, the Center for a New American Security, and the Center for Strategic and International Studies (CSIS). Each team considered the strategic trade-offs they would make in light of constraints imposed by sequestration. Of the four groups, all but one reduced the size of the army's reserve components, with cuts ranging from 19,000 to 84,000 soldiers. The exception, a group from CSIS, increased the reserve component by 100,000 while reducing the active component by 163,000 below the projected 490,000 end strength in 2017. Although the exercise did not allow a more precise rebalancing of forces across the active and reserve components, the results suggest that the exercise's participants generally believed that reducing personnel—in both the active and reserve components—would sustain readiness and allow the military to invest in new and emerging technologies.[23]

All of this leaves the reserve component in an awkward position. On the one hand, reserve-component leaders understand the need to balance active-component and reserve-component capabilities. They understand the nation's fiscal situation and accept that force reductions may be on the horizon across components. Returning the reserve component to its historical role as a strategic reserve—one called upon only in times of national crisis—is a real possibility. On the other hand, reserve-component leaders are loath to relinquish the hard-fought advances in personnel and equipment readiness that they achieved over a decade of continuous warfare. Unlike during the post-Vietnam era, the drawdowns in Iraq and Afghanistan find the reserve component at its highest state of readiness. Many reserve-component leaders argue that maintaining this state of readiness and parity with active-component units is vital for both domestic response and national security missions. Advocates of using the reserve component as an operational reserve—one that is exercised on a regular basis through consistent deployment and increased training and funding—have been particularly vocal in the debate over the active/reserve-component force mix.

The tension between the active and reserve components over roles and missions has been exacerbated by the lack of clear guidance from either the legislative or executive branch. Congress and the president have not expressed the extent to which the reserve component should revert to being a strategic reserve rather than an operational one. In the absence of such guidance, active- and reserve-component leaders have become increasingly wary of each other's intentions. Journalist Sydney J. Freedberg Jr. of the online defense magazine *Breaking Defense* best captures the zeitgeist: "Such a conflict would be damaging for all involved and counterproductive for the country. No one I interviewed actually seems to want that war. Instead, everyone is watching the other side warily for budget grabs—and perhaps sometimes seeing malice where there might be none."[24] Senior military leaders will have to navigate carefully through this delicate and politically charged atmosphere when making decisions about striking the optimal active/reserve-component balance.

Congress is the only branch that can play a credible role in adjudicating between the services and components. Members of Congress face considerable challenges in doing so. Legislators must understand that any significant decision regarding force mix can have consequences that stretch out for years to come. Changing the military's force structure—by changing its role or moving different types of formations from one component to another—has long-term, strategic implications—particularly for the reserve component. The pipeline of qualified reservists in an increasingly technology-dependent military is already lengthy for active-component units. It is even longer in the reserve component. For example, converting an artillery battalion into a civil affairs unit means that the army loses the capabilities of not one battalion but two. The artillerymen who turned in their howitzers will not become experienced civil affairs experts in short order. Conversely, the army will not be able to put that new battalion into the field because it is untrained. Just because it exists on paper does not make it a formation ready to perform its mission. In some cases, not changing a reserve-component unit may be wiser than divesting the army of two capabilities for a long time period.

Members of Congress will need to develop a more nuanced understanding of the military to look across components to retain, expand, or even discontinue military capabilities as required. These capabilities may exist in traditional units (military police and civil affairs) and nontraditional domains (such as the National Guard's Agribusiness Development Teams and the State Partnership Program). Not every organization in the military is truly interchangeable, even if some perform the same general function. Adjustments to the force mix must also be made in light of current, potential, and emerging threats. The Russian invasion of Crimea in February 2014 illustrates the unpredictability of threats to US interests abroad. The military's leadership also has a role in the force mix debate. Active- and reserve-component leaders must also develop their understanding of and appreciation for each other's capabilities. Promoting a constructive dialogue in the face of fiscal austerity is a significant challenge for senior military leaders. Yet doing so will help each component to support each other while assisting members of Congress in determining the best way to utilize the components. Sun Tzu's axiom—to know your enemy and know yourself—is particularly apt.

Conclusion

The relationship between Congress and the reserve component differs from its relationship with the active component in important ways that affect how lawmakers behave and how legislation is crafted. The reserve component wields its political influence—both in uniform and through its associated lobbying activities—much more skillfully than its active-component counterparts. The local connection between members and reservists creates more opportunities for applying this influence. The case of the seat on the JCS illustrates how members can take positions that favor the reserve component—and the National Guard in particular—as a low-cost way to take a position that demonstrates support for the reserve component.

The ongoing debate over the active/reserve-component force mix takes place in the context of the relationship between Congress and the reserve component. Decisions over the active component's and reserve component's roles and missions, manning and equipment, and, ultimately, their relative budget share reflect more than the result of defending against national security threats. These decisions are heavily influenced by local concerns over what state governors and members of Congress consider to be "their" military

—the National Guard and Reserves—and how best to craft legislation that serves national defense requirements both at home and abroad.

Notes

1. Timothy J. Lowenberg, "The Role of the National Guard in National Defense and Homeland Security," National Guard Association of the United States, 2009, www.ngaus.org.

2. William H. Riker, *Soldiers of the States: The Role of the National Guard in American Democracy* (Washington, DC: PublicAffairs, 1957).

3. Martha Derthick, *The National Guard in Politics* (Cambridge, MA: Harvard University Press, 1965).

4. Sydney J. Freedberg Jr., "Budgets and 'Betrayal': National Guard Fights to Keep Apache Gunships," *Breaking Defense*, January 23, 2014, http://breakingdefense.com/2014/01/budgets-betrayal-national-guard-fights-to-keep-apache-gunships/.

5. "Pa. National Guard Opposes Army Proposal to Take Apache Helicopters," *Patriot-News/PennLive.com*, January 14, 2014, www.pennlive.com/midstate/index.ssf/2014/01/pennsylvania_national_guard_op.html.

6. Charles A. Stevenson, *Congress at War: The Politics of Conflict since 1789* (Washington, DC: Potomac Books, 2007).

7. US Congress, Senate, Committee on Homeland Security and Governmental Affairs, *Hurricane Katrina: A Nation Still Unprepared: Katrina Investigation Report*, 109th Cong., 2nd sess., 2006.

8. Author interview with Washington state adjutant general Timothy J. Lowenberg, Camp Murray, WA, 2011.

9. Christopher Cooper and Robert Block, *Disaster: Hurricane Katrina and the Failure of Homeland Security* (New York: Times Books, 2006), 126.

10. Commission on the National Guard and Reserves, *Commission on the National Guard and Reserves: Transforming the National Guard and Reserves into a 21st-Century Operational Force* (Washington, DC: Government Printing Office, 2008).

11. Ibid., 358.

12. US Congress, Senate, Committee on Armed Services, *Hearing to Receive Testimony on Whether the Chief, National Guard Bureau, Should Be a Member of the Joint Chiefs of Staff*, 112th Cong., 1st sess., 2011, 1.

13. Ibid.

14. Ibid., 16.

15. Ibid., 19.

16. Ibid., 40.

17. Ibid., 37.

18. Ibid., 33.

19. Anthony J. Nownes, *Total Lobbying: What Lobbyists Want (and How They Try to Get It)* (New York: Cambridge University Press, 2006).

20. David R. Mayhew, *Congress: The Electoral Connection* (New Haven, CT: Yale University Press, 1974).

21. Gary Roughead and Kori Schake, *National Defense in a Time of Change* (Washington, DC: Brookings Institution, 2013), 13, www.brookings.edu/research/papers/2013/02/us-national-defense-changes.

22. Ibid., 14.

23. Center for Strategic and Budgetary Assessments, *Strategic Choices Exercise Outbrief* (Washington, DC: Center for Strategic and Budgetary Assessments, 2013), www.csbaonline.org/publications/2013/05/strategic-choices-exercise-outbrief/.

24. Sydney J. Freedberg Jr., "Active vs. Guard: An Avoidable Pentagon War," *Breaking Defense*, June 28, 2013, http://breakingdefense.com/2013/06/28/active-vs-guard-an-avoidable-pentagon-war/.

6

Legislating "Military Entitlements"

A Challenge to the Congressional Abdication Thesis

ALEXIS LASSELLE ROSS

Since the 1990s, military pay and benefits have experienced several aspects of expansion. Such policy changes have contributed to significant growth in military personnel costs per service member. If left unchecked, this cost growth could induce one of three outcomes. One possibility is that the overall defense budget could expand to accommodate increasing costs, which is unlikely. Alternatively, if the defense budget and the size of the military remain constant while compensation continues its current budget trajectory, personnel costs could consume the entire defense budget by the year 2039.[1] This scenario is also unlikely. Under a third possibility, policymakers could be forced to decrease manpower levels to accommodate compensation costs, which could consequently reduce US military capabilities. Evidence suggests this third scenario is already occurring.[2]

Concerned senior officials in the executive branch have called previously sacrosanct military pay and benefits unsustainable. These officials have attempted to work with Congress to control compensation costs. However, Congress often rejects the president's proposals, as its members generally consider the current costs a necessary expense to support an all-volunteer military. This chapter does not attempt to solve this costly and increasingly debated issue or prescribe the "right" level of compensation for troops who have sacrificed a great deal, particularly over the last decade. Rather, it examines an underlying factor in the current landscape of military pay and benefits: Congress's involvement.

The views expressed in this chapter are those of the author and not necessarily those of the Military Compensation and Retirement Modernization Commission or any other entity of the US government.

Most scholars who study the balance of power between Congress and the executive in national security policymaking assert that the president commands while Congress most often yields. However, such a conclusion overlooks policymaking on military pay and benefits. This chapter argues that Congress does indeed assert its policy agenda when it passes legislation on military compensation and that these entitlements have important implications. Using a case study on TRICARE-for-Life (TFL), a policy that provides military retirees over the age of sixty-five access to military health care, known as TRICARE, the chapter examines how Congress established this policy despite the objections of the executive branch. It also explores the profound budgetary, political, and manpower ramifications of congressionally mandated "military entitlements."

Congress and National Security Policymaking

Much of the literature that interprets the national security authorities within the Constitution asserts that the framers allocated more powers to Congress than the executive.[3] However, following World War II, Congress has not exercised its full constitutional authority and usually defers to the president to establish military policy. Although many make the case that the executive has employed an excessively strong presidential prerogative, there is reasonable evidence that Congress's diminution is a result of both presidential initiative and congressional inaction.[4] In fact, some scholars argue that Congress's approach at times is characterized by deference, ambivalence, and abdication.[5]

This diminished level of congressional involvement is not without fluctuation. A variety of research has shown the legislative and executive branches' relative power waxes and wanes based on numerous variables: times of war and peace, the country's perceptions of the president, and other political, personal, legal, and institutional conditions.[6] Notably, many scholars believe there was a resurgence of congressional participation in the 1970s prompted by the Vietnam War and the Watergate scandal and facilitated by changes in the resources and organization of Congress. This predominant school acknowledges that Congress's power remains eroded but contends that congressional actors are now less deferential to the executive.[7] Of course, the cyclic pattern continues, and many scholars argue the post-9/11 period consists of a typical wartime relationship: a strong executive and an overly accommodating legislature.[8]

Although Congress has attempted to take a more active role since the 1970s, legislators' increased involvement is usually through means that are indirect (e.g., hearings, letters to executive branch officials, and required reports) rather than direct (i.e., substantive legislation). Research that demonstrates exceptions to Congress's usual deference often reflects legislators' use of indirect methods to shape defense policy.[9] Still, subtly guiding policy using indirect tools is a less powerful method than direct action via substantive legislation. Additionally, it is believed that when Congress does act on military matters, its interest and participation is limited more often to structural policy concerning the distribution of resources and involving domestic stakeholders (e.g., earmarks for weapon systems and opposition to base closures). Otherwise Congress continues to yield to the president during times of crisis when our national interests are threatened and also when crafting strategic policies that affect military force structure.[10] Even with the various nuances, academia generally regards Congress as a secondary player.

However, current scholarship often focuses on the use of military force, which represents only a fraction of defense policy. In the infrequent cases when other defense policy is studied, research centers on subjects such as weapons acquisition and base closures and neglects military compensation, another equally important subset of defense policy.[11] Furthermore, studies on the legislature's participation often conclude that Congress relies mostly on indirect, rather than the more authoritative direct, methods, but they do not take into account Congress's use of entitlements to direct military compensation. Considering the intensity of congressional involvement in the creation and expansion of military pay and benefits in the 2000s and how consequential these policies have been on defense budgets and force structure, Congress has had great influence in national security policymaking.

Recent Trends in Military Compensation

The objective of the military personnel compensation system is to attract, motivate, retain, and ultimately manage the departure of service members. To meet these goals, the military establishes compensation policies based on the unique needs and characteristics of the organization. For example, the military is a hierarchical organization without lateral entry that attempts to manage the supply and demand of military personnel through manpower policies such as its retirement system.[12] Military compensation today is a combination of multiple types of pay and benefits, as outlined in table 6.1.

Service members' basic pay, or income earned based on rank and years of service, is only one part of his or her total compensation package. Other regular cash pay includes allowances for housing and food as well as the economic advantage from nontaxable portions of cash pay. In particular circumstances, military members additionally receive special and incentive (S&I) pay to encourage them to enter or continue service. Aside from purely monetary compensation, troops also receive nonmonetary benefits called noncash pay.

Table 6.1. Types of Military Compensation

CASH PAY	NONCASH PAY
Regular Military Compensation	In-Kind Benefits
• Basic pay	• Health care for current members and dependents
• Basic Allowance for Housing	• Family housing and barracks
• Basic Allowance for Subsistence	• Subsistence in kind (i.e., dining halls)
• Tax advantages	• Installation services (e.g., child care, DOD-run schools, commissaries, exchanges, recreational facilities and programs)
	• Educational benefits
Special and Incentive (S&I) Pays	Deferred Benefits
• Payment for hazardous or difficult conditions (e.g., hostile fire pay)	• Retirement pay
	• Health care for retirees and dependents
• Payment for particular duties or occupations (e.g., aviation continuation pay)	• Other veterans' benefits (e.g., disability pay, educational benefits, mortgage assistance)
• Payment for needed skills or ranks (e.g., reenlistment bonuses)	

This includes in-kind benefits, which are goods or services provided to current members for free or at subsidized prices, and deferred benefits, which comprise retirement annuity, health care, and other benefits available at a later date to veterans, retirees, and their families.

Different types of compensation deliver varying levels of effectiveness.[13] For example, in-kind benefits offer reliable goods and services for military members who are frequently away from home and families that habitually relocate to often unfamiliar and remote areas. Indeed, military members' lifestyle necessitates easy access to consistent, quality services such as child care and housing. Furthermore, health and dental benefits are required to ensure the readiness of troops, and after decades of physically rigorous and dangerous work, deferred benefits such as retiree health care are helpful in caring for former service members.

Conversely, noncash benefits, and particularly deferred ones, have several disadvantages. Investments in fixed on-base services do not reach the population living farther from installations and are largely unresponsive to changing military missions and force composition. In-kind benefits often are provided inefficiently by the Department of Defense (DOD), whose primary mission is not education and retail, for example. Also these benefits are not targeted to those who most need or want them. Moreover, noncash compensation, in general, does not allow service members to determine for themselves how to fulfill their needs.

Issues of perceived value also affect the utility of noncash benefits. First, troops cannot easily recognize the value of noncash benefits and often conclude, incorrectly, their compensation package is less than that of their civilian counterparts.[14] Second, deferred benefits received later in one's life offer less perceived value to younger individuals due to the concept of the personal discount rate.[15] As such, deferred benefits have a minimal impact on recruitment and a small effect on retention until the tenth through twentieth years of service, when the impact is great.[16] Deferred benefits motivate only a small portion of the military because just 17 percent of the force serves long enough to qualify for benefits provided during military retirement.[17]

Most important, noncash benefits do not provide the same flexibility as cash benefits to reward individuals based on performance and necessary skill sets. Ultimately cash pay, and special and incentive pay in particular, can readily target the military's recruiting and retention needs. In fact, S&I pays are the most cost-effective compensation tool for dealing with supply-and-demand conditions throughout the force, as they can be adapted for specific force-management needs and can help to manage the flow of personnel throughout the manpower system.[18] This is critical, since compensation in the all-volunteer force is intended to aid in the supply of high-quality military forces. For all the reasons stated above, noncash compensation, particularly deferred benefits, is the least effective compensation tool for achieving manpower objectives, while cash pay, especially S&I pay, is the most effective.

Military Compensation Expands in the 2000s

Since 1999 several policy changes pertaining to cash and noncash pay have increased both the amount of compensation available and the population eligible for them. They include adjustments in annual pay, increased housing allowances, extra S&I pays, expanded health care, and additional benefits for retirees. These policy changes caused strategic implications in both the defense budget and the military's manning goals.

According to the DOD, in the years from 2002 to 2012 the cost for military pay and benefits increased nearly 90 percent, while the size of the military grew only about 3 percent.[19] This means that the military force itself remained almost constant while the cost to compensate it nearly doubled in a decade. David Chu, the undersecretary of defense for personnel and readiness from 2001 to 2008, when much of the expansion in pay and benefits occurred, stated, "The amounts have gotten to the point where they are hurtful. They are taking away from the nation's ability to defend itself."[20] Former defense secretary Leon Panetta has acknowledged that these costly, yet typically sacrosanct, personnel programs are no longer safe from impending budgetary trade-offs: "The fiscal reality facing us means that we must also look at the growth of personnel costs, which are a major driver of budget growth and are, simply put, on an unsustainable course."[21] This looming resources challenge within the defense budget is likely to pit personnel costs against spending on other programs such as weapon modernization.[22]

In addition to the budgetary implications, another important impact of recently expanded pay and benefits is their effect on new accessions or reenlistments. Ultimately compensation must aid the military organization in meeting its manpower goals. There are a variety of factors that cause people to serve in the military, among them patriotic duty and monetary incentives. The post-1973 all-volunteer force is motivated more by pecuniary incentives than it was in previous eras.[23] Not all pay and benefits, though, are equally effective in recruitment and retention. Research generally shows that increased compensation helped mitigate challenges in filling the ranks amid ongoing combat operations and growth in the size of the army and Marine Corps in the 2000s.[24] Note, however, that accession and reenlistment studies usually measure the impact of cash pays, not deferred or in-kind benefits. As explained above, cash compensation has more advantages than noncash benefits, and current remuneration is valued higher than deferred benefits.

An important factor in the recent increase in compensation is the role Congress played and the effects of its actions. Congress initiated many of the most costly and least effective compensation policies of the 2000s, sometimes despite objection from the executive.[25] Congress's approach to military compensation has been unsystematic. Its pay and benefits initiatives were taken over several years and with little attention to how each policy would affect the efficiency or effectiveness of the comprehensive military personnel system. In correlation, there are generally four causes of recent military compensation cost growth: changes in the composition of the force, increases in the costs that the DOD incurred when providing a benefit, an upsurge in the amount of benefits available, and increases in users and usage rates.[26] Half of the four causes—expanded benefits and greater eligibility—are associated with legislative changes. To examine more closely Congress's influence in military compensation, the following section presents a case study on TRICARE-for-Life.

TRICARE-for-Life: Congress Legislates a "Military Entitlement"

During the wave of military compensation expansion in the 2000s, Congress not only refrained from the deferential behavior or secondary status characterized in the literature—it led. In the case of TRICARE-for-Life specifically, Congress advanced its policy agenda despite the objections of the executive. In fact, the intensity of both branches' actions increased as the legislative process progressed. Using historical legislative documents and official communications between the branches on the development of the TFL policy, this case study presents evidence that it was the legislative branch, not the executive, that ultimately dictated the pace and form of this important policy change.

Prior to congressional action in 2000, military retirees over the age of sixty-five obtained health care in two ways. They received medical and dental care at military medical facilities when space and resources were available. However, as established in law, priority at military treatment facilities (MTFs) was given to active-duty military members and their dependents before retirees.[27] This "space-available" arrangement was not meant to be older retirees' primary health coverage. Rather, it was intended that retirees would transition to the Medicare system upon turning sixty-five.[28] However, a combination of Medicare and space-available access to MTFs was proving problematic for older retirees. Starting in the 1980s, the Department of Defense downsized its health-care network, and the number of retirees aged sixty-five and older grew exponentially. To address the issue, Congress passed legislation between 1997 and 2000 to authorize four demonstration programs to test and analyze the viability of different options of enhanced health care for retirees over sixty-five.

With the demonstration programs under way, the executive branch's preferred approach for dealing with the retiree health-care challenge was to resource and execute the pilot projects, study their results, and then explore options to provide better health-care access for older retirees. The DOD understood there were problems throughout the military health-care system, particularly in its administration and customer support. The DOD sought, first, to improve care for active-duty troops and their families and then address Medicare-eligible retirees' access. This prioritization is evident in the fiscal year 2001 budget request, legislative proposals, and public statements. Although senior military and DOD officials pledged commitment to retirees during hearing testimony, they cautioned lawmakers on the substantial costs associated with any additional benefits and endorsed the pilot programs already under way.[29] The cochair of the Defense Medical Oversight Committee, Adm. Donald L. Pilling, testified, "We support the demonstration programs funded in the President's budget and will continue to pursue the definition and financing of a stable long-term benefit for retirees."[30] "We discourage any provisions to expand these programs prior to the completion of congressionally required studies and reports," the chief of staff of the army, Gen. Eric K. Shinseki, stated.[31]

Despite the executive branch's preference to proceed pragmatically, most members of Congress were eager to deliver a swift solution to the issue of retiree health care. The moment was opportune. In 2000 there was a national budget surplus, campaigning for congressional and presidential elections was under way, and momentum had built from earlier actions to catch military pay and benefits up after decades of neglect.[32] More important, legislators were motivated by the passions of constituents and interest groups.[33] Many members of Congress believed military retirees who had served their country honorably were being denied the medical care they expected in the older stages of their lives.

There has been great debate about whether retirees have a legitimate claim to free lifetime health care through the military medical system. Extensive legal research demonstrates that no statutory entitlement to free, lifetime, on-base health care ever existed—only permissive law that allows retirees access to military treatment facilities if space and services are available. Furthermore, even if recruiters promised this benefit, the DOD cannot establish such benefit without explicit authorization; only Congress holds that constitutional authority (Article I, Section 8, Clause 14). Finally, federal courts have ruled consistently that claims of promised free health care for life have no legal standing.[34] However, the perception persists. Lawmakers and DOD officials alike noted an implied contract or a moral, although not legal, commitment to retirees.[35] Thus there was great interest among members of Congress to improve access to quality health care for Medicare-eligible retirees, preferably quickly.

This strong congressional interest developed into a new benefit during action on the Floyd D. Spence National Defense Authorization Act for Fiscal Year 2001 (FY 2001 NDAA). As the legislative cycle advanced, each branch's position, as well as its actions and responses to the other, intensified. Both the House and Senate Armed Services Committees reported out bills, H.R. 4205 and S. 2549, that included a pharmacy benefit for retirees and extended the three existing demonstration programs for retiree health care. The executive branch registered its concerns several times as the FY 2001 NDAA advanced through the legislative cycle and Congress grew closer to a health-care benefit for Medicare-eligible retirees. Initially, in response to the committee-reported version of the House measure, President Bill Clinton's statement of administration policy (SAP) reiterated his administration's preference that demonstration programs be completed and studied before expanding benefits. It also noted that demonstrations should not be extended longer than one or two years.[36] In the SAP on the committee-passed S. 2549, the president maintained his position that demonstration programs must run their course and be evaluated before considering longer-term options.[37]

Interestingly, almost immediately after receiving the SAP warning against a long-term extension, the full House passed by a vote of 406 to 10 an amendment to extend nationwide and make permanent the TRICARE Senior Prime demonstration program, or Medicare subvention.[38] In similar fashion to the House, a day after receiving the SAP for its legislation, the Senate amended its bill on the floor by a vote of 96 to 1 to include a provision that would offer Medicare-eligible military retirees access to TRICARE. The amendment only authorized coverage for two years (FY 2002 and FY 2003) to keep the bill within the mandatory spending caps established under that year's budget resolution.[39]

Once the full House and Senate acted, each converting a different demonstration project into a health-care program for older retirees, the executive branch grew more concerned. The SAP to the committee-passed FY 2001 Department of Defense Appropriations Bill conveyed disapproval of the House appropriations bill not funding the expanded and extended Medicare subvention program in the House-passed authorization bill as well as the program's sizable costs and prematurity.[40] Additionally, in a letter to the Senate Armed Services Committee, Secretary of Defense William Cohen warned that congressionally initiated health benefits "create billions of dollars of new unfunded discretionary as well as mandatory pay-as-you-go (PAYGO) costs. Unless the PAYGO costs of this bill are reduced or offset, its enactment could result in an across-the-board sequester of mandatory programs, including Medicare, veterans, and agricultural programs." Regarding the expanded retiree benefits in both bills, he pleaded that "more work is needed on these proposals before deciding which, if any, should be pursued and how to fund those without hurting our overall health care operations or other defense priorities. *I urge the Congress to proceed with caution and refrain from mandating new unfunded benefits* [emphasis added]."[41]

Finally, the DOD also submitted an official appeal for the conferees' consideration during the House-Senate conference on the FY 2001 NDAA. It argued the initiatives in the House and Senate bills were premature and costly: "The Department urges deferral of the expanded benefits for military retirees over sixty-five in Senate section 701 and House section 725 pending further evaluation and full funding of any expanded benefit."[42]

Despite the executive's official statements of reservation, the conference committee agreed to a program now commonly known as TFL. The conference report on the FY 2001 NDAA essentially included a permanent version of the Senate floor amendment. It allowed individuals who are entitled to Medicare upon turning sixty-five to continue using the TRICARE system.

Medicare would be the first payer for services provided, and TRICARE would supplement coverage. The conference report was adopted in both chambers by wide margins.[43]

TRICARE-for-Life was signed into law on October 30, 2000.[44] In his signing statement, President Clinton expressed satisfaction that the NDAA included several policies to improve military compensation but noted concern with one: TRICARE-for-Life. President Clinton stated he agreed with the essence of Congress's intention but had reservations about how the benefit is structured and its consequent expense: "The Act provides comprehensive health care coverage to military retirees over the age of sixty-five. Although I am concerned that the Congress fails to deal fully with the high, long-term cost of this new benefit, I am pleased overall with the way the Act supports individuals, who dedicated so much to the service of our country."[45] The TFL provision was one of hundreds of policies contained in the more than five-hundred-page National Defense Authorization Act that year. Although the executive branch earlier had urged Congress to exclude the provision, the president ultimately accepted it as part of a larger package of important policies.

Since the enactment of TFL, Congress has acted to protect the policy. In the late 2000s and early 2010s, the president argued, mostly unsuccessfully, for various changes in military compensation to slow cost growth. Specific to TFL, the president's budget requests for FY 2013 and FY 2014 sought to introduce an annual premium for TFL, which has been free to retirees since its creation.[46] The DOD described these fees as modest and advocated them by comparing TFL to "Medigap" health-care coverage, which many seniors buy to supplement Medicare.[47] Congress, however, viewed the imposition of fees as reducing the TFL benefit. In both years, Congress not only rejected the proposals and the budgetary savings they would have created, it also expressly forbade the DOD from taking any action to implement TFL premiums. First, the National Defense Authorization Act for FY 2013 included a sense-of-Congress statement expressing that the unique and extraordinary demands required of a career in the military have earned retirees a quality health-care benefit during retirement.[48] Later, in the Consolidated and Further Continuing Appropriations Act of 2013, Congress prohibited the DOD from spending any appropriated funds to implement an annual fee for TFL.[49] Congress repeated this moratorium the following year when the president again requested an annual TFL premium in FY 2014.[50]

In summary, legislators progressed from expanding demonstration programs by one to two years and to a few more locations to, ultimately, a permanent and nationwide program. Along the way, the executive's official statements grew more direct in their disapproval. By the time the bills went to conference, the secretary of defense had argued that initiatives in the

House and Senate bills were premature and costly. Specifically they would create billions of dollars of new unfunded discretionary and mandatory costs and would threaten the overall health-care program, as well as other critical defense priorities elsewhere in the budget. Congress passed TRICARE-for-Life anyway, and the implications have been significant.

Strategic Implications of TRICARE-for-Life

When legislators mandated a nationwide and permanent TRICARE-for-Life benefit before the demonstration programs were complete, they essentially gambled on an untested and costly policy that is extraordinarily hard to revise due to its traits as an entitlement (to be discussed in detail below). Legislative action occurred despite the warnings of the DOD and even a few members of Congress.[51] Of note, even the House Armed Services Committee, just five months before supporting the enactment of TFL, questioned the prudence of converting a pilot project into a permanent program.[52] In the end, what were the effects of TFL on the military health-care system, the DOD's manpower goals, and the defense budget? Furthermore, how do the strategic implications of congressional action on TFL alter the common perception that Congress does not influence defense policymaking in a significant way?

Effects of TRICARE-for-Life on Military Health-Care and Manpower Goals

When Congress mandated TRICARE-for-Life, it dramatically changed the landscape of the military health-care system. Prior to 2001 and the creation of TFL, roughly 88 percent of military retirees over sixty-five used Medicare supplemental insurance or were covered by Medicaid. By 2011 this figure dropped below 20 percent as older retirees flocked to the new military-provided system.[53] By 2012 Medicare-eligible retirees and their dependents accounted for 22 percent of eligible TRICARE users in the United States, while active-duty personnel represented only 14 percent.[54] All told, the DOD spends more on medical care provided to former service members and their families than to actual troops in uniform. Retirees sixty-five and older are the most expensive beneficiaries per capita and have the highest usage rates by far of any other group.[55]

TRICARE is attractive due to its low cost-sharing rates for users. Since 2000, national health-care fees surged while the out-of-pocket costs for participants of the military health-care system went down slightly.[56] In the mid-1990s, the military's user fees were specified in law, which is a highly inflexible practice made more restrictive because the statute did not allow the fees to adjust with inflation. Because the face value of most out-of-pocket costs did not change, they lost 41 percent of their real value between 1997 and 2010 due to inflation. As beneficiaries paid less in real value, the DOD was forced to pay more to cover the expenses. Occasionally Congress even decreased or eliminated user fees.[57] Not only do low user fees draw retirees to TRICARE, they also encourage higher usage rates among participants, which in turn increases government spending on the program.

Additionally, TRICARE-for-Life is only slightly effective in increasing the supply of manpower. TFL provides military retirees access to health care upon turning sixty-five. Accordingly, it is a noncash, deferred benefit. As described above, this kind of benefit has limited utility in retaining troops during the first half of their careers and a very small effect on attracting new recruits. Furthermore, new survey data show the relative importance service members place on different types of compensation. The results found that troops do not value the level of the TFL benefit commensurate with the amount of funding required to provide it.[58]

While noncash compensation and deferred benefits are found to have limited positive effect on recruitment and retention, this is only one, albeit the primary, purpose of military compensation. Many advocates believe the intangible effect associated with increases in any type of compensation has helped preserve the all-volunteer force. Those who sought greater pay and benefits in the 2000s usually were motivated by perceived insufficiencies and a moral obligation to military members to repay them for their service, especially frequent, lengthy deployments to Iraq and Afghanistan. This is valid reasoning, although data measuring the ability of TFL, in particular, to affect people's willingness to volunteer and serve is not readily available.

Budgetary Implications of TRICARE-for-Life

During debate on the final outcome of TRICARE-for-Life, Sen. Phil Gramm (R-TX) said, "Not only is this bill a budget buster—it will win the blue ribbon . . . of fiscal irresponsibility and lack of financial discipline."[59] The amount spent each year on health care for retirees sixty-five and older and their dependents has been growing steadily and reached $9.8 billion in FY 2012.[60] Several factors contribute to the increase in overall military health-care spending, including the rise in benefits available and the number of claimants to them, low cost-sharing for beneficiaries and excessive utilization of services, and general medical inflation. However, TFL has been the largest single factor contributing to the recent cost growth in the military's medical program. Excluding TFL, the DOD's health-care costs have increased 90 percent between FY 2000 and FY 2012. However, when TFL's accrual fund is included, spending grew roughly 150 percent over the same period.[61]

Currently health care represents nearly one-quarter of total compensation costs, but it is expected to swell to one-third by 2021.[62] Overall, the military health-care system makes up 9 percent ($47 billion) of the DOD's non-war-related budget request in FY 2013. The Congressional Budget Office estimates the DOD medical budget will roughly double ($95 billion) by FY 2030.[63] Note, however, that there are health-care-related costs in other areas of the defense budget, such as military construction, which makes it difficult to get a full accounting of the true cost of military health care.

Another budgetary impact of TFL is that its funding qualifies as mandatory spending, which forces the internal allocation of DOD funds. Mandatory spending typically results in opportunity costs that affect other programs, particularly if the size of the overall defense budget is limited. In summary, given its high costs and overall small effect on achieving manpower goals, TFL yields a low return on investment.

Implications of "Military Entitlements"

When Congress passed TRICARE-for-Life in the FY 2001 NDAA, it created an entitlement with profound implications. Entitlements are obligations established in law that require the government to disburse a benefit to any individual or unit of government that meets the eligibility requirements. As such, they are legally required, open-ended, quasi-permanent benefits that are highly sensitive to politics.[64] Current scholarship on entitlements does not explore fully defense policies; similarly, the field of Congress and national security neglects entitlements. To address this gap, I suggest the concept of *military entitlement*, a term that applies to some congressionally mandated benefits such as TFL. Its meaning is simple: a legal obligation that the government provide a benefit to eligible members of the armed forces, former members, or their families. However, its implications are nuanced. In many ways, military entitlements operate like traditional entitlements; in other ways, they are unique.

TRICARE-for-Life has the same political effect as other entitlements. It is difficult to reverse or reduce obligations provided in law, because it is unpopular to deprive a group of something to which the law states they are entitled.[65] The strong support that older military retirees have in the DOD, on Capitol Hill, and in interest groups exemplifies the program's susceptibility to politics. Senior officials of the executive branch have routinely faced insurmountable political challenges in attempting to persuade lawmakers to alter military benefits. Former defense secretary Robert Gates described this experience: "The proposals routinely die an *ignominious* death on Capitol Hill [emphasis added]."[66]

Political sensitivity for a military entitlement, however, is even more complex than traditional entitlements. According to the literature on political parties' issue ownership, Americans typically perceive the Republican Party as more skillful in handling issues such as national defense and taxes, while they tend to regard Democrats as more adept at working social welfare and social group relations issues.[67] This issue identification is blurred, however, for military entitlements. National security and social welfare issues overlap in TRICARE-for-Life. The program is believed to strengthen the all-volunteer military and honor veterans, as well as expand medical assistance to senior citizens. Consequently TFL appeals to both parties. As a result, there are concurrent claims to the policy, instead of the traditional issue ownership of each party. This "concurrent issue ownership" will ensure long-lasting support for TFL.

It is not enough to say that TRICARE-for-Life is expensive. Rather, because it is an entitlement that legally obligates the government to provide a service, total costs are open-ended. The amount of resources required to sustain an entitlement depends on the number of people collecting the benefits and the amount of benefits to which they are entitled, not agencies' management of the programs or annual appropriations bills. Furthermore, entitlements, as previous claims on government resources, must be satisfied before all other claims can be fulfilled. Hence, a rise in military entitlements, and their associated mandatory spending, is closely followed by budgetary compromises. As combat operations conclude causing war-related costs to decline, and as discretionary programs are reduced to accommodate deficit-reduction techniques and typical postwar cost-cutting measures, the total defense budget will likely decrease.[68] However, military entitlements and the funding they require will remain fixed, causing their portion of the declining defense budget to increase. Leon Panetta put it simply: "If we fail to address [the growth in personnel costs], then we won't be able to afford the training and equipment our troops need in order to succeed on the battlefield. There's a tradeoff here."[69]

Because of the nature of entitlements, mandatory spending carries on indefinitely. In fact, the only factors capable of altering the trajectory of entitlement programs are demographics, the economy, and congressional changes to underlying program law.[70] The president's budget requests and even long-term national security planning have little control over these programs. Rather, the benefits will continue to exist until Congress changes them. This gives the congressionally mandated policy a greater sense of permanence than if it were an internal DOD policy and hence secures the legislature's continued participation in policy decisions. Altogether, this indicates that when Congress utilizes entitlements, it strengthens its influence over defense policymaking.

Generalizing the TRICARE-for-Life Case to Military Compensation

The case study on TRICARE-for-Life yields findings that can be generalized to Congress's involvement in military compensation overall. The following are two examples of instances when Congress used its legislative power to mandate its policy preferences and override the executive's initiatives. In doing so, Congress protected its role in the defense policymaking process.

For years the DOD attempted to contain rising health-care costs by introducing fee increases for retirees under sixty-five who were not yet eligible for Medicare and TFL. The DOD budget requests in 2006, 2007, and 2008 included such proposals. In each year, Congress not only rejected the proposals, it also passed legislation prohibiting fee increases for beneficiaries. In 2009 and 2010 the DOD did not attempt to adjust cost-sharing. Nonetheless, Congress forestalled it by passing moratoriums on fee increases in those years. It was not until 2011 that the DOD proposed, and Congress allowed, higher fees for retirees.[71] Congress's actions in military health-care policy—both expanding the benefit and later preventing the DOD from restricting it—have significantly affected military health care and military compensation in general.

Furthermore, Congress has taken unequivocal action to protect its role in the policymaking process. For example, in 2012 the president's budget request proposed a commission similar to those used for base realignment and closure (BRAC) in order to consider changes to military retirement. Using a BRAC-like construct, "Congress would have to vote up or down on the [military retirement] recommendation without amendment and under expedited procedures."[72] Congress rejected this proposal and, instead, directed a commission to recommend options to both the legislative and executive branches.[73] By doing so, Congress has retained control of military compensation reform and will legislate only the changes it considers appropriate.[74]

In both examples, the executive required congressional action to achieve its goals. In each instance, the president either underwent a long struggle to win support from lawmakers (i.e., increased fees) or he did not get the exact outcome he desired (i.e., a commission with the authority to present policy changes to Congress for an up-or-down vote).

Conclusion

The evidence demonstrates Congress proactively pursued its own policy agenda when it mandated and later protected TRICARE-for-Life, a military entitlement. Obviously, the legislature is meant to pass laws, but the particulars of this case are important for three reasons. First, when Congress legislated, it disregarded the executive's official objections regarding the cost and prematurity of the program. Such action does not match the deference, abdication, ambivalence, and other passive behaviors scholars commonly use to describe the legislative branch. Second, TFL is a military entitlement, which intensifies its significant impacts. Also, because the policy is an entitlement, Congress will remain in control of its future. Third, the effects of TFL will reverberate throughout the military's health-care system and defense budget for decades. The many strategic implications of this legislation demonstrate the real but underappreciated effect of congressional influence in defense policymaking.

Overall, military pay and benefits increased dramatically in recent years. Many are congressionally directed; some are military entitlements. These policy changes were sometimes a result of piecemeal actions taken to "fix" certain elements of pay and benefits while failing to see their overarching, long-term implications for the remarkably complex military compensation system. Consequently, the rate of military compensation cost growth and its effect on the rest of the defense budget is alarming, presenting the executive and legislative branches with a policy dilemma.

Ideally, any efforts to make pay and benefits more effective in fulfilling manpower needs, more valuable to service members, and more affordable to the DOD should be designed comprehensively and undertaken systematically. Since much of the expansion in compensation is a result of congressional action and because military entitlements cannot be altered without amending the underlying program law, Congress has played and will continue to play an important part in this public policy area. Congress is a large, decentralized, deliberative body that must build consensus to achieve action.[75] As such, Congress usually operates incrementally, with a near-term focus and a limited scope. Institutionally, Congress's traits make comprehensive reform based on a long-term perspective difficult. Politically, asking legislators to repeal or reduce the benefits they initiated presents an additional challenge.

Nevertheless, Congress is, constitutionally, an equal branch to the executive and has responsibility for raising and supporting military forces. If the executive is to limit escalating costs and invest more resources in the most constructive and efficient benefit types, it must effectively engage Congress to do so. Only legislators can affect the course of military entitlements.

Notes

1. Todd Harrison, *Rebalancing Military Compensation: An Evidence-Based Approach* (Washington, DC: Center for Strategic and Budgetary Assessment, 2012), i. This projection assumes

that the budget trajectory continues its current course and the DOD budget remains flat with inflation.

2. Military Compensation and Retirement Modernization Commission, *Interim Report* (Washington, DC: Military Compensation and Retirement Modernization Commission, June 2014), 18, 21–22, www.mcrmc.gov/public/docs/reports/MCRMC-Interim-Report-Final-HIRES-L.pdf. From 2001 to 2012, pay and benefits per active-duty service member increased by 42 percent in real terms. Bipartisan Policy Center and American Enterprise Institute, *Trends in Military Compensation: A Chartbook* (Washington, DC: Bipartisan Policy Center and American Enterprise Institute, 2014), http://bipartisanpolicy.org/sites/default/files/BPC%20AEI%20Military%20Compensation%20Chartbook%20July%202014.pdf.

3. James P. Pfiffner, *Power Play: The Bush Presidency and the Constitution* (Washington, DC: Brookings Institution Press, 2008); Louis Fisher, *Presidential War Power*, 2nd ed. (Lawrence: University Press of Kansas, 2004); and Paul E. Peterson, "The International System and Foreign Policy," in *The President, the Congress, and the Making of Foreign Policy*, ed. Paul E. Peterson (Norman: University of Oklahoma Press, 1994).

4. Arthur M. Schlesinger Jr., *The Imperial Presidency*, (New York: Popular Library, 1974); Louis Fisher, *Congressional Abdication on War and Spending* (College Station: Texas A&M University Press, 2000); and Christopher J. Deering, "Congress, the President, and Military Policy," *Annals of the American Academy of Political and Social Science* 499 (September 1988): 136–47.

5. James M. Lindsay, "Deference and Defiance: The Shifting Rhythms of Executive-Legislative Relations in Foreign Policy," *Presidential Studies Quarterly* 33, no. 3 (September 2003): 530–46; Jasmine Farrier, *Congressional Ambivalence: The Political Burdens of Constitutional Authority* (Lexington: University Press of Kentucky, 2010); and Fisher, *Congressional Abdication*.

6. Farrier, *Congressional Ambivalence*; Lindsay, "Deference and Defiance"; and Andrew Rudalevige, "'The Contemporary Presidency': The Decline and Resurgence and Decline (and Resurgence?) of Congress: Charting a New Imperial Presidency," *Presidential Studies Quarterly* 36, no. 3 (September 2006): 506–24.

7. Barry M. Blechman, *The Politics of National Security: Congress and U.S. Defense Policy* (New York: Oxford University Press, 1990); and Randall B. Ripley and James M. Lindsay, ed., *Congress Resurgent: Foreign and Defense Policy on Capitol Hill* (Ann Arbor: University of Michigan Press, 1993).

8. Pfiffner, *Power Play*; and Thomas E. Mann and Norman J. Ornstein, *The Broken Branch: How Congress Is Failing America and How to Get It Back on Track* (New York: Oxford University Press, 2006).

9. William G. Howell and Jon C. Pevehouse, *While Dangers Gather: Congressional Checks on Presidential War Powers* (Princeton, NJ: Princeton University Press, 2007); and Robert David Johnson, *Congress and the Cold War* (New York: Cambridge University Press, 2006); and Douglas L. Kriner, *After the Rubicon: Congress, Presidents, and the Politics of Waging War* (Chicago: University of Chicago Press, 2010).

10. James M. Lindsay and Randall B. Ripley, "How Congress Influences Foreign and Defense Policy," in *Congress Resurgent: Foreign and Defense Policy on Capitol Hill*, ed. Randall B. Ripley and James M. Lindsay (Ann Arbor: University of Michigan Press, 1993), 17–35.

11. Note the research presented here focuses on military and defense policy rather than foreign policy. For a good example of Congress's assertiveness in foreign policy, see the research on arms control treaties and the Senate's use of its advice-and-consent authority in David P. Auerswald, "Arms Control," in *Congress and the Politics of National Security*, ed. David P. Auerswald and Colton C. Campbell (New York: Cambridge University Press, 2012), 189–212.

12. Beth J. Asch and John T. Warner, *A Theory of Military Compensation and Personnel Policy* (Santa Monica, CA: Rand Corp., 1994); and Paul F. Hogan, "Overview of the Current Personnel and Compensation System," in *Filling the Ranks: Transforming the U.S. Military Personnel System*, ed. Cindy Williams (Cambridge, MA: MIT Press, 2004), 29–53.

13. The debate on the effectiveness and efficiency of the compensation types is summarized in Carla Tighe Murray, "Transforming In-Kind Compensation and Benefits," in *Filling the Ranks: Transforming the U.S. Military Personnel System*, ed. Cindy Williams (Cambridge, MA: MIT Press, 2004), 189–212; and Steven M. Kosiak, *Military Compensation: Requirements, Trends and Options* (Washington, DC: Center for Strategic and Budgetary Assessments, 2005).

14. The Department of Defense estimated in 2008 that when some of the military's benefits are included with pay, 80 percent of the analogous civilian population earned less than the comparable military population. Brenda S. Farrell, *Military Personnel: Comparisons between Military and Civilian Compensation Can Be Useful, but Data Limitations Prevent Exact Comparisons*, written testimony before the Subcommittee on Personnel, Committee on Armed Forces, Senate, 111th Cong. (Washington, DC: Government Accountability Office, April 28, 2010), www.gao.gov/products/GAO-10-666T.

15. Individuals tend to value compensation received in the future much lower than the same amount received today.

16. Hogan, "Overview of the Current Personnel and Compensation System."

17. Defense Business Board, *Modernizing the Military Retirement System*, report to the secretary of defense (Washington, DC: Defense Business Board, October 2011), 3, http://dbb.defense.gov/Reports.aspx. Retirement statistics vary between officer and enlisted personnel. Forty-three percent of officers and 13 percent of enlisted troops historically qualify for retirement.

18. Beth J. Asch et al., *Cash Incentives and Military Enlistment, Attrition, and Reenlistment* (Santa Monica, CA: Rand Corp., 2010).

19. Leon Panetta, *Department of Defense Authorization for Appropriations for Fiscal Year 2013 and the Future Years Defense Program, Hearings Before the Committee on Armed Services, Senate*, hearings held February 14, 28, March 1, 6, 8, 13, 15, 20, and 27, 2012, 112th Cong., S. Hrg. 112-590, pt. 1 (written testimony of the secretary of defense, February 14), 8. A 90 percent increase is roughly 30 percent above inflation.

20. David Chu, quoted in Greg Jaffe, "As Benefits for Veterans Climb, Military Spending Feels Squeeze," *Wall Street Journal*, January 25, 2005, http://webreprints.djreprints.com/1156160669825.html.

21. Leon Panetta, "Defense Priorities: Today and Tomorrow," speech presented at the Woodrow Wilson International Center for Scholars, Washington, DC, October 11, 2011, www.wilsoncenter.org/event/defense-priorities-today-and-tomorrow.

22. For an overview of this policy debate, see Todd Harrison, *The New Guns versus Butter Debate* (Washington, DC: Center for Strategic and Budgetary Assessments, 2010), 2–3.

23. David R. Segal, *Recruiting for Uncle Sam: Citizenship and Military Manpower Policy* (Lawrence: University Press of Kansas, 1989); and Charles C. Moskos, *A Call to Civic Service: National Service for Country and Community* (New York: Free Press, 1988).

24. Asch et al., *Cash Incentives*; Steven M. Kosiak, *Military Manpower for the Long Haul, Strategy for the Long Haul Series* (Washington, DC: Center for Strategic and Budgetary Assessments, 2008), 26.

25. For example, the repeal of the REDUX retirement system that would have offered a more modest annuity, Concurrent Receipt that allows service members to collect retirement pay without an offset for veterans' disability payments, removal of the Social Security offset for the Survivors' Benefits Plan, and TRICARE-for-Life.

26. Maren Leed and Brittany Gregerson, *Keeping Faith: Charting a Sustainable Path for Military Compensation* (Washington, DC: Center for Strategic and International Studies, 2011), 6, http://csis.org/publication/keeping-faith.

27. 10 U.S.C. 1074; 10 U.S.C. 1076.

28. Department of Defense, *Military Compensation Background Papers: Compensation Elements and Related Manpower Cost Items, Their Purposes and Legislative Backgrounds*, 7th ed., November 2011, 675, http://militarypay.defense.gov/Reports/backgroundpapers.html; and Don J. Jansen and Katherine Blakeley, *Military Medical Care: Questions and Answers*, RL33537 (Washington, DC: Congressional Research Service, October 4, 2012), 19. Realizing that military retirees under sixty-five were left in a gap following the creation of Medicare in 1965, Congress authorized these retirees access to health care through the DOD until age sixty-five (Military Medical Benefits Amendments of 1966, Pub. L. No. 89-614). At such time, they were to participate in Medicare.

29. Several senior military leaders, including the then chairman of the Joint Chiefs of Staff, Gen. Henry Shelton, publicly stated their belief that the country should provide health care to older retirees. Shelton recommended swift action to create a retiree health-care entitlement during a House Armed Services Committee hearing a month after the committee received official communication from the secretary of defense urging Congress to refrain from expensive, premature retiree health-care mandates. See Henry H. Shelton, *Military Services' Posture, Readiness, and Budget Issues, Hearing before the Committee on Armed Services, House,* hearing held September 27, 2000, 106th Cong., House Armed Services Committee No. 106-44 (Statement of the Chairman, Joint Chiefs of Staff), 92-96. Note, however, that senior military officers are required to provide their honest professional opinion to Congress even if it conflicts with the policies of a president's administration. See Pat Towell, "Congress and Defense," in *Congress and the Politics of National Security*, ed. David P. Auerswald and Colton C. Campbell (New York: Cambridge University Press, 2012), 83. In fact, military officers do not represent the president or his administration. The research in this chapter focuses instead on the interaction between the executive and legislative branches.

30. Donald L. Pilling, *Hearings on National Defense Authorization Act for Fiscal Year 2001—H.R. 4205 and Oversight of Previously Authorized Programs: Hearings on Title IV— Personnel Authorizations; Title V—Military Personnel Policy; Title VI—Compensation and Other Personnel Benefits; Title VII—Health Care Provisions, before the Military Personnel Subcommittee, Committee on Armed Services, House of Representatives,* held February 25, 28, and March 8, 15, and 17, 2000, 106th Cong., House Armed Services Committee No. 106-41 (statement of the cochair, Defense Medical Oversight Committee, March 15), 761.

31. Eric K. Shinseki, *Department of Defense Authorization for Appropriations for Fiscal Year 2001 and the Future Years Defense Program, Part 1, Hearings before the Committee on Armed Services, Senate,* held February 8, 10, 29, and March 1, 7, and 9, 2000, 106th Cong., S. Hrg. 106-609, pt. 1 (statement of the chief of staff, US Army, March 1), 561.

32. For example, Congress passed comprehensive reform of the military retirement system in the National Defense Authorization Act for Fiscal Year 2000 (Pub. L. No. 106-65).

33. Military retirees fervently urged lawmakers to take immediate action. A cautious, incremental approach was unacceptable. One constituent confronted the then Senate majority leader, Trent Lott (R-MS): "You should be leading the fight. Instead, it is widely reported that you favor a bite-size approach to nibble by bits and pieces at the problem rather than meeting it head on." A retired master sergeant said, "I cannot understand why the Congress of the United States cannot understand the urgency. To us, they're playing a game

for crying out loud and they're playing a game with our lives." Quoted in Betsy Rothstein, "Sen. Lott Besieged by Angry Military Retirees," *The Hill*, February 23, 2000.

34. David F. Burrelli, *Military Health Care: The Issue of "Promised" Benefits* (Washington, DC: Congressional Research Service, January 19, 2006).

35. *Hearings on National Defense Authorization Act for Fiscal Year 2001—H.R. 4205 and Oversight of Previously Authorized Programs: Hearings on Title IV—Personnel Authorizations; Title V— Military Personnel Policy; Title VI—Compensation and Other Personnel Benefits; Title VII—Health Care Provisions, before the Military Personnel Subcommittee, Committee on Armed Services, House of Representatives*, held February 25, 28, and March 8, 15, and 17, 2000, 106th Cong., House Armed Services Committee No. 106-41, March 15, 123-24, 178; *Department of Defense Authorization for Appropriations for Fiscal Year 2001 and the Future Years Defense Program, Part I, Hearings before the Committee on Armed Services, Senate*, held February 8, 10, 29, and March 1, 7, 9, 2000, 106th Cong., S. Hrg. 106-609, pt. 1, February 8 and March 1, 13, 30, 435.

36. William J. Clinton, "Statement of Administration Policy on H.R. 4205, Floyd D. Spence National Defense Authorization Act for Fiscal Year 2001," May 17, 2000, www.presidency .ucsb/ws/index.php?pid=74810.

37. William J. Clinton, "Statement of Administration Policy on S. 2549, National Defense Authorization Act for Fiscal Year 2001," June 6, 2000, www.presidency.ucsb/ws/index .php?pid=74899.

38. *Congressional Record*, H3377–H3392 (daily ed., May 18, 2000), amendment of Rep. Gene Taylor (D-MS), Roll No. 207. Under the Medicare subvention demo, military retirees over sixty-five received health care from the military system, and the Health Care Financing Administration (the agency that administered Medicare at the time) reimbursed the DOD for a portion of the costs.

39. *Congressional Record*, S4525–S4536, S4541–S4542, S4627 (daily ed., June 6–7, 2000), amendment, as modified, of Sen. John Warner (R-VA), Roll No. 117. Sen. Tim Johnson (D-SD) also offered an extensive retiree medical program. However, his policy to allow older military retirees permanent, full access to the Federal Employees Health Benefits Program violated the Budget Act. See *Congressional Record*, S4620–S4633 (daily ed., June 7, 2000).

40. William J. Clinton, "Statement of Administration Policy on H.R. 4576, Department of Defense Appropriations Bill, FY2001," June 6, 2000, www.presidency.ucsb/ws/index.php ?pid=74827.

41. William Cohen, "Letter to Senator Warner, Chairman, Committee on Armed Services, Senate," August 7, 2000, Record Group 233, Box 106-188, National Archives.

42. Department of Defense, "TRICARE Expansion of Health Care Coverage for Over 65 Military Retirees," in *DOD Appeal to the FY2001 Defense Authorization Bill (August 31, 2000): O-70*, Record Group 233, Box 106–188, National Archives.

43. *Congressional Record*, H9647–H9666 (daily ed., October 11, 2000), conference report agreed to, 382 to 31, Roll No. 522; *Congressional Record*, S10299, S10334–10394 (daily ed., October 12, 2000), conference report agreed to, 90 to 3, Roll No. 275.

44. Pub. L. No. 106-398, sec. 712.

45. William J. Clinton, "Statement on Signing the Floyd D. Spence National Defense Authorization Act for Fiscal Year 2001," *Weekly Compilation of Presidential Documents* 36, no. 44 (October 30, 2000): 2690.

46. Military retirees do, however, pay an annual fee for the Medicare Part B program.

47. Office of the Undersecretary of Defense (Comptroller), *United States Department of Defense Fiscal Year 2013 Budget Request Overview* (February 2012), 5-4, http://comptroller.defense.gov /Portals/45/Documents/defbudget/fy2013/FY2013_Budget_Request_Overview

_Book.pdf; Office of the Undersecretary of Defense (Comptroller), *United States Department of Defense Fiscal Year 2014 Budget Request Overview* (April 2013), 5-6, http://comptroller .defense.gov/Portals/45/Documents/defbudget/fy2014/FY2014_Budget_Request _Overview_Book.pdf.

48. Pub. L. No. 112-239, sec. 707.

49. Pub. L. No. 113-6, sec. 8128.

50. Consolidated Appropriations Act, 2014, Pub. L. No. 113-76, sec. 8137.

51. Sen. Bob Kerry (D-NE) led the opposition, albeit small, to TFL during debate on the conference report. He argued the program's expense was exorbitant, the promise of free lifetime health care had been exaggerated, and the TFL policy was an admission that Medicare was an inadequate program. See *Congressional Record*, S10365–S10369 (daily ed., October 12, 2000).

52. "Neither the Department of Defense, nor Congress, had sufficient information to move the currently running health care demonstration programs for the military Medicare-eligible beneficiaries from the demonstration to the permanent program stage." House Committee on Armed Services, *Floyd D. Spence National Defense Authorization Act for Fiscal Year 2001*, H. Rept. 106-616 (May 12, 2000), 381.

53. Department of Defense, *Evaluation of the TRICARE Program: Fiscal Year 2012 Report to Congress*, February 28, 2012, 82, http://tricare.mil/hpae/studies/reports.cfm.

54. Department of Defense, *Evaluation of the TRICARE Program: Fiscal Year 2013 Report to Congress*, February 28, 2013, 11, http://tricare.mil/tma/dhcape/program/evaluation.aspx.

55. Brittany Gregerson, "Curing Military Health Care," *Armed Forces Journal* (May 2012), www.armedforcesjournal.com/2012/05/10122465.

56. Congressional Budget Office, *Costs of Military Pay and Benefits in the Defense Budget*, Pub. No. 4234 (Washington, DC: November 2012), 28–30. Premiums in the private sector have increased roughly 80 percent in real terms. To illustrate the contrast in cost-sharing between TRICARE and private sector plans, the total out-of-pocket costs for families of working-age retirees enrolled in the TRICARE Prime plan is merely 18 percent of what families pay in employer-provided plans. In the FY 2001 NDAA, Congress eliminated many fees for families of active-duty service members enrolled in TRICARE Prime. Consequently, they receive free health care with no out-of-pocket costs except for small co-pays for prescription drugs.

57. Gregerson, "Curing Military Health Care."

58. Harrison, *Rebalancing Military Compensation*. Harrison's survey sample was not random, introducing self-selection bias. Representation of the ranks in the sample does not accurately correspond to the proportion in the full military population.

59. *Congressional Record*, S10370 (daily ed., October 12, 2000).

60. Department of Defense, *Fiscal Year 2012 Medicare-Eligible Retiree Health Care Fund Audited Financial Statements*, November 7, 2012, http://comptroller.defense.gov/cfs/fy2012.htm #medicare.

61. Leed and Gregerson, *Keeping Faith*, 17. Congress required in the FY 2001 NDAA that the DOD use accrual budgeting for the TFL program beginning in FY 2003. When the DOD began to account for future TFL liabilities in current budgets, it made deferred costs immediately evident and dramatically increased the DOD medical budget.

62. Ibid., 26.

63. Congressional Budget Office, *Long-Term Implications of the 2013 Future Years Defense Program* (Washington, DC: Congressional Budget Office, July 2012), 20.

64. Aaron Wildavsky and Naomi Caiden, *The New Politics of the Budgetary Process*, 5th ed. (New York: Longman, 2004); and Allen Schick, *The Federal Budget: Politics, Policy, Process*, 3rd ed. (Washington, DC: Brookings Institution Press, 2007).

65. Wildavsky and Caiden, *New Politics of the Budgetary Process*, 132.

66. Robert M. Gates, "Eisenhower Library (Defense Spending)," speech presented at the Eisenhower Library, Abilene, KS, May 8, 2010, www.defense.gov/speeches/speech .aspx?speechid=1467.

67. Danny Hayes, "Candidate Qualities through a Partisan Lens: A Theory of Trait Ownership," *American Journal of Political Science* 49, no. 4 (October 2005): 909.

68. A recent example of a deficit-reduction technique that greatly impacted the defense budget is sequestration, an automatic reduction in federal government outlays to occur over ten years starting in 2013, as required by the Budget Control Act of 2011 (Pub. L. No. 112-25).

69. Panetta, "Defense Priorities."

70. Joseph White, "Entitlement Budgeting vs. Bureau Budgeting," *Public Administration Review* 58, no. 6 (December 1998): 512.

71. Congressional Budget Office, *Costs of Military Pay and Benefits*, 33, 41–42.

72. Office of the Undersecretary of Defense (Comptroller), *United States Department of Defense Fiscal Year 2013 Budget Request Overview* (February 2012), 5-5, http://comptroller.defense .gov/Portals/45/Documents/defbudget/fy2013/FY2013_Budget_Request_Overview _Book.pdf.

73. Pub. L. No. 112-239, sec. 671.

74. This example is inconsistent with the delegation and regret Farrier found in her case study on Congress and BRAC commissions. See Farrier, *Congressional Ambivalence*.

75. David P. Auerswald and Colton C. Campbell, "Congress and National Security," in *Congress and the Politics of National Security*, ed. David P. Auerswald and Colton C. Campbell (New York: Cambridge University Press, 2012), 12.

Part II

Parochial versus National Interests

7

Defense and the Two Congresses

Parochialism Balance

CHUCK CUSHMAN

There have always been two Congresses—one that focuses on national poli-cymaking and one that serves local, constituency interests.[1] Defense policy, though, emerged during the Cold War as a bit of a special case: The defense policy consensus that led to the creation of a powerful Department of Defense (DOD) and a global strategy of containment protected defense policy from being overrun by local interests. Until the Cold War ended in 1991, even the most constituency-minded members of Congress wrapped their efforts to support local interests in the language of strategy.

In parallel with the emergence of the Cold War defense consensus, Congress developed an institutional approach to lawmaking that defined how Congress balances its two roles of national lawmaker and local representa-tive. This system of "regular order" helped Congress function: It gave power to committees (and their chairs) to shape policy proposals and linked policy decisions to budget choices contained in the annual appropriations bills.

Defense policy was the poster child for regular order. The powerful House and Senate Armed Services Committees produced a comprehensive autho-rization bill every year, guaranteed by tradition to come to the floor of each chamber for debate, and the policy decisions in the annual defense bill, the National Defense Authorization Act (NDAA), would inform the annual de-fense appropriations act that would follow it to the floor in each chamber.

Regular order is more than a process—it is as much about the underly-ing policy consensus as it is about rules or floor procedure. Defense policy achieved a protected status because there was a strong bipartisan consensus about its importance to the nation and about how to guarantee the effective-ness of the containment strategy. Until the Cold War's end, defense came the closest of any policy area to defining how regular order was supposed to be. And once the Cold War ended, so did defense policy's privileged position.

Since the end of the Cold War, successive Congresses and administrations have groped toward a defense strategy that makes sense in the emerging world. The task has been complicated by the fluidity of world events and the stark difference between contemporary reality and that of the Cold War. The institutions that make policy in Washington are largely themselves a product of the Cold War, so adapting to new challenges is very difficult.

Nationally politics in the United States has also changed dramatically since the end of the Cold War. The emergence of a competitive Republican Party (the GOP) that has won the majority in House elections regularly and the accompanying shift toward a more ideologically coherent political struggle between the two parties have led to a decline of the old regular order system in Congress (which, after all, was largely the product of forty years of Democratic control of the Congress).

And these changes have impacted on defense policy. Not only is the strategic consensus gone—the preferred position of defense policy in regular order is also gone. That means that defense policy is treated more like other policy issues than it used to be, which means that members are freer to inject local concerns into defense than they were during the Cold War. Certainly members during the Cold War worked to protect bases and defense industry in their home districts, but they felt the need to defend their efforts as serving the larger need of national defense. The erosion of regular order has allowed members to treat the defense budget as just another pork barrel to be haggled over.

Seeing defense budgets as acceptable targets for the traditional tools of policymaking—trades, logrolling, and the like—is more a change of emphasis than a new thing. Deals have always been part of defense budgeting. But the rebalancing that is occurring makes members feel that they can seek to advance constituency ends on an equal basis with serving national policy goals. How has this emerged, and what does it mean for defense budgeting? The answers to those questions become clear after reviewing the emergence of regular order along with the development of the Cold War consensus, the evolution of defense budgeting after the Cold War, and the emergence of the Tea Party caucus in the Republican Party, which has replaced strong defense with budget discipline as a defining pillar of GOP politics.

Cold War Defense Politics: Regular Order Personified

In the postwar years of the mid-twentieth century, congressional policymaking evolved into a highly organized process that allowed Congress to play a key role in shaping national policy. Regular order empowered the oversight committees to define policy goals for federal agencies, with the appropriations committees producing spending bills that supported those congressional policies. Congress's approach to defense policy defined regular order in its complex intertwining of policy set in bills from the Armed Services Committees and defense budgets passed by the Appropriations Committees in an annual process that has brought an authorization and appropriations bill to the floor in each chamber every year since 1961.

During the Cold War, Congress played a decisive role in shaping the US defense establishment. Foreign and defense policies fall into three types, with different roles of the key policy players.[2] In crisis policies, the demand for rapid response centers most decision making on the White House and senior agency officials (the Department of State and the DOD being the major players), with Congress playing no real role during the crisis due to its slower internal processes. In strategic policy, where major goals and efforts are outlined, the executive branch again takes the lead due to its deep reserves of expertise in the DOD and State and its centralized management from the White House; congressional leaders play a key role in accepting or revising strategic proposals, which they then pass on to the relevant committees for action.

Actually building the capabilities needed to achieve those strategic goals is the focus of structural policy, where agency staff and the committees take the lead in selecting weapons, designing force structures, and sustaining bases. During the early years of the Cold War, Congress embraced its structural role by building the executive branch agencies needed to manage the new role of the United States as global superpower, and throughout the Cold War Congress devised and then followed a set of procedures and practices that allowed it to retain a role as partner with the presidency in crafting and executing the Cold War strategy of containment. Congress wrote the laws that created the DOD, the National Security Council, the Central Intelligence Agency, and the other components of the Intelligence Community.

At the same time, Congress reformed its own committee structure to make it better suited to oversee the emerging national security establishment, and it devised a new process for passing defense authorization bills that placed Congress squarely in the center of defense decision making. Prior to the Second World War, Congress passed naval and military authorizations and spending bills that were very broad, leaving a great deal of leeway for the leaders in the War and Navy Departments. With the adoption of the Russell Amendment in 1959, which would take effect for the fiscal year (FY) 1962 budget cycle (bills passed in 1961), Congress required itself to authorize DOD spending on a program-by-program basis, giving the House and Senate Armed Services Committees comprehensive oversight responsibilities that reached down into every aspect of the nation's military.[3]

By reviewing every defense weapon program annually, as well as reviewing force structure and other key policy guidance, the House and Senate Armed Services Committees ensured that Congress would be an equal partner with the White House in setting US national security strategy. The defense committees' power was recognized by other committees and the prestige of serving on them was clear.[4]

In addition to giving Congress a forum for examining policy guidance for the DOD every year, the House and Senate Armed Services Committees' annual passage of the NDAA became an expected part of the annual legislative cycle—so much so that the NDAA was the only nonappropriations bill guaranteed significant floor time every year.[5] In addition the NDAA became the guidance for crafting of the annual defense appropriations bills—with the chair of the House Armed Services Committee regularly winning support on the floor for cutting items from the spending bill that had not been authorized in the NDAA. The sequence of these bills is the perfect embodiment of the idea of regular order: The oversight committee does thorough investigation of the issues through hearings and reports ordered from the DOD, which inform the policy guidance issued by Congress in the NDAA, and the appropriations bills then pay for weapons, troop levels, and bases that sustain the strategy laid out in the NDAA.

The regular-order process was successful in keeping Congress at the center of defense policy debates from 1961 through the end of the Cold War and in placing the defense committees in charge of congressional policymaking on defense matters. The end of the Cold War did not do much to change either arrangement: During the contentious 1990s, Congress was the forum for the difficult debate over downsizing the Cold War military, and the NDAA remained the vehicle for managing defense policy in Congress.

The House and Senate Armed Services Committees oversaw policy for the largest, and most expensive, parts of the executive branch. Their dominance over defense policy also influenced foreign policy oversight in Congress. While service on the Senate Foreign Relations Committee had long been held in high esteem, membership on the Senate Armed Services Committee came to equal, and then outshine, a seat on Foreign Relations.[6] In fact, by the late 1970s, the Senate Armed Services Committee was powerful enough to insert itself into foreign policy in a very dramatic fashion by issuing a report to the Senate on the second Strategic Arms Limitations Treaty (SALT II) in 1979, which recommended voting against the treaty—this despite having no formal jurisdiction over treaties.[7] Such a move could not have happened if Foreign Relations had been strong enough to beat back this intrusion by the Senate Armed Services Committee into its business.

But the Foreign Relations Committee was then in the midst of bruising internal battles that lowered its prestige within the Senate and allowed the Senate Armed Services Committee to poach on its territory so successfully. Years of disagreement among the Republican senators serving on the Foreign Relations Committee came to a head in 1979 when hard-line conservatives, led by North Carolina Republican senator Jesse Helms, made use of the committee's rules to demand that their party be given control over one-third of the committee's budget.

This allowed the GOP to hire its own committee staffers, which enabled it to do more work to advance the GOP's policy arguments but at the expense of ending any hopes that the whole committee could present a united front on any issue before the Senate. While this gave the conservatives more capability in making their case, the formation of separate majority and minority staffs for the committee eroded the ability of the committee to sway the Senate on foreign policy topics. And into that policy vacuum swept the Senate Armed Services Committee.[8]

On the House side, the Committee on Foreign Affairs was never as prestigious as its Senate counterpart—it did not have a role in considering treaties, nor did it examine nominees for senior State Department positions and ambassadorships. The House Armed Services Committee was therefore able to move into a position of power and prestige within the House much more easily. Thus, in both chambers, the Cold War pressed Congress to build policymaking processes that helped move the defense committees to positions of prominence, which they were able to maintain throughout the Cold War. Their prominence would come under question as the Cold War ended, though.

Post–Cold War Reality: Regular Order Evolving

The 1990s saw two enormous changes in Congress that eroded regular order and undercut Congress's traditional approach to being a full partner in setting defense policy. First was the end of the Cold War and, with it, the foreign and defense policy consensus.

Cold War congressional processes and staffs were designed around the assumption of a clear, lasting strategy for policymaking to follow. The strategy of containment based on deterrence had been constructed by leaders in both the executive and legislative branches in the late 1940s and the 1950s, and it would remain the guide to US foreign policy until the end of the Cold War. Without a strong consensus driving the annual defense authorization and spending bills, members of Congress would be likely to default to their normal way of dealing with issues: Local concerns dominate their thinking.[9]

This is not to suggest that parochialism played no role in defense policymaking during the Cold War—it was just better kept in check by broad agreement on US national security strategy.[10]

American leaders in both branches struggled to articulate a new strategic framework throughout the 1990s, with little success. While the White House and the DOD struggled to deal with the collapse of the USSR and the many global challenges that erupted as the Soviet Union was slowly fading from the scene (including the Iraqi invasion of Kuwait in 1990 and the subsequent Operation Desert Shield and Operation Desert Storm), the administration of George H. W. Bush also proposed its first take on a post–Cold War approach to defense, the Base Force.[11] Defense-minded legislators also made several efforts to offer new ideas, such as the proposal on force structure by House Armed Services Committee chair Les Aspin (D-WI), which called for a significant reduction in, and reorganization of, US military forces.[12] Aspin's work would later become the basis of the DOD's Bottom-Up Review when he served as President Bill Clinton's first secretary of defense.[13]

The end of the Cold War allowed both branches to take fresh looks at other aspects of defense policy, also with no promise of consensus between Congress and the White House. Clinton's first defense policy issue is a case in point. As a candidate for the presidency, he had announced his support for allowing gay and lesbian personnel to serve openly. Before his transition into office was complete, opposition to a change in the DOD's policy was already mounting in Congress, led in part by Senate Armed Services Committee chair Sam Nunn (D-GA). The new president could not overcome foes of his idea, which led to the requirement for the Pentagon to produce the Don't Ask, Don't Tell, Don't Pursue (DADT) policy being included in H.R. 2401, the National Defense Authorization Act for Fiscal Year 1994.[14]

The second major change in Congress was the Republican victories in the 1994 elections—bringing to power a party with a new set of policy priorities and a new approach, top-down legislating. After a forty-year stint in the minority, the GOP had a long list of goals it had not been able to advance under Democratic control. GOP leaders also took a different approach to managing the House. Where Democratic speakers had deferred to committee chairs, incoming speaker Newt Gingrich (R-GA) imposed term limits on chairs, and during the hectic first year they were in the majority, the members of Gingrich's leadership team directed committees to produce specific bills or wrote the bills themselves and sent them directly to the floor. The GOP majority was generally prodefense, but they could still find policy fights with the Clinton White House. For instance, Clinton's efforts to reduce spending on missile defense found few takers in the Congress, which kept funding the programs throughout Clinton's terms in office.[15]

The 1994 GOP victories highlight a long-emerging change in American politics that shapes how Congress now responds to issues. Starting in the 1960s, individual candidates for public office began to capitalize on mass media (newspapers, radio, and especially television) to market their campaigns.[16] Coupled with an increasing reliance on primaries to select candidates, direct marketing by campaigns has shifted American politics from a party-centered system to a candidate-centered one that places very high demands on each candidate to raise money for future races. It also pushes incumbents to show their voters constantly how they work to advance their constituents' interests. In a candidate-centered system, parochial concerns will trump party leaders' policy preferences—and defense policy was no longer immune from this after the Cold War.[17] Primaries also help drive the two parties toward more extreme ideologies, as voters respond to extreme politicians by picking more partisan candidates.[18] Polarization and the continuing ideological sorting of voters into the two political parties means more fractious policy debates—and without a strategic consensus, this affects defense as much as any other issue Congress has to confront.[19]

How does this affect Congress and defense policy? Under the old system of regular order, the defense committees reviewed the president's annual budget submission in February–April, using a series of hearings with senior DOD civilian and military officials to study the strategic situation and the administration's policy proposals. Following this intense study period, the committees would produce their draft versions of the NDAA for the next fiscal year, with those bills usually coming to the floor in June (House) and July (Senate). The two chambers would reconcile their differences and produce a final compromise version by early September. The House and Senate Appropriations Committees would follow a similar schedule, with their spending bills following NDAA to the two chamber floors about two weeks later—with the goal of finalizing the spending bill for passage at the end of September. Republican majorities largely followed this pattern in the 1990s and early 2000s, but the process began to fray under the pressure of wartime expenditures to support the operations in Afghanistan and Iraq.

Under the 1997 budget deal, defense spending had to meet budget targets, which did help in getting bills completed. Following the 9/11 attacks, defense spending skyrocketed as the United States entered the wars in Afghanistan and Iraq. Wartime commitments dramatically increased defense spending—through the mechanism of supplemental spending bills. These measures were passed as stand-alone efforts, not subject to the regular budget process and so not part of the normal negotiations and trade-offs that the annual defense bill faces.[20]

The arrival of the Barack Obama administration in January 2009 led to the end of supplemental bills, as the president moved the war spending into the annual defense appropriations bill. The return of GOP control in the House after the 2010 midterms added pressure to defense budgeting, as the Tea Party–inspired Republicans worked to reduce the federal budget—and this time the budget hawks were as powerful as the war hawks in Republican ranks.

Defense Policymaking in the Age of the Tea Party

The rise of the Tea Party in the 2010 midterms has helped to bring all the trends that have shaped American politics since the 1970s into sharp relief. For defense policy, that means the end of the privileged position it had before 1991. Not only have the leadership changes in Congress centralized power and eroded committee control of their issue spaces, the independence and hard-line positions of the Tea Partiers have also undercut the defense committees' ability to shape policy in the old way, using regular order. Newer members now have no loyalty to their party labels or to their leaders or to the norms of the Congress; many of them came to Washington to stop business as usual, and they prioritize budget cuts over defense spending. With their strong support from activists back home, Tea Party Republicans do not have to accommodate themselves to the traditional norms of Congress—evidenced most clearly by their clear preference to work in their district offices instead of Washington, wanting to stay closely connected to their constituents. This means much less time in Washington and much less time for working in committee to produce popular bills and significantly reduced floor time to finalize bills.[21]

The Tea Party's insistence on budget discipline added to a difficult situation. After his election in 2008, President Obama had ended the practice of paying for wartime activities through supplemental appropriations bills, bringing contingency funding back into the regular budget process. While this helps Congress make more realistic budget decisions, it also adds to the pressure on the appropriators. They must include wartime spending in their debates, all the while accommodating the Tea Party's demands for lower overall spending.

In the years following the 9/11 attacks, Congress had very little trouble passing the annual NDAA. The fact that the United States was at war made passage of this legislation fairly straightforward, and the pressure to ensure that the DOD had all the resources it needed for its operations in Afghanistan and Iraq meant that NDAA authorizing levels were very generous—thus avoiding any hard choices in the annual bill.

While avoiding hard choices was easy from 2001 to 2009, the earlier practice became a problem for both authorizers and appropriators once the Iraq War began its drawdown and the Tea Party arrived in Washington. The annual debates over the NDAA have been used to deal with several contentious issues, such as rescinding the DADT policy in December 2010 and keeping open the detention facilities at Guantánamo Bay, Cuba (in both the FY 2013 and FY 2014 NDAA bills).[22] But generally the program levels authorized for major weapon systems have been so high that the House and Senate Appropriations Committees found themselves forced to make the hard decisions about the actual spending levels without any useful guidance from the NDAA. As reported in the defense blog of *Politico* regarding the 2014 NDAA:

> The new compromise legislation might keep Congress' record alive of 52 straight years having a defense authorization bill, but its usefulness is limited, says Gordon Adams, a national security budget official during the Clinton administration.
>
> "Authorizing defense funding at a level that bears no relationship to the budget reality around them reflects that they continue to play inside baseball when the crowd has left the stadium," Adams told Morning D. "By pretending there would be more money, the authorizers managed to evade tough choices, and even left themselves room to push for special interests that will make the Pentagon's planning problems even worse."[23]

One counterexample, though, illustrates that the defense committees can use their NDAA debates to send strong signals, which are very difficult to ignore. In the FY 2013 NDAA, the Senate took a recorded vote on the Senate Armed Services Committee's decision to cancel spending for a second engine for the F-35 fighter program. Supporters of the second engine (including the congressional delegations of the states where that engine was to have been built) could not muster the votes to keep the spending in the appropriations bill later that year—a roll call vote in opposition to the second engine was too strong a message to overcome.[24]

One key tool used by the leaders to get defense spending bills passed quickly became politically poisonous by 2010—the earmark. In the late 1990s, GOP leaders began urging the appropriations committees to sweeten their bills with earmarks to make sure the bills would have enough votes to pass. While the 1997 budget agreement was popular in itself, making it work was a painful process. Every year spending bills had to meet its budget targets, meaning that many popular programs were cut and few new initiatives could be launched. Using earmarks to guarantee legislators favored projects in the bills meant that the leaders could feel confident that their troops would still support the bills at lower total levels, if only to preserve their favorite projects. Without them, passage of appropriations bills is much tougher; the FY 2014 transportation bill failed in the House because its low total spending, set by the House-approved budget resolution, did not gain enough votes on the floor.[25] Earmarks were enormously popular and very effective at gaining support for spending bills. At their high points in 2009 and 2010, "appropriations bills contained 9,499 congressional earmarks worth $15.9 billion. This compares with 11,286 congressional earmarks worth $19.9 billion in FY09."[26]

Budget talks aimed at agreeing on a new budget deal like the 1997 deal proved impossible. The distance between the White House and the House GOP was too great, leading to a compromise in the 2011 Budget Control Act designed to force Congress and the White House to devise a workable budget or face across-the-board budget cuts—including defense spending. Failure of the "super committee" in late 2011 to craft such a budget deal caused the sequester to take effect. The impact of sequestration on the DOD was regarded as very harmful, both in direct consequences and in preventing any long-term budget planning from occurring at the Pentagon.[27]

As President Obama and Congress plan for the remainder of his term in office, Congress finds itself with less capability to act as a partner in defense policymaking than it has been since the start of the Cold War. The old system of regular order, devised during the postwar years, was the embodiment of the broad policy consensus held by American policymakers, and nowhere was this more clear than in defense policy. Cold War defense policymaking was the best example of regular order in connecting the policy guidance of the House and Senate Armed Services Committees with defense spending bills that funded the programs approved by House and Senate Armed Services Committees. While there were arguments on specifics throughout the 1950s to the 1990s, the system largely operated well and allowed Congress to play a key role in defining US defense policy for decades.

That process began to break down as the Cold War ended and new challenges presented themselves to the United States around the globe. With no overarching strategy in place any more, Congress found it harder to connect authorizing and appropriating, but it managed to work out policy difference internally and with the White House, with some success in the 1990s. The 9/11 attacks galvanized the government into an aggressive response, and Congress played a vital role from 2001 to 2009 in that response, in providing resources to the DOD for its wars in Afghanistan and Iraq but also by reorganizing key parts of the federal government to allow it to work more effectively to defend US national interests—both by creating the new Department of Homeland Security and by reorganizing the sixteen intelligence agencies into a more cooperative system under the office of a national intelligence director.

While Congress has been able to play a role, all has not gone well. Congress's authorizing committees have not wrestled with budget reality, leaving the hard decisions to the appropriations committees. While the appropriators understand defense budgets intimately, their expertise does not extend to strategy, and without that guidance from the defense committees, all they can do is assess individual programs according to their own progress or failures. The NDAA bill, which had gone to the floors of both chambers and been passed in an almost automatic process every year since 1961, suddenly confronted tremendous difficulties in 2012 and 2013. House and Senate legislators struggled to craft an agreeable compromise in both years, just managing to get the bill passed at the end of each year.[28] Near-failure to pass the NDAA suggests that policy differences between the chambers (and within each body) are now so great that the old system may not be able to bridge current partisan gaps.

Defense policy is in far better shape than the related fields of homeland security and intelligence, however. Congress has not been able to resolve its own internal disagreements over how to manage homeland security, leaving the department under the supervision of over eighty committees and subcommittees—a decade after the department's founding. And intelligence oversight has been fraught with internal disagreement since the late 1990s, when failures to anticipate Pakistani and Indian nuclear tests began a long roster of intelligence problems that culminated in the 2004 intelligence reorganization act, which created the Office of the Director of National Intelligence.[29] Partisan bickering in both chambers reduced the effectiveness of the two intelligence committees, impairing their reputations within the Congress and derailing their efforts to produce an annual intelligence authorization bill. While this had been repaired by the leaders of the two committees by 2009, lingering disagreements over how to produce effective spending bills continue to limit congressional efforts to drive intelligence policy.[30] One key issue that rankles the intelligence committees is that the Appropriations Committees manage intelligence spending through the defense bill (not a stand-alone intelligence bill), and they frequently "deem" programs they want to support as having been authorized, regardless of what the committees may have enacted.[31]

Conclusion

Defense is no longer a special issue area that gets bipartisan support. Emerging political trends affect it as much as any other issue area Congress works on and all issues have been subordinated to harsh ideological differences between the parties—at the same time as policymaking has been trumped by the need of most members to work directly with constituents in their districts.

In each party there are factions that see no reason to treat defense any differently than other issue areas. In the GOP, budget policy has become a central focus. Until the ideological polarization calms and the fear of primary challenges abates, there is no reason to imagine that defense will return to anything like the privileged position it held in the Cold War. Budget hawks seem to have the upper hand in the Republican ranks, and there is little evidence to suggest that the Tea Party faction is going to disappear in the near future. As long as hard-line Republicans have some sway in internal party debates, the war hawks who were able to preserve higher levels of defense spending will not be able to restore the Pentagon to its former protected status.

Democrats have favored the idea of a "peace dividend" (reduced defense spending in times of reduced tension), and the combination of GOP budget hawks and Democratic calls to reinvest in domestic priorities is likely to spur continued reductions in the defense budget. Overreach by the intelligence community in the name of protecting the United States from terrorists has spurred a broad debate on the scale and propriety of national intelligence efforts at the same time. All of this suggests that the conditions that led to the creation of the Cold War consensus in the late 1940s and early 1950s are not likely to reoccur. Defense is slowly turning into just another policy issue.

And if it is just another issue, it will be handled using the traditional congressional methods for making policy: deals, trades, logrolling, and posturing. Regular order emerged as a system for using these tools to move legislation, and defense policy became the epitome of regular order in action. What has changed is the emphasis. Where Congress used regular order in service of a national policy consensus that blunted some of the impact of local concerns on defense policy, Congress in the Tea Party era seeks a new balance between lawmaking and constituency service. Congress has a long history demonstrating that it can achieve legislative success in domestic policy using these tools; in the absence of a new defense consensus that would again protect or privilege defense policymaking, those tools will surely help Congress find its way with defense policy, as well. Congress will find a way to manage its twin responsibilities of national lawmaking and local constituency service.

Notes

1. Roger H. Davidson and Walter J. Oleszek, *Congress and Its Members*, 9th ed. (Washington, DC: CQ Press, 2004), 3–12.

2. Randall B. Ripley and Grace A. Franklin, *Congress, the Bureaucracy, and Public Policy*, 5th ed. (Pacific Grove, CA: Brooks/Cole, 1990).

3. Robert David Johnson, *Congress and the Cold War* (New York: Cambridge University Press, 2006).

4. Steven S. Smith and Christopher J. Deering, *Committees in Congress*, 2nd ed. (Washington, DC: Congressional Quarterly, 1990), 87, 101. Smith and Deering note that the House and Senate Armed Services Committees are treated as both policy and constituency committees. The foreign policy committees serve no constituency needs.

5. The Senate did not consider its NDAA on the floor in 2013, for the first time. Scheduling conflicts and arguments between Majority Leader Harry Reid (D-NV) and Minority Leader Mitch McConnell (R-KY) on a number of issues pushed the bill to late in the year. The rush of budget deals pushed the bill off the calendar entirely as a result of the delay. The Senate eventually took up the compromise version already passed by the House and passed it without amendments. See Juana Summers and Austin Wright, "Senate Sends Defense Bill to Obama," *Politico*, December 19, 2013, www.politico.com/story/2013/12/senate-national-defense-authorization-act-barack-obama-101364.html.

6. Forrest Maltzman, *Competing Principals: Committees, Parties, and the Organization of Congress* (Ann Arbor: University of Michigan, 1997), 165–66.

7. Donald T Critchlow, *The Conservative Ascendancy: How the GOP Right Made Political History* (Cambridge, MA: Harvard University Press, 2007), 169.

8. Johnson, *Congress and the Cold War.*

9. Davidson and Oleszek, *Congress and Its Members*. In his *Home Style: House Members in Their Districts* (Boston: Little, Brown, 1978), Richard Fenno explores the goals that drive member behavior and points out that while power and good policy are important, reelection drives most decisions, as it must, since members cannot achieve their other goals without getting reelected.

10. The DOD eventually succeeded in obtaining funding for the B-1 bomber even after program cancellation by President Jimmy Carter in 1977, by identifying subcontractors and contractors for the program in congressional districts across the country. Stephen E. Frantzich and Claude Berube describe the tactic of distributing subcontractors into many districts in their work *Congress: Games and Strategies* (Lanham, MD: Rowman & Littlefield, 2010), 330. See also "The B-1 Comes Home to Roost," *New York Times*, July 17, 1988, www.nytimes.com/1988/07/17/opinion/the-b-1-comes-home-to-roost.html.

11. Lorna Jaffe, *The Development of the Base Force, 1989–1992* (Washington, DC: Joint History Office, Office of the Chairman of the Joint Chiefs of Staff, 1993).

12. John T. Correll, "Washington Watch: The Base Force Meets Option C," *Air Force Magazine* 75, no. 6 (June 1992), www.airforcemag.com/MagazineArchive/Pages/1992/June%201992/0692watch.aspx.

13. Les Aspin, *Report on the Bottom-Up Review* (Washington, DC: Government Printing Office, 1993).

14. Pub. L. No: 103-160, signed November 30, 1994, Library of Congress, http://thomas.loc.gov/cgi-bin/bdquery/z?d103:HR02401:@@@D&summ2=m&.

15. Bradley Graham, "Congress to Push for a National Missile Defense," *Washington Post*, September 5, 1995, A01.

16. Dennis W. Johnson, *No Place for Amateurs: How Political Consultants Are Reshaping American Democracy*, 2nd ed. (New York: Routledge, 2007); Paul S. Herrnson, *Congressional Elections: Campaigning at Home and in Washington*, 6th ed. (Washington, DC: Sage / CQ Press, 2012); Jason Johnson, *Political Consultants and Campaigns: One Day to Sell* (Boulder, CO: Westview, 2012).

17. John H. Aldrich, "Political Parties in a Critical Era," *American Politics Research* 27, no. 1 (January 1999): 9–32.

18. James Druckman, Erik Peterson, and Rune Slothus, "How Elite Polarization Affects Public Opinion Formation," *American Political Science Review* 107, no. 1 (February 2013): 57–79.

19. Bill Bishop, *The Big Sort: Why the Clustering of Like-Minded Americans Is Tearing Us Apart* (Boston: Mariner Books, 2008).

20. Congress agreed to supplemental appropriations for wartime expenses every year from 2001 to 2006 and from 2008 to 2009. Border protection received additional funds through supplemental appropriations in 2010. See http://thomas.loc.gov/home/approp/app14 .html for full details on appropriations legislation passed by Congress.

21. Thomas E. Mann and Norman J. Ornstein, *The Broken Branch: How Congress Is Failing America and How to Get It Back on Track* (New York: Oxford University Press, 2006); Thomas E. Mann and Norman J. Ornstein, *It's Even Worse Than It Looks: How the American Constitutional System Collided with the New Politics of Extremism* (New York: Basic Books, 2012).

22. Don't Ask, Don't Tell Repeal Act of 2010, Pub. L. 111-321, December 22, 2010, http:// thomas.loc.gov/cgi-bin/bdquery/z?d111:HR02965:@@@D&summ2=m&.

23. Kate Brannen, "An Insider's Bill in an Outsider's World?" *Morning Defense* (blog), *Politico*, December 11, 2013, www.politico.com/morningdefense/1213/morningdefense12457.html.

24. Christopher Drew, "House Votes to End Alternate Jet Engine Program," *New York Times*, February 16, 2011, www.nytimes.com/2011/02/17/us/politics/17-f-35-engine.html?_r=0.

25. Kerry Young, "Once the Deciders on Spending, Appropriators Now Follow the Leaders," *Roll Call*, October 4, 2013, www.rollcall.com/news/once_the_deciders_on_spending _appropriators_now_follow_the_leaders-228166-1.html.

26. Taxpayers for Common Sense, *TCS FY2010 Earmark Analysis: Apples-to-Apples Increase in Earmarks*, February 18, 2010, www.taxpayer.net/library/article/tcs-fy2010-earmark -analysis-apples-to-apples-increase-in-earmarks.

27. Kate Brannen, "Chuck Hagel Issues New Dire Warning on Sequestration," *Politico*, August 1, 2013, www.politico.com/story/2013/08/chuck-hagel-defense-budget-sequestration -95016.html.

28. Spencer Ackerman, "Senate Approves US Defence Budget Plan with Sexual Assault Reforms," *The Guardian*, December 20, 2013, www.theguardian.com/world/2013/dec/20 /congress-passes-ndaa-defense-budget-sexual-assault-reform.

29. David Stout, "Bush Signs Bill to Revamp U.S. Intelligence Community," *New York Times*, December 17, 2004, www.nytimes.com/2004/12/17/politics/17cnd-intel.html.

30. Amy B. Zegart, "The Domestic Politics of Irrational Intelligence Oversight," *Political Science Quarterly* 126, no. 1 (Spring 2011): 1–25.

31. Jennifer Kibbe, "Congressional Oversight of Intelligence: Is the Solution Part of the Problem?" *Intelligence and National Security* 25, no. 1 (February 2010): 24–49.

8

Congress and New Ways of War

CHARLES A. STEVENSON

I built the United States Navy right here in this room.

—*Rep. Carl Vinson (D-GA), chair, House Naval Affairs Committee*

The most effective form of lobbying in Washington . . . is not conducted by a private interest but by two of the executive departments of the government itself, that of the army and navy.

—*Rep. Fiorello La Guardia (R-NY)*

Congress is a necessary partner with the US military in developing new ways of war because it must approve the development of new capabilities, create military institutions, fund operations, and agree to the promotion of senior leaders. The Constitution gives Congress broad powers not only to build and equip the armed forces but also to micromanage them. The empowering phrases are "To raise and support Armies," "To provide and maintain a Navy," and "To make Rules for the Government and Regulation of the land and naval Forces."

Throughout the nineteenth century, Congress worked directly with army and navy leaders to set force size and spending levels. Except in wartime, presidents were largely out of the loop. Only in the twentieth century, with larger standing forces and White House–led budget processes, did presidents play a significant role in preparing the military for future wars.

Congress also treated the armed forces as part of its patronage system, appointing young men to the service academies at West Point and Annapolis and often intervening to support their later promotions and assignments. Lawmakers also sought and protected military installations in their home areas as part of their regular political activities.

This chapter discusses the congressional role in military innovation, a factor often overlooked by writers focusing on technology or its use in combat.

From the earliest days of the republic, Congress has often been a key supporter of new technologies as well as of US grand strategy in dealing with the rest of the world. Without congressional intervention, America would likely have been much slower to develop steam-powered warships as well as submarines and military aircraft. Without congressional support, the United States could not have become a global superpower with a diversity of nuclear and conventional weapons and a network of alliances and installations.

This chapter identifies five major ways that Congress acts to shape new ways of war. Lawmakers tend to embrace promising technologies especially when they offer dramatic improvements in military capability or local economic benefits. They are often key supporters of military innovators in their struggles with resistant military leadership, and they occasionally empower new organizations to take advantage of new ways of war. On the other hand, they often rush to investigate problems and failures. And they tend to question military innovations that raise significant domestic issues—for example, the growing use of drones for civilian as well as military purposes and the increased importance of cyber operations for both defense and offense.

How the United States responds to new ways of war depends in large part on how individual lawmakers, and Congress as an institution, respond to those threats and opportunities.

Divided Sources of Civilian Control

The US Constitution provides civilian control of the military but through two separate chains of command: from the president as commander in chief of military operations and from the Congress with the power of the purse and the authority to regulate the size, organization, and weaponry of the armed forces. Lawmakers do not always agree with the chief executive on how best to prepare for or fight conflicts that may arise.

In dealing with the new ways of war, the main lines of friction are rarely between civilians in Congress and the military but rather between civilian-military coalitions that differ over the best ways to prepare for future conflicts. Sometimes members of Congress ally with dissidents in uniform whose innovative views have been rejected by their superiors. Sometimes they form what turn out to be short-lived coalitions to support particular programs or policies. Often "iron triangles" develop, linking congressional, military, and contractor personnel in common cause, regardless of the views of more senior leaders. At other times, Congress ends up taking sides in disputes among military factions and forcing its own solutions. Rarely does Congress act on these matters with a strong, consistent, and unified voice.

Support for New Military Technologies

Congress has often asserted its civilian control over the military by endorsing or blocking new military technologies. From Benjamin Franklin and Eli Whitney to Thomas Edison and Alexander Graham Bell, Americans have embraced inventiveness and fostered innovation. The framers of the Constitution gave Congress specific powers "to promote the progress of science and useful arts" by granting authors and inventors "exclusive right to their respective writings and discoveries." Many of these inventions, of course, had military applications. Congress played a key role in supporting military innovation in some areas and thwarting it in others.

Warships

Congress changed course during the nineteenth century on the kind of navy it wanted to provide. Robert Fulton had already developed several commercial steamships when he approached the US government in 1813 with ideas for a steam-powered floating battery for harbor defense of New York. The James Madison administration and Congress eagerly approved funds as part of the war with Great Britain. By the time of the vessel's sea trials, however, the war was over and Fulton had died. In 1816 Congress authorized another steamship, but no action was taken until 1835.[1] Only in the 1840s did Congress regularly vote to build additional steam-powered warships.

In the retrenchments following the Civil War, the Navy itself was divided over which technologies to pursue. It decommissioned large numbers of its ships, including the *Wampanoag*, which had been the fastest warship ever built, a title it held until the 1880s. The ship was not favored by the Navy's leadership, however, which continued to insist that new ships have sails and use their engines only on rare occasions.[2]

Starting in the 1880s, groups formed to push for naval modernization and a more assertive US policy overseas. Navy leaders found support in Congress in both parties and in the executive branch and won support for newer, bigger warships. Naval modernization was especially welcomed by coastal representatives, who helped forge what one historian has called a new "military-industrial complex" of sailors, shipbuilders, and steel manufacturers with members of Congress.[3]

The war with Spain in 1898 marked a strategic turning point, leading to US acquisition of Caribbean territories and the distant Philippines. Annexation of Hawaii at the same time created a powerful argument for a far-flung blue water navy with coaling stations and overseas bases.

Submarines

Congress pressured the navy to study the use of submarines, which held little interest for traditional sailors. In 1862 and 1864 Congress specifically added funds for the navy to develop "submarine inventions." Although the Confederate navy had a submarine that sank a Union navy ship in 1864, the US Navy failed to develop a successful submersible for three more decades.

The ultimate winner, John P. Holland, had initially approached the US Navy with detailed plans in 1875. In subsequent years he built six prototypes, largely financed by Fenians who wanted to sink a British ship in New York harbor in support of Irish independence. Holland won a design competition in 1888, but the incoming Benjamin Harrison administration decided to shift the money to surface ships. In 1893 Congress approved $200,000 for a design competition in response to lobbying by a Chicago businessman, George Baker. A selection board chose Holland's design over Baker's, but the navy dithered until 1895 before finally awarding the contract to Holland, whose company became Electric Boat, later the builder of nuclear-powered submarines.[4]

Airpower

Members of Congress also spurred the development of military aircraft. Orville and Wilbur Wright tried for several years, starting in 1905, to interest the army in buying and testing its aircraft, but nothing happened until they approached a leading Republican senator, Henry Cabot Lodge of Massachusetts, who contacted the War Department on their behalf. Test flights were finally held in September 1908, leading to the Wright brothers' initial contracts. Despite their success, Congress did not appropriate funds specifically for aviation until 1911.[5]

The Wrights also had competition from gas-filled aircraft, which had been advocated by some army officers as early as the 1890s. In fact, the army created its first balloon detachment in 1902 and sent officers to participate in balloon sports racing in subsequent years. The army's Aeronautical Division was established in 1907 and acquired its first dirigible a year later.[6]

With war threatening in Europe in 1914, Congress became more supportive of military airpower. It created an aviation section of the Signal Corps with 320 men and in March 1915 created the National Advisory Committee for Aeronautics with military and civilian members.[7] The navy also created separate aviation units in 1914.

In the 1920s a congressional faction arose to champion an independent air force. Members seized upon reports of dishonest procurement practices to get the House of Representatives to create a select investigative panel, named the Lampert Committee after its chairman Floriam Lampert (R-WI), which conducted a year-long series of hearings in 1924 and 1925. The committee was a forum for airpower advocates, notably Brig. Gen. Billy Mitchell, who is regarded as the father of the US Air Force. Although the panel recommended several pieces of legislation, including ones to create a unified air service and to create a Department of National Defense with land, sea, and air components, the Military Affairs Committee rejected the bills, and no further legislative effort was made until after World War II.[8]

Army Weaponry

The army was ridden with factions, each of which had its congressional supporters. The airpower faction was most successful in promoting its new way of war. The cavalry maintained strong support throughout the period between the world wars. The soldiers urging exploitation of tank warfare, however, lost out to those supporting the army leadership and the infantry. Congress disbanded the separate Tank Corps in 1920, folding it into the infantry. When the then captain Dwight Eisenhower wrote an article on the advantages of armored warfare, he was told that his ideas were "not only wrong but dangerous," and he was threatened with a court-martial. With few lawmakers supporting the armor advocates, Congress sided with the army leadership in blocking innovative tank design in the 1920s.[9]

Support for Executive Branch Grand Strategies

Congress also exercised civilian control over the military through its influence on America's grand strategies. Until the 1890s American leaders shared a consensus based on George Washington's Farewell Address and the Monroe Doctrine that sought to avoid foreign wars and entanglements, kept the armed forces small, and used navy and Marine Corps units to police US interests abroad, mostly in the Western Hemisphere.[10] Except during the expansionist war with Mexico, the army was used mainly against Native Americans on behalf of encroaching settlers. The army also maintained coastal defense batteries and, through the Corps of Engineers, built federally funded roads, canals, and bridges and did projects relating to navigation and flood control. Until the Industrial Revolution and the adoption of a more global foreign policy, there were few opportunities or a need to develop major new military technologies.

Despite vigorous debates and spirited opposition, Congress endorsed US imperialism and funded the forces to carry it out. In a notable example of self-restraint, however, that illustrates how Congress lets domestic interests shape foreign policy, sugar interests added a provision to the declaration of war against Spain forbidding annexation of Cuba. Congress also resisted calls from some members to end the guerrilla war in the Philippines and to withdraw from any of the many Latin American and Caribbean nations where US troops intervened between 1907 and 1930.

Throughout the twentieth century, Congress frequently debated and sometimes modified but ultimately supported executive branch policies committing US forces to the defense of European allies—notably in 1917, 1940, and 1950. Congress also supported presidential policies to oppose communist expansion in Europe, Korea, the Middle East, and Southeast Asia. Majorities in Congress regularly rejected most efforts to restrict military operations abroad, such as in Vietnam until 1973, in Lebanon, in Haiti, and in the Balkans. It formally authorized the use of force against Iraq in 1991 and 2002 and against Afghanistan and al-Qaeda in 2001.[11] The one major effort to assert its constitutional role in major military operations, the War Powers Act of 1973, has never been accepted by any subsequent president as binding. Though in legal limbo, the law has succeeded in practice because no major military operation not formally authorized by Congress has in fact lasted more than about three or four months.

Congress also supported major strategic shifts by various administrations, such as the development of a triad of nuclear retaliatory forces, the original nuclear arms limitation agreements with the Soviet Union, the Richard Nixon and Jimmy Carter agreements with China, and the 2001 abrogation of limits on missile defense. After the 9/11 attacks, Congress supported a massive counterterrorism effort and, by voting for war against Iraq, implicitly supported the George W. Bush administration's strategy of preventive war. And while Congress has on occasion voted specific limits on what the intelligence community can do, it has formally approved a process allowing clandestine operations provided there is presidential approval and congressional notifications.

Congressional Tactics, Techniques, and Procedures

As the following examples will show, Congress often deals with these momentous issues relating to future wars and capabilities in the same way it handles ordinary domestic matters—with parochialism, concerns regarding jobs, emphasis on efficiency more than effectiveness, and with optimism as an answer to doubts. It rushes to investigate failures but rarely studies successes. Lawmakers often swing between excitement over promising technologies and concern over high or unanticipated costs. When they encounter resistance, they are quite willing to empower new organizations to exploit the new ways of war. They are quickest to embrace ideas that offer dramatic improvements in military capability and local economic benefits.

Congress as an institution has enormous power when it writes laws and appropriates funds. But committees of jurisdiction also have great power over their domains, both as initiators of legislation and as powers whom others wish to please. The House and Senate Armed Services Committees have gained enormous influence because they have regularly passed defense authorization bills, now numbering in the hundreds of pages, each year since 1961. The defense appropriations subcommittees have the ultimate power of the purse, and they regularly exercise it in numbing detail. Individual members can also have great power over the Pentagon and its component parts because officials want to do favors or avoid punishments. Executive branch officials do not need a law signed by the president or an order from the White House to make them solicitous of congressional views and responsive to mere suggestions from lawmakers. Each of these civilian power centers can influence the military. Following are five broad patterns describing congressional responses to new ways of war.

Embracing Promising Technologies

Lawmakers tend to embrace promising technologies, especially when they offer dramatic improvements in military capability or local economic benefits. We have seen this in the development of warships and airplanes prior to World War II. The development of nuclear weapons led to interservice rivalries after 1945 in which Congress was a significant participant. Airpower advocates won most of those early battles, while the navy struggled to turn itself into a nuclear war fighting force, despite the vulnerability of surface ships. Congress tended to side with the newly independent air force, boosting its budget beyond what the Harry Truman administration proposed while cutting the army and navy. The Marine Corps defeated Truman's effort to dismantle it by getting congressional supporters to guarantee a three-division force in permanent law. The army drastically reduced its size but readily embraced nuclear weapons and worked to build missiles and artillery to deliver them.

The 1950s and early 1960s were a time of rampant interservice rivalries, with each group corralling support on Capitol Hill for its pet projects. Congress made few changes in the defense budgets during the Dwight Eisenhower administration and did not challenge the shift to a strategy of nuclear deterrence. But Congress seized upon evidence of Soviet military advances in the late 1950s to add funds for strategic programs. Lawmakers continued to boost the budget through 1963, then became more cost-conscious as the United States got more deeply involved in Vietnam.[12]

Secretary of Defense Robert McNamara imposed some order on the process but succeeded only partially. He killed a new long-range bomber but had to set high limits on the number of air force missiles and bombers. Many senior military leaders were quite open about their disdain for McNamara's number-crunching and tight civilian control.

Following the Vietnam War, Congress regularly debated but ultimately approved the strategic modernization programs for the nuclear triad of missiles, submarines, and bombers. One exception was the B-1 bomber, killed in the Carter administration and resurrected by President Ronald Reagan. Congress also defeated a missile accuracy program that critics said would have led to an unstable US first-strike posture. Congress later supported the missile defense programs of the Reagan administration, especially the Strategic Defense Initiative (SDI), but slowed funding after an initial burst of enthusiasm. The B-2 bomber was criticized for its high cost but ultimately approved because of its revolutionary stealth characteristics.[13]

When major weapon programs have been challenged in Congress, the most active and vocal defenders tend to be those lawmakers who have constituents who benefit from the programs. Most of the members of the defense committees have military installations or contractors that they defend and promote because of the local economic benefits that come with the bases and contracts. The major defense contractors spread the work around the country to gain political support: The B-1 bomber program had subcontracts in forty-eight states, the F-22 fighter in forty-four, and the F-35 fighter in forty-six, according to contractor estimates.

The V-22 Osprey, a transport aircraft with a revolutionary tilt-rotor design, was strongly supported by the Marine Corps because it went "twice as far, twice as fast" as its helicopter fleet. When Secretary of Defense Dick Cheney tried to cancel the program, Congress fought back, led by the delegations from Texas and Pennsylvania, where the system was built. The struggle lasted four years until shortly before the 1992 elections, when Cheney conceded defeat. By then there were subcontracts in forty-two states, thus securing strong legislative support for the program.[14]

In addition to this parochialism, some members of Congress have pushed innovative ideas on their own merits. The Military Reform Caucus in the 1980s, a bipartisan group including both liberal senator Gary Hart (D-CO) and conservative representative Newt Gingrich (R-GA), criticized the Pentagon's search for costly and complex weapons and urged instead simpler systems such as F-16 fighters that would be more reliable and affordable in larger numbers. These ideas were widely circulated, but the dollars continued to flow into the traditional programs.[15]

In the 1990s a group of futurist members advocated a broad range of technology efforts under the label Revolution in Military Affairs (RMA) to develop weapons with precision accuracy and sensors that would give commanders situational awareness over a huge geospatial area. Although the Bill Clinton administration embraced the rhetoric of the RMA, its civilian and military leaders fell short in practice, leading lawmakers to force the creation of a National Defense Panel filled with RMA zealots.[16]

Supporting Military Innovators

Lawmakers are often key supporters of military innovators in their struggles with resistant military leadership. Military mavericks have often found allies on Capitol Hill, either because they agree with their recommendations or they welcome the criticism of current leaders and policies. Billy Mitchell first found Hill support when he wanted to demonstrate that aerial bombardment could sink battleships. The navy strongly opposed letting the army conduct such tests until members of Congress threatened the service with mandatory legislation. The sinking of the former German battleship *Ostfriesland* in 1921 was a turning point for airpower. Mitchell continued his advocacy in later congressional hearings. In 1925, however, he went too far, seizing upon two aviation accidents to say they were "the direct result of the incompetency, criminal negligence and almost treasonable administration of the national defense by the Navy and War Departments." He was court-martialed for bringing discredit on his service and chose a pro-airpower member of Congress as his lawyer. Meanwhile, Rep. Fiorello La Guardia (R-NY)—himself a former bomber pilot—introduced three bills to protect Mitchell by forbidding reprisals against officers who testify before Congress. They were not voted on. Though Mitchell was found guilty and later resigned, President Calvin Coolidge felt compelled to reduce his sentence of five years without pay to half pay. Congress then passed a compromise measure making the Air Corps a coequal combat branch of the army, adding an assistant secretary of war for air, mandating an expansion in personnel and equipment, and directing that only air officers could command air units.[17]

When in 1952 the navy tried to force the then captain Hyman Rickover into retirement by not promoting him to rear admiral, enough powerful members of Congress, led by Sen. Henry "Scoop" Jackson (D-WA), came to his defense that the navy convened a new selection board with instructions to include someone with his credentials. Rickover had such strong Hill support for his development of nuclear-propulsion systems for the navy that no one was able to force his retirement until President Reagan finally did in 1982.[18]

Senator Jackson also conspired with air force general Bernard Schriever in 1955 to pressure President Dwight D. Eisenhower to accelerate and give special budget protection for the air force intercontinental ballistic-missile program.[19]

Perhaps the most significant assertion of congressional power against a reluctant executive was the Goldwater-Nichols Act of 1986. Several members of Congress joined with some reform-minded senior officers to develop the public case for changes in the Pentagon and to fashion legislation that won broad approval despite vigorous opposition from the navy and the Reagan administration.[20]

Empowering New Organizations

Lawmakers occasionally empower new organizations to take advantage of new ways of war. New ways of war often require new organizations, both to overcome bureaucratic resistance to the innovation and to fully exploit its advantages. This was the pattern in the long struggle by American aviators for an independent air force, by submariners for special status, by marines for exclusive rights to amphibious assault, and by special operations forces (SOF) for an independent command.

Congress played a significant role in resolving many of these disputes. It created an independent air force in 1947, supported a special fleet of nuclear-powered submarines, guaranteed the marines three divisions and longevity in 1952, and voted to create the Special Operations Command (SOCOM) in 1986. Still unresolved is how to organize and assign responsibilities for cyber operations and some aspects of defense within national borders. On the other hand, Congress determined in 1946 to keep nuclear weapons development in a civilian organization—and President Truman refused to transfer physical control of those weapons to the military until the Korean War. Congress also made a conscious decision in 1958 to separate military space programs from the civilian ones run by the National Aeronautics and Space Administration.

Creation of SOCOM was a vivid example of Congress imposing its will on a reluctant military establishment. President John F. Kennedy strongly supported the expansion of the Army Special Forces—the Green Berets—in 1961, but Congress remained lukewarm to the effort. Many military leaders blamed the enthusiasm for counterinsurgency for problems in the Vietnam War, calling counterinsurgency another means of civilian interference. The failed Iranian hostage rescue mission in 1980 (Operation Eagle Claw) led to a military reform effort in Congress that sought to promote interservice co-operation rather than rivalry and in particular urged the creation of antiter-rorist units that could perform "special operations." Reagan administration officials gave lip service to the idea but worked bureaucratically to oppose any significant changes. Stung by increased terrorist acts such as the bombing of the US embassy in Beirut in 1983, appropriators demanded that the Pentagon create a separate funding program for SOF in order to make it harder for the services to shift money into other areas. In 1986 House and Senate authorizers passed a law creating an independent SOCOM and guaranteeing a separate budget, despite the continued opposition of the civilian and military leadership of the Pentagon.[21]

When SOF proved especially agile and effective in the early stages of the war in Afghanistan, Congress strongly supported the expansion of SOCOM, which grew from 38,000 people in 2001 to 63,000 in 2012, heading toward a planned 71,000. In 2013, however, key congressional committees complained about inadequate justification of some SOCOM expansion plans and made slight budget cuts.[22]

The Central Intelligence Agency (CIA) also has developed paramilitary forces and other means of covert action, a secret new way of war for the United States. The few members of Congress privy to the activities of the CIA prior to the 1970s supported the agency's programs. When some of its operations were disclosed, notably domestic spying, assassination attempts on foreign leaders, and secret support for unsavory foreign leaders, Congress set up a formal system for accountability, requiring the president to personally authorize the program and to notify Congress regarding the plans. This led to the creation of House and Senate Intelligence Committees that oversee the intelligence community on behalf of Congress as a whole.[23]

After the 9/11 attacks, Congress forced a reluctant George W. Bush administration to create a formal Department of Homeland Security (DHS) and later reorganized the intelligence community by creating a new top post of director of national intelligence (DNI) as well as an interagency body, the National Counterterrorism Center (NCTC), for joint operational intelligence and joint planning against terrorism.

Investigating Problems and Failures

Congress has a long history of investigating military problems, especially major failures. The very first congressional investigation, in 1792, targeted the disastrous defeat of the forces of Gen. Arthur St. Clair in a battle with Indians in the Northwest Territory. In fact, about half the investigations conducted by Congress over the next century were related to activities of the armed forces. Following the capture and burning of Washington in 1815, Congress first demanded reports from the Madison administration and later launched its own investigations of what went wrong. During the Civil War, the Joint Committee on the Conduct of the War met almost daily—though in secret—when Congress was in session, holding 272 formal hearings. Its members traveled widely to battlefields and elsewhere and later issued eleven reports.

Logistical problems in the war with Spain in 1898 and soldier complaints about things such as the "embalmed beef" they were fed prompted congressional investigations that laid the groundwork for the army reforms instituted in the following years.

Congress also held major investigations of the military disaster at Pearl Harbor, the firing of Gen. Douglas MacArthur in 1951, and the failure to prevent the 9/11 attacks in 2001. Hearings on cost overruns and performance problems with new weapon systems were a routine part of congressional oversight of the annual defense budgets. Some gained widespread notoriety; others merely affected funding levels.

During US operations in Iraq and Afghanistan, members of Congress held extensive hearings and often criticized some aspects of the conduct of those wars, usually the political-military strategy rather than military operations. As the military situation in Iraq worsened in 2005 and 2006, members of Congress gave vocal support to military officers such as Gen. David Petraeus, who was leading his own internal fight to get military support for counterinsurgency (COIN) doctrine and strategy.[24] COIN was seen as a better way of war in both Iraq and Afghanistan. The Barack Obama administration's 2012 strategic guidance reemphasized the importance of COIN forces but declared that "U.S. forces will no longer be sized to conduct large-scale, prolonged stability operations."[25]

Questioning Military Innovations

Lawmakers tend to question military innovations that raise significant domestic issues. Most military activities have little spillover into domestic civilian life. But when they do, Congress has a struggle balancing competing concerns. The most significant, of course, are major military operations and conscription. Wars cost money and threaten funds for domestic programs. Conscription disrupts the lives of voters, who may take their anger out at the polls.

Some preparations for future wars do spill over and provoke domestic reactions. Many lawmakers supported the 1963 nuclear test ban treaty precisely because it removed radioactive materials from the food supply, regardless of its impact on the development of new weapons. And while most lawmakers fight to keep open military bases in their home areas, few would welcome a large new installation unless the Pentagon paid for new roads and otherwise mitigated the environmental impact.

Civil defense was an appealing response to the threat of nuclear war for military planners and was pushed for a while by the Kennedy administration, but the general public never embraced the idea. During the 1961 Berlin Crisis, Congress approved President Kennedy's request for $107 million for civil defense, but a year later the defense committees opposed a request to provide subsidies for construction. Missile defenses around cities also made strategic sense until the public decided it didn't want its own neighborhoods to be nuclear targets.

A growing controversy surrounds how far to go in homeland security. Most passengers resent intrusive Transportation Security Administration inspections at airports even if they appreciate the results. Many local police organizations welcome the addition of military equipment but then face public anger when excessive force is used against innocent people.

The domestic use of drones has sparked another controversy. In 2012 Congress passed a law pushing the Federal Aviation Administration to accelerate the integration of unmanned aerial vehicles (UAVs) into the national airspace system by 2015, but a backlash developed among members of Congress raising privacy and civil liberties concerns.[26]

Domestic concerns have also arisen to challenge the adoption of weaponized drones and offensive cyber operations as new ways of war. Congress is divided over how to balance activities to combat terrorist and cyber attacks with the legal protections afforded US citizens and their rights and expectations of privacy.

The Fight over Drones

Drones are a rapidly expanding form of technology with numerous military and civilian uses. American lawmakers, and the public at large, have begun vigorous debates over drones precisely because these systems raise domestic policy concerns, including privacy and legal protections against government actions as well as foreign policy concerns.

UAVs were developed and tested over the years of the Cold War, but by the start of the twenty-first century had become, in journalist Mark Mazzetti's phrase, "the ultimate weapon for a secret war."[27] Both the intelligence community and the Defense Department saw remotely piloted weapons as an ideal new way of fighting the war on terrorists. They reduced the risks to pilots, offered greater accuracy and thus less collateral damage and fewer casualties, and they had the advantage of greater secrecy.

UAVs raised a series of issues for Congress, both as weapon programs and as tools for a new way of war. In the early decades when the aircraft were developed for intelligence and surveillance missions, lawmakers questioned

A weaponized US Air Force Reaper drone in flight. *Courtesy of General Atomics Aeronautical Systems, Inc. All rights reserved.*

the multiplicity of programs that never seemed to go into production and into operation. UAVs struggled for many decades to achieve the support and acceptance they have today largely because they lacked strong sponsors and a friendly organizational home. Both the intelligence community and the military's operational commands wanted collection platforms like UAVs, but each had their own needs and doctrine for making use of them. Predator surveillance aircraft were used by the CIA in the Balkans early in the Clinton administration after the intelligence committees approved money for their development. Reportedly, the agency resisted embracing armed drones, however, because of concerns that their use might conflict with the longstanding ban on assassinations.[28]

For a long time the US Air Force appeared to resist unmanned reconnaissance aircraft because of the "white scarf syndrome," the preference for men in the cockpit of any flying machine. Dozens of UAV programs were started in the 1970s and 1980s, but only Pioneer and Predator made it into the operational inventory by the late 1990s. The air force also insisted that only rated pilots be allowed to operate the UAVs. Congress repeatedly complained about the lack of results from the numerous research programs and forced the creation of a central management office. In 1996, over Pentagon opposition, Congress approved $10 million for the Pentagon to begin development of a weaponized UAV system. The Clinton administration ordered the testing of armed Predators in response to the bombing of two embassies in Africa in 1998.[29]

Congressional enthusiasm for UAVs grew in the late 1990s. In 2000 Congress ordered that "within ten years, one-third of U.S. military operational deep strike aircraft will be unmanned." The 9/11 attacks gave added impetus to the effort to put precision-guided missiles on reconnaissance drones, which were first utilized in Afghanistan. Both the Pentagon and the intelligence community rapidly increased their numbers of UAVs. In the case of the Department of Defense (DOD), the inventory grew from about fifty in 2001 to over 7,500 by 2012, of which about 5 percent are armed. The budget jumped from $667 million in 2001 to $3.9 billion in 2012. The fraction of manned aircraft in the DOD inventory dropped from 95 percent in 2005 to 69 percent in 2011, and Congress in 2007 ordered a policy of giving "a preference for unmanned systems in acquisition programs for new systems."[30]

While using UAVs for overseas surveillance had drawn little opposition, weaponized drone strikes became much more controversial as the use of drones became more frequent and more public. Lawmakers and others raised questions about the programs and about the legal authority for targeted killings, especially when at least four US citizens were among the victims. Some people argued that drones had become a new form of secret war that should be carefully overseen, that their very advantages made it too easy to get involved in wars. Others argued that targeted killings raised profound moral and legal issues. Critics claimed that many innocent civilians were dying in the drone attacks and cited the backlash in Pakistan and elsewhere as a result of civilian casualties.

In 2012 President Obama publicly acknowledged the drone program, and gradually the administration made additional disclosures about its rules of operation. In 2013 he announced that the targeted killing program was being reduced and would eventually shift from the CIA and be consolidated in the Pentagon. Congress blocked the transfer, however, with secret restrictions added to the 2014 omnibus appropriations bill.[31]

Critics claimed that Congress had failed to oversee the drone programs. Members of the intelligence committees defended their efforts, noting that they were notified of all CIA armed strikes and regularly reviewed the justifications for them. Members of the defense committees said that they received periodic reports and briefings of DOD-run operations. The members and staff of the foreign policy and judicial committees, however, were denied access to the reports and to the classified legal opinions justifying them.[32]

While the Obama administration sought to quell the criticism with greater transparency about drone operations and more elaborate procedures to make targeting decisions, some in Congress sought to prevent or restrict lethal strikes. One idea was to apply to Pentagon-run operations—both drone strikes and major SOF raids—a legal regime similar to that in law for CIA-run covert actions, whereby the president must make a formal finding and Congress must be promptly notified. To limit the reporting to major activities, the criterion could be that if the president has to decide on an action, that was something Congress needed to be informed about.

Confusion over Cyber Operations

As with drones, both offensive and defensive cyber operations raise domestic policy issues that force lawmakers to weigh competing interests and values. They also raise important questions about which organizations in government should be given authorities and responsibilities for cyber activities. There is far from a consensus on how to resolve these conflicting issues.

Computers opened the door to many new ways of war, from better weapon design and testing to more precise control and targeting and now to where adversaries of many different types—civilian, military, individual, corporate, governmental—can attack the computer systems of others and must constantly be on the defensive against attacks on themselves.

Congress played a role in supporting cyber activities from the 1960s when the Defense Advanced Research Projects Agency (DARPA) developed the technology for what became the internet. The Pentagon spurred the development of faster and more capable computers for military purposes even before the private sector began selling games and personal devices. By the late 1990s, military planners saw offensive possibilities in what was originally called "information warfare." Meanwhile, the news media regularly reported hacking of government computers, and Congress began pressing for better computer security.

Congress quietly supported cyber capabilities for covert warfare and responded more openly to warnings of the threat of cyber attacks on domestic economic systems—"a digital Pearl Harbor." President Clinton created a commission in 1996 that warned of major vulnerabilities in what was beginning to be called "critical infrastructure," such as the electric grid and air traffic control systems. He issued a formal directive in 1998 requiring federal agencies to develop plans for protection of those systems through consultations with industry. The fact that 85–90 percent of crucial computer systems are in the private sector meant that any government policy had to deal with issues of regulation, costs of compliance, proprietary information, and personal privacy. Although cyber attacks were recognized as a possible new way of war, the battlefield was seen as primarily on American soil. From the start, Congress focused more on cyber defense than offense.[33]

After the 9/11 attacks, many federal agencies rushed to develop programs for cyber security. More than twenty-one federal organizations now have some kind of cyber mission, and each probably has some congressional patrons to defend its budget and its bureaucratic standing.[34] In addition to the turf wars between the Pentagon and the intelligence community, there are now bureaucratic fights among various military organizations and among many civilian organizations—the crime fighters at the Federal Bureau of Investigation, the critical infrastructure panels in the DHS, and the domestic agencies that deal with aviation, energy, banking, and so forth. The beleaguered DHS complains that it must report to over a hundred congressional panels.

The clashing perspectives on how to manage federal cyber security programs has prevented Congress from agreeing to basic legislation. One of the main differences has been between lawmakers who want to require industry to adopt certain security procedures and those who want to make adherence voluntary. Another has been between privacy advocates and supporters of information sharing with the federal government and between agencies. These differences prevented any major congressional action from 2011 to 2013.[35]

Disclosures of classified information regarding the extent of US government surveillance of telecommunications, and admission that the government regularly collects vast amounts of data on US citizens as well as potential terrorists, led to a firestorm of criticism and further investigations by Congress in 2013. While the intelligence committees generally defended the agencies they oversee, other committees raised personal privacy and domestic legal concerns in their own investigations. Congress seemed likely to try to impose tougher restrictions on the intelligence agencies from collecting information on people within the United States both to protect privacy and to rein in a bigger, badder, more intrusive government than they had realized.

Rules and responsibilities for offensive cyber warfare remain obscure. President Obama released a paper titled *International Strategy for Cyberspace* in May 2011. It said little about offensive cyber operations but reiterated the right of self-defense using "all necessary means." The paper promised that the United States would develop "a range of credible response options" and would seek "stability through norms"—that is, diplomatic efforts to build an international consensus on proper conduct in cyberspace. The administration subsequently had talks with the Russians and Chinese about these matters.[36]

Reports have surfaced of an October 2012 presidential directive that orders government agencies to identify potential targets and plan for and coordinate offensive cyber operations but requires presidential approval for any operation likely to result in "significant consequences," such as loss of life or serious responsive consequences to the United States. About the same time, the chairman of the Joint Chiefs of Staff, Gen. Martin Dempsey, said, "We now have a playbook for cyber . . . [and] we're updating the rules of engagement." Additional reports suggested that US intelligence organizations had carried out 231 offensive cyber operations in 2011, mostly against targets in Iran, Russia, China, and North Korea and against nuclear proliferation.[37]

For the US military, cyberspace is another "domain" for operations and thus for planning, training, and equipping. Congress has probed for further information and received a DOD report emphasizing defensive activities and promising quarterly briefings of cyber operations. Meanwhile, Congress began reviewing a proposed $5.1 billion budget for cyber operations as well as plans to increase the size of the Cyber Command from 900 personnel to 4,900 over the next few years. The Defense Science Board (DSB) in January 2013 declared that "cyber attacks are expected in every future conflict" and urged developing "world-class cyber offensive capabilities." In order to ensure the professionalization of this new type of warfare, the DSB recommended recruiting a class of cyber warriors with career paths, training expectations, and appropriate incentives.[38]

Cyber issues confront Congress with legal and jurisdictional questions as well as policy ones. This new way of war involves a broader range of agencies with missions and capabilities than traditional conflict as well as hard questions such as when a cyber problem constitutes an act of war. The Obama administration sidestepped that question in a report to Congress by noting that the War Powers Act only relates to the introduction of armed forces "into hostilities." Electrons are not troops equipped for combat.

After considering splitting control of the National Security Agency (NSA) and the Cyber Command because those organizations have separate legal authorities and budgets and are overseen by different congressional committees, President Obama decided to maintain dual-hatted leadership.

Since the American public is concerned about NSA access to domestic communications, it will be harder for Congress to handle the management of cyber activities dispassionately. One suggestion for oversight is similar to that for drones. The presidential directive on cyber operations already requires presidential approval of all actions with significant consequences. If time does not allow obtaining that approval, the secretary of defense is empowered to conduct "emergency cyber actions" but only if they are "limited in magnitude, scope, and duration" and do not result in deaths. Congress could demand notification of those activities approved by the president as well as timely notification of any emergency actions.

Conclusion

History shows that Congress, as an institution, has often been a key sup-porter of new ways of war. But individual members have varied widely in their views, some advocating and others strongly opposed to the technolo-gies, organizations, operations, and strategies used to pursue them. Rather than imposing a civilian perspective on the US military, Congress has usually been a partner with military factions that advocate those new ways of war.

Analysts have identified five "game-changing" technologies that could have revolutionary impacts on warfare. These are additive manufacturing (often called "3-D printing"), autonomous systems such as drones and ro-bots, directed energy, cyber capabilities, and human performance modifica-tion. Within the Pentagon, these technologies have generated opponents as well as supporters for predictable reasons. "Large organizations tend to resist technologies that may disrupt core ways of doing business," a recent study notes, also citing former defense secretary Robert Gates's comment that the military services have "nostalgia" for their "traditional orientation."[39]

Congress has a similar tendency to resist major change. As a study of DARPA's role in developing revolutionary technology noted, "disruptive ca-pabilities will also face an uphill battle in Congress if they must compete with large platform acquisitions. One reason is jobs. For example, UAVs require few people to build them and only a few billion dollars to deploy, whereas production of fighter aircraft keeps thousands of people employed and in-fuses hundreds of billions of dollars into congressional districts."[40]

As the discussion of drones and cyber operations shows, there is no solid consensus in Congress on the military value of those technologies, com-pared with the costs, risks, and domestic impacts. There are not yet strong and visible advocates and sponsors on Capitol Hill. Until and unless that oc-curs, these possible new ways of war will remain underdeveloped.

Notes

1. Frank M. Bennett, *The Steam Navy of the United States* (Pittsburgh: W. T. Nicholson, 1896), 11, 16.
2. Lance C. Buhl, "Mariners and Machines: Resistance to Technological Change in the American Navy, 1865–1869," *Journal of American History* 41 (1974): 703–27.
3. Benjamin Franklin Cooling, *Gray Steel and Blue Water Navy: The Formative Years of America's Military-Industrial Complex, 1881–1917* (Hamden, CT: Archon Books, 1979), 85–109.
4. Jacob Goodwin, *Brotherhood of Arms: General Dynamics and the Business of Defending Amer-ica* (New York: Times Books, 1985), 26, 28, 34–35, 38–39.
5. Thomas P. Hughes, *American Genesis: A Century of Innovation and Technological Enthusiasm, 1870–1970* (New York: Viking, 1989), 101–3; Wayne Biddle, *Barons of the Sky: From Early Flight to Strategic Warfare* (New York; Simon & Schuster, 1991), 43.

6. Carroll V. Glines, *The Compact History of the United States Air Force* (New York: Hawthorn Books, 1963), 41–46, 52.

7. Biddle, *Barons of the Sky,* 78.

8. Rondall R. Rice, *The Politics of Air Power* (Lincoln: University of Nebraska Press, 2004), 34–35, 69, 175.

9. David E. Johnson, *Fast Tanks and Heavy Bombers: Innovation in the U.S. Army, 1917–1945* (Ithaca, NY: Cornell University Press, 1998), 29, 51, 75; George F. Hofmann, "The Demise of the U.S. Tank Corps and Medium Tank Development Program," *Military Affairs* (February 1973): 20–25.

10. Barbara Salazar Torreon, *Instances of Use of United States Armed Forces Abroad, 1798–2013,* CRS Report for Congress (Washington, DC: Congressional Research Service, May 3, 2013).

11. Charles A. Stevenson, *Congress at War: The Politics of Conflict since 1789* (Dulles, VA: Potomac Books, 2007).

12. Arnold Kanter, *Defense Politics: A Budgetary Perspective* (Chicago: University of Chicago Press, 1979), 40–41.

13. James M. Lindsay, *Congress and Nuclear Weapons* (Baltimore: Johns Hopkins University Press, 1991), 10, 36, 98–99.

14. Christopher M. Jones, "Roles, Politics, and the Survival of the V-22 Osprey," in *The Domestic Sources of American Foreign Policy,* 4th ed., ed. Eugene R. Wittkopf and James M. McCormick (Lanham, MD: Rowman & Littlefield, 2004), 283–302.

15. Thomas Mahnken, *Technology and the American Way of War since 1945* (New York: Columbia University Press, 2008), 125–26.

16. Ibid., 177–78.

17. Douglas Waller, *A Question of Loyalty: Gen. Billy Mitchell and the Court-Martial That Gripped the Nation* (New York: HarperCollins, 2004), 7, 20, 37, 145, 324, 329–30; Rice, *Politics,* 45, 71.

18. Theodore Rockwell, *The Rickover Effect: The Inside Story of How Adm. Hyman Rickover Built the Nuclear Navy* (Annapolis, MD: Naval Institute Press, 1992), 154–57.

19. Neil Sheehan, *A Fiery Peace in a Cold War* (New York: Random House, 2009), 268–99.

20. James R. Locher III, *Victory on the Potomac: The Goldwater-Nichols Act Unifies the Pentagon* (College Station: Texas A&M University Press, 2002).

21. David Tucker and Christopher J. Lamb, *United States Special Operations Forces* (New York: Columbia University Press, 2007), 93, 96–99; Thomas K. Adams, *U.S. Special Operations Forces in Action* (New York: Frank Cass, 1998), 67, 70, 186, 189, 201.

22. Jim Thomas and Chris Doherty, *Beyond the Ramparts: The Future of U.S. Special Operations Forces* (Washington, DC: Center for Strategic and Budgetary Assessments, 2013); Nick Schwellenbach, "Congress Says Special-Ops Budget Too Top Secret," *Time,* June 26, 2013.

23. Amy B. Zegart, *Eyes on Spies: Congress and the United States Intelligence Community* (Stanford, CA: Hoover Institution Press, 2011), 20–30.

24. Fred Kaplan, *The Insurgents: David Petraeus and the Plot to Change the American Way of War* (New York: Simon & Schuster, 2013).

25. White House, "Sustaining U.S. Global Leadership: Priorities for 21st Century Defense," January 2012, 6.

26. Richard M. Thompson II, *Drones in Domestic Surveillance Operations: Fourth Amendment Implications and Legislative Responses,* CRS Report for Congress (Washington, DC: Congressional Research Service, September 6, 2012).

27. Mark Mazzetti, *The Way of the Knife: The CIA, a Secret Army, and a War at the Ends of the Earth* (New York: Penguin Press, 2013), 99.

28. Ibid., 91, 97–98.

29. Jeremiah Gertler, *U.S. Unmanned Aerial Systems*, CRS Report for Congress (Washington, DC: Congressional Research Service, January 3, 2012); Mazzetti, *Way of the Knife*, 91–93.

30. Gertler, *U.S. Unmanned*, 9.

31. See Adam Entous, "U.S. Acknowledges Its Drone Strikes," *Wall Street Journal*, June 15, 2012, http://online.wsj.com/news/articles/SB10001424052702303410404577746898191601145 6; Eric Holder, "Letter to Patrick Leahy," May 22, 2013, http://msnbcmedia.msn.com/i /msnbc/sections/news/AG_letter_5-22-13.pdf; "Remarks by the President at the National Defense University," May 23, 2013, http://www.whitehouse.gov/the-press-office/2013 /05/23/remarks-president-national-defense-university; and Eric Schmitt, "Congress Restricts Drones Program Shift," *New York Times*, January 16, 2014.

32. Michael Hirsh, "The NSA's Future: A Tale of Two Committees," *National Journal*, August 2, 2013; Tony Romm, "Intelligence Oversight Has Some Limits in Congress," *Politico*, October 10, 2013, http://www.politico.com/story/2013/10/intelligence-oversight-has -some-limits-in-congress-98099.html.

33. Rita Tehan, *Cybersecurity: Authoritative Reports and Resources*, CRS Report for Congress (Washington, DC: Congressional Research Service, July 18, 2013); John T. Moteff, *Critical Infrastructures: Background, Policy, and Implementation*, CRS Report for Congress (Washington, DC: Congressional Research Service, July 11, 2011).

34. Dana Priest and William M. Arkin, *Top Secret America: The Rise of the New American Security State* (Boston: Little, Brown, 2011), 88.

35. Tim Starks, "2012 Legislative Summary: Cybersecurity," *CQ Weekly*, January 14, 2013, 92; Tony Romm, "Cybersecurity Reform Going Nowhere Fast," *Politico*, October 9, 2013, http://www.politico.com/story/2013/10/cybersecurity-reform-going-nowhere-fast -98027.html

36. White House, *International Strategy for Cyberspace: Prosperity, Security, and Openness in a Networked World*, May 2011, 14, www.whitehouse.gov/sites/default/files/rss_viewer /international_strategy_for_cyberspace.pdf.

37. Robert O'Harrow and Barton Gellman, "Secret Cyber Directive Calls for Ability to Attack without Warning," *Washington Post*, June 7, 2013; Thom Shanker, "Pentagon Is Updating Conflict Rules in Cyberspace," *New York Times*, June 27, 2013.

38. Ellen Nakashima, "Pentagon to Boost Cybersecurity Force," *Washington Post*, January 27, 2013; Barton Gellman and Ellen Nakashima, "U.S. Spy Agencies Mounted 231 Offensive Operations in 2011, Documents Show," *Washington Post*, August 30, 2013; Defense Science Board, *Resilient Military Systems and the Advanced Cyber Threat*, January 2013, www.defense .gov/pubs/2013_China_Report_FINAL.pdf.

39. Shawn Brimley, Ben FitzGerald, and Kelley Sayler, *Game Changers: Disruptive Technology and U.S. Defense Strategy* (Washington, DC: Center for a New American Security, September 2013).

40. Richard H. Van Atta, Michael J. Lippitz, Jasper C. Lupo, Rob Mahoney, and Jack H. Nunn, *Transformation and Transition: DARPA's Role in Fostering an Emerging Revolution in Military Affairs, Volume 1: Overall Assessment* (Alexandria, VA: Institute for Defense Analyses, April 2003), 69.

9

Closing Guantánamo

A Presidential Commitment Unfulfilled

LOUIS FISHER

After the terrorist attacks of September 11, 2001, the George W. Bush administration brought almost eight hundred suspects from around the world to the Guantánamo Bay Naval Station in Cuba. The administration claimed authority to hold these individuals indefinitely without charging them of a crime and giving them the opportunity to demonstrate their innocence. It was well known that many were captured without any evidence of being linked to terrorist operations against the United States. Instead, American forces accepted judgments from members of the Northern Alliance (Tajiks, Uzbeks, and others) who had been fighting the Taliban in a civil war. Newspaper stories reported a bounty-hunter system, with members of the Northern Alliance given $5,000 if they identified someone as a Taliban and $20,000 if they associated someone with al-Qaeda.[1] According to reports, Pakistani officials were paid as much as $10,000 to turn over a suspect.[2]

Over the years, US officials in Guantánamo recognized that detainees held at the naval base represented a mix of terrorist fighters and innocent people erroneously swept up. Hundreds would be released without apology from the US government or financial compensation. Moazzam Begg, seized in Pakistan in January 2002, was held at Guantánamo and at Bagram and Kandahar in Afghanistan for three years. Initially labeled an "enemy combatant," he was eventually released without explanation, apology, or any type of reparation.[3] By the end of the Bush administration, the number of detainees at Guantánamo had fallen to about 248.[4]

Obama's Public Commitment

One of Barack Obama's first pledges during his presidential campaign in 2007 and 2008 was to close the detention facility at Guantánamo.[5] On January 22,

2009, his second day in the Oval Office, he issued Executive Order 13492 to close it "as soon as practicable, and no later than 1 year from the date of this order."[6] His decision to sign the order marked an extraordinary lack of political judgment, damaging his administration from the start and revealing no understanding of how to exercise presidential power effectively. Putting his signature on an executive order could never by itself change detention policy at the naval base.

Remarkably, none of Obama's presidential advisers seemed to warn him of the political downsides. Releasing terrorist suspects to other countries or transferring them to the United States was immensely controversial. The administration needed to first meet with lawmakers, learn about their concerns, fashion a reasonable compromise, and locate a secure facility on the mainland to house the detainees. It failed to take any of those elementary steps. If Obama had asked Congress to help create the legislative framework for the closure, progress would have been possible. His executive order was the type of unilateral action that had backfired repeatedly on George W. Bush.

To the surprise of White House officials, Obama's announcement to close Guantánamo and transfer detainees abroad was not broadly interpreted as taking the moral high ground. Instead, the executive order provoked sustained criticism from members of Congress and the public.[7] The criticism seemed fueled more by fear than fact. Many terrorists had been prosecuted in federal court, found guilty, and placed in super-maximum-security ("supermax") prisons in the United States without incident. Thirty-three international terrorists, many with ties to al-Qaeda, were placed in a single federal prison in Florence, Colorado, with little public notice.[8] Convicted terrorists were held at Fort Leavenworth, Kansas, and other federal prisons. Some states opposed having detainees housed within their borders, following the "not in my back yard" attitude, but an economically pressed community in Montana volunteered to open its unused 464-bed Two Rivers Regional Detention Facility to detainees from the naval base.[9]

In a major national security speech on May 21, 2009, President Obama reviewed the record of holding detainees at Guantánamo. Over a period of seven years, the system of military commissions at the naval base had "succeeded in convicting a grand total of three suspected terrorists." Over that time, the Bush administration had released 525 detainees after concluding there was no basis to hold them. To Obama the procedures in place at Guantánamo "set back the moral authority that is America's strongest currency in the world. Instead of building a durable framework for the struggle against al Qaeda that drew upon our deeply held values and traditions, our government was defending positions that undermined the rule of law." Rather

Guards from the US Navy Expeditionary Guard Battalion at Guantánamo Bay, Cuba, escort a detainee to the medical facility in Camp Four, November 23, 2007. *Department of Defense*

than serving as a tool to combat terrorism, the naval base "became a symbol that helped al Qaeda recruit terrorists to its cause. Indeed, the existence of Guantanamo likely created more terrorists around the world than it ever detained."[10]

On August 24, 2009, the Justice Department announced that a special task force on interrogations and transfer policy, created by President Obama on January 22, 2009, had proposed a number of recommendations. With regard to detainees at Guantánamo, the United States would transfer some to other countries after receiving assurances of a capacity to hold detainees until they could be safely released. The United States would also seek to monitor the treatment of individuals transferred to other countries.[11]

Congress Responds

The mood on Capitol Hill turned strongly against Obama's decision to close the base. Opposition was voiced by both Democrats and Republicans. Senate Democratic Leader Harry Reid of Nevada stated, "We will never allow terrorists to be released into the United States."[12] On May 12, 2009, the House Appropriations Committee reported a bill providing for supplemental appropriations. The committee report stated that the bill "has not provided

$50,000,000 requested to support implementation of a future decision by the Administration on the disposition of individuals currently detained at the Guantanamo Bay Naval Base."[13] Instead, it would await a proposal from the Defense Department to consider shifting funds through the reprogramming process (moving money from one purpose to another within an appropriations account), including possible relocation of detainees and closing the facility.[14] Later in the report the total dollar amount requested by the administration to close Guantánamo was placed at $80 million.[15] That total consisted of $50 million for the Defense Department and $30 million for the Justice Department.

As explained in the committee report, the bill required President Obama to submit a plan regarding the proposed disposition of detention facilities at the naval base.[16] Rep. Frank Wolf (R-VA) offered an amendment in committee to place a moratorium on releasing or transferring any Guantánamo detainees to the United States until the administration submitted a plan for the disposition of each detainee, including how security risks would be addressed and also a certification of the consent of state governors and state legislatures. The amendment was defeated on a party-line vote of 20 to 32.[17]

House debate on the supplemental appropriations bill highlighted several key issues. Rep. David Dreier (R-CA) objected that the administration had not presented to Congress a "clear plan as to how the facility will be closed and, most important, what will be done with the detainees. Will they be moved to American soil? Tried in jail or—God forbid—released here in the United States?"[18] The administration had not provided Congress with an analysis of security risks in releasing detainees and how that would be handled. Dreier thought that governors and state legislators should have the final say on whether detainees would be housed in their states.[19] He said a number of states "have already indicated an interest in having an opportunity to receive these detainees."[20] The bill deleted the $80 million the administration requested to transfer the detainees to the United States.

House Republican Leader John Boehner of Ohio expressed his pleasure at having the $80 million removed from the bill. He asked, "What is the administration's plan for those prisoners who are being held at our detention facility? Will they release or transfer them to American soil? I don't know of any community or neighborhood in America that would want them."[21] He pointed to the Republican solution: the Keep Terrorists Out of America Act.[22] An amendment by Rep. Todd Tiahrt (R-KS) to prohibit detainees from being transferred or released to the United States was rejected by the House Rules Committee.[23]

Further raising legislative concerns was a White House decision on April 14, 2009, to resettle eight of seventeen Uighurs from the naval base into the

United States, most of them placed in Virginia. Uighurs are an ethnic group of western China, and some are members of the Eastern Turkistan Islamic Movement, considered by the Beijing government to be a terrorist group. The Obama administration believed that releasing Uighurs from Guantánamo into the United States would encourage European and other governments to accept some of the detainees.

According to the administration's plan, the Uighurs would simply show up in American communities, free to move around. Supposedly a swift, secretive operation would preempt any political outcry and interference by Congress.[24] That project failed also. Before the detainees could leave the naval base, Representative Wolf learned about the scheduled transfers. He had not been briefed by the White House. His angry outburst forced the administration to shelve the plan.[25] The House voted to accept the rule agreed to by the House Rules Committee, denying supplemental funds to transfer detainees from the naval base, 247 to 178.

Although Congress often divides along partisan lines in supporting or opposing presidential actions, the vote count on Guantánamo was overwhelmingly bipartisan. In acting on the supplemental appropriations bill, the Senate on May 20, 2009, voted 90 to 6 to prohibit funds to transfer or release detainees to the United States. The six voting no were Democrats: senators Dick Durbin of Illinois, Tom Harkin of Iowa, Patrick Leahy of Vermont, Carl Levin of Michigan, Jack Reed of Rhode Island, and Sheldon Whitehouse of Rhode Island. The three senators deciding not to vote were Democrats: Robert C. Byrd of West Virginia, Ted Kennedy of Massachusetts, and Jay Rockefeller of West Virginia.[26]

Statutory Limitations in 2009

As enacted on June 24, 2009, the supplemental appropriations bill provided that none of the funds made available in the bill or any prior statute "may be used to release an individual who is detained as of the date of enactment of this Act, at Naval Station, Guantanamo Bay, Cuba, for the purpose of detention in the continental United States, Alaska, Hawaii, or the District of Columbia, except as provided in subsection (c)."[27] Subsection (c) provided that none of the funds made available in that or any prior act may be used to transfer an individual detained at the naval base into the continental United States, Alaska, Hawaii, or the District of Columbia "for the purposes of prosecuting such individual, or detaining such individual during legal proceedings, until 45 days after the plan detailed in subsection (d) is received." That subsection required President Obama to submit to Congress, in classified form, a plan regarding the transfer of Guantánamo detainees to the United

States.[28] In signing the bill, Obama offered no objections to the language on Guantánamo.[29] The statute provided a way for Obama to move detainees to the United States. However, he never submitted a plan to Congress.

The lopsided Senate vote on May 20, 2009, should not have surprised President Obama or his advisers. On July 19, 2007, the Senate had taken a vote on a sense-of-the-Senate resolution stating that detainees housed at Guantánamo "should not be released into American society, nor should they be transferred stateside into facilities in American communities and neighborhoods." The sponsor of the resolution, Sen. Mitch McConnell (R-KY), explained that his amendment "does not prohibit moving the terrorists elsewhere," nor did it "rule out closing Guantanamo Bay, although my personal view is that is a bad idea."[30] The resolution was accepted on a vote of 94 to 3.[31] Three senators did not vote. One was Barack Obama of Illinois.

Five other statutes in 2009 included limitations on releasing detainees from Guantánamo into the United States. Language in a bill enacted on October 28, 2009, stated that none of the funds available in that statute or any other act may be used to release a Guantánamo detainee into the continental United States, Alaska, Hawaii, or the District of Columbia or into the US territories of Guam, American Samoa, the US Virgin Islands, the Commonwealth of Puerto Rico, or the Commonwealth of the Northern Mariana Islands.[32] A separate statute enacted on that same day provided that transfers may not occur until forty-five days after the president submits to Congress a comprehensive plan described in the bill.[33] Before a transfer may occur, the president must consult with the chief executive of the state, the District of Columbia, or the territory or possession of the United States that receives a detainee.[34] Similar language appears in statutes enacted on October 30, December 16, and December 19, 2009.[35]

Prosecuting Detainees in New York City

Congressional suspicions were further heightened in November 2009 when the administration announced its decision to try Khalid Sheikh Mohammed (aka KSM), the most senior al-Qaeda detainee, in a federal courthouse in New York City. As with the decision to close Guantánamo by executive order, the administration failed to reach out effectively to members of Congress and political leaders in New York. Critics asked why a self-proclaimed terrorist such as KSM should receive procedural safeguards available to defendants in federal court while detainees at the naval base accused of less serious offenses should face trial by military commission.[36] Efforts to prosecute KSM faced difficulties, particularly if a federal judge excluded his confessions coerced by torture. If by some chance he were acquitted, the administration suggested that he would not be released but instead be held indefinitely in military detention.[37] What would that result tell other nations about the American system of justice?

After initially pledging support for Attorney General Eric Holder's plan for KSM, New York City mayor Michael Bloomberg raised numerous objections, including the financial cost of holding a trial in Manhattan. Estimated costs of security expenses began at $75 million a year and escalated sharply upward to $1 billion a year. Sen. Charles E. Schumer (D-NY) at first agreed with Bloomberg on holding the trial in Lower Manhattan.[38] With Schumer and other early allies withdrawing their support, the Obama administration recognized it would lose this battle as well. Eventually KSM would be tried by a military commission in Guantánamo. The rejection of the trial in New York City was humiliating to President Obama and particularly to Attorney General Holder.[39]

On November 4, 2013, Attorney General Holder announced he had been correct four years earlier in attempting to put KSM and four other suspects on trial in New York City. He estimated that the trial would not have cost $200 million a year and that the five defendants would have been found guilty and placed on death row. He noted that the military commissions were still in pretrial hearings in prosecuting the five men, with no estimate when the trials might start. Holder said, "If you look at the history of the Article III prosecutions, you will see that they don't take nearly as long as those that occur in the military system."[40] A law review article in 2012 explored the constitutional issues of Congress deciding to prohibit the prosecution in civil court of KSM and the other four defendants.[41]

Actions in 2010

Subsequent legislation by Congress continued to place restrictions on Obama. The administration asked Congress to appropriate about $350 million to buy and renovate a nearly empty prison in Thomson, Illinois. The White House planned to transfer all the Guantánamo detainees there. But on May 19, 2010, the House Armed Services Committee voted unanimously to approve a bill that banned spending any funds to build or modify any facility inside the United States to house detainees from the naval base. The committee explained that it wanted to see "a thorough and comprehensive plan" that outlined the merits, costs, and risks involved in using such a facility, but no such plan was submitted by the administration.[42]

In June 2010, the Obama administration decided to release Mohammed Odaini from Guantánamo and return him to Yemen. A federal district judge had ordered his release after finding he had no connection to al-Qaeda. Odaini had been recommended for release by the Bush and Obama administrations. They recognized that he was a student in Pakistan and had just happened to visit a guesthouse known to be a haven for al-Qaeda operatives. He was arrested with them and held at the naval base from age eighteen to twenty-six.[43]

A decision by the Obama administration led to a detainee at Guantánamo, Ahmed Khalfan Ghailani, being tried not at the naval base by a military commission but by federal court in Manhattan in 2010. Charged with assisting in the 1998 bombings of the American embassies in Kenya and Tanzania, Ghailani was the first Guantánamo detainee moved to the civilian system. The trial was controversial because both the administration and the trial judge indicated that if he were somehow acquitted, he would not be released but returned to military custody.[44] In November 2010 a jury found Ghailani guilty of conspiracy to damage or destroy US property but acquitted him of 284 other counts, including all murder charges.[45]

American and Canadian lawyers worked to reach a plea deal for Omar Khadr, the youngest detainee at Guantánamo. He was sent to the naval base shortly after he turned sixteen, accused of killing a US soldier with a grenade in Afghanistan in 2002 when he was fifteen. By October 2010 he had already spent more than eight years at the naval base. His attorneys described him as a child soldier who should be rehabilitated rather than prosecuted.[46] Later that month he pled guilty, an agreement that allowed the Obama administration to avoid a military trial. Under the plea deal, he served a reduced sentence, much of it in his home country of Canada.[47]

Developments in 2011

Legislation passed in December 2010 and submitted to President Obama in January 2011 flatly prohibited the use of funds to transfer or release detainees to the United States. During consideration of the bill, Attorney General Holder advised Congress that the limitation would "set a dangerous precedent with serious implications for the impartial administration of justice" and would take away "one of our most potent weapons in the fight against terrorism."[48] Facing this congressional restriction, the administration considered a signing statement by President Obama insisting that, as head of the executive branch and commander in chief, he had prosecutorial discretion and wartime powers giving him independent authority to bring detainees into the United States for trial or to transfer them to other countries.[49]

The bill prohibited the use of funds for the transfer or release of detainees from Guantánamo Bay, either within the United States and its territories or to foreign countries.[50] When President Obama received the bill, instead of vetoing it he issued a signing statement, stating that the language "represents a

dangerous and unprecedented challenge to critical executive branch authority to determine when and where to prosecute Guantanamo detainees, based
on the facts and the circumstances of each case and our national security
interests." He vowed to "seek repeal of these restrictions," to seek to mitigate
their effects, and to "oppose any attempt to extend or expand them in the
future."[51] Notwithstanding these objections, the administration accepted the
statutory restrictions.

Regarding transfers to other countries, the bill authorized the secretary
of defense to certify in writing, with the concurrence of the secretary of
state, that the government willing to receive detainees was not a designated
state sponsor of terrorism and maintained effective control over the facility
to house detainees.[52] As to this language about certification, Obama said in
his signing statement it would "interfere with the authority of the executive
branch to make important and consequential foreign policy and national security determinations" and "hinder the conduct of delicate negotiations with
foreign countries." However, Obama had little choice but to accept statutory policy. A political price had to be paid for attempting to act unilater-
ally through an executive order rather than working jointly and openly with
lawmakers.

In limiting Obama's options, the bill also provided a way for the administration to transfer Guantánamo detainees to other countries if the secretary
of defense provided the necessary certification. Interestingly, this statutory
authority was rarely exploited by the Obama administration. Congress provided the means. The administration chose not to use the clear statutory
authority made available to it. Obama did appoint Daniel Fried, a career dip-
lomat, to travel the world finding countries willing to take Guantánamo detainees. He was able to transfer several dozen detainees from the naval base
to other countries.[53]

On March 7, 2011, President Obama issued an executive order to provide
periodic review of individuals detained at the naval base. For each detainee,
an initial review would commence as soon as possible "but no later than 1
year from the date of this order." Detainees would receive a hearing before
a periodic review board (PRB). Each detainee would be provided, in writing
and in a language he could understand, the reasons for being held at the naval
base. A detainee would be assisted by a government-provided personal representative who would possess the security clearances necessary for access to
information about the detainee. In addition, a detainee could be assisted by
private counsel, at no expense to the government.[54] Nothing was done by the
Obama administration to implement the PRBs until October 2013.

Legislation enacted on April 15, 2011, added new restrictions on transferring
detainees to the United States, its territories, or possessions.[55] Discretionary

authority to the secretary of defense remained. No funds could be used to transfer a Guantánamo detainee to another country unless the secretary of defense submitted to Congress a certification not later than thirty days before the transfer. The country could not be a designated state sponsor of terrorism, would have to maintain effective control over its detention facility, could not face a threat of being unable to exercise control over the individual, and must have agreed to take effective steps to ensure that the detainee cannot act to threaten the United States, its citizens, or its allies.[56]

The secretary could waive the statutory restrictions if he determined that a transfer would be in the "national security interests of the United States" and included that judgment in his certification.[57] Significantly, the Obama administration—after objecting to congressional limitations on executive authority—never used the waiver authority. This statute continued the prohibition on the use of any funds to construct or modify any facility in the United States, its territories, or possessions to house any detainee in Guantánamo or any person under the effective control of the Department of Defense.[58]

In signing the bill, Obama repeated his objections that statutory limitations on transferring detainees represent "the continuation of a dangerous and unprecedented challenge to critical executive branch authority to determine when and where to prosecute Guantanamo detainees." However, he did not acknowledge that the legislation offered a number of discretionary powers to the executive branch to transfer detainees from the naval base. Those powers would not be used by his administration.

On April 24, 2011, the *Washington Post* published a lengthy article titled "How the White House Lost on Guantanamo." For more than two years, the White House's plans to close the detention center at the naval base "had been undermined by political miscalculations, confusion and timidity in the face of mounting congressional opposition," according to some administration officials and members of Congress.[59] The failed effort reflected Obama's leadership style: "a passivity that at times permits opponents to set the agenda." Other than his major speech at the National Archives on May 21, 2009, he did not "raise the issue on his own."[60] The problem was not just opposition from the Republican Party. Democrats also deserted Obama, "sometimes in droves."[61]

As the year 2011 drew to a close, there was little movement toward closing Guantánamo. Senate Minority Leader Mitch McConnell (R-KY) proposed that detainees in Iraq suspected of killing Americans be brought to the naval base.[62] The administration, however, was determined not to add other individuals to Guantánamo. Senate Majority Whip Dick Durbin (D-IL) compared the record of military tribunals at the naval base with the prosecution of terrorists in civil courts. "More than 300 terrorists have been successfully prosecuted in our courts," he said. "The same courts that Sen. McConnell questions whether they could adequately protect America. . . . How many have been prosecuted in military tribunals in that same period of time? Three."[63]

Limited Progress in 2012

A story in the *New York Times* on February 9, 2012, described a Republican House Armed Services Committee report as criticizing the Obama administration for taking too many risks in releasing detainees from Guantánamo. It said that of sixty-six detainees transferred under Obama, five (about 7.6 percent) were "suspected" of having reengaged in terrorist activity. That percentage compared to 11.5 percent of detainees released by the Bush administration. Democrats on the panel criticized the report for failing to appreciate the strategic and national security interests in releasing low-risk detainees as part of a process to close the facility.[64]

A statute enacted on January 2, 2013, prohibited the use of funds to construct or modify US facilities to house the detainees at the naval base.[65] However, the bill authorized the secretary of defense to issue a certification thirty days in advance before transferring detainees to foreign countries. Various conditions would have to be met.[66]

As in the past, Obama raised constitutional objections to these limitations on his authority, but this time he conceded: "Our Constitution does not afford the President the opportunity to approve or reject statutory sections one by one. I am empowered either to sign the bill, or reject it, as a whole." He made a general observation about a provision that limited his authority to transfer third-country nationals held at a detention facility in Parwan, Afghanistan, to the government of Afghanistan or to other nations: "Under certain circumstances, the section could violate constitutional separation of powers principles." This argument was too vague. Under *what* circumstances? He offered no explanation. On four other occasions, the signing statement referred generally to separation of powers principles without providing any specific analysis.

On July 11, 2012, the Pentagon announced it had sent Ibrahim al-Qosi, convicted at Guantánamo by a military commission, to Sudan. It was the first time a detainee convicted under the Obama administration version of a military tribunal had been sent back to his native country. He was among the first detainees brought to the naval camp in 2002. On July 7, 2010, he pled guilty to conspiracy and supporting terrorism. His guilty plea stated that he had performed a number of tasks for Osama bin Laden, including running the kitchen and serving as driver. He said he also fired a mortar for a militia helping the Taliban against the Northern Alliance. The transfer reduced the camp's population to 168.[67] On September 29, 2012, the Obama administration transferred Omar Khadr to Canada.[68]

The Obama administration sustained a serious setback in federal court when the DC Circuit ruled that Salim Ahmed Hamdan, bin Laden's former bodyguard and driver, had been improperly prosecuted by a military tribunal for a war crime (material support) that did not exist at the time he was accused of having committed it. The opinion relied largely on the legal principle of ex post facto, which protects defendants from being charged retroactively for crimes that were not considered legal offenses when allegedly committed.[69] All three judges of the appellate panel, including Brett M. Kavanaugh, David B. Sentelle, and Douglas H. Ginsburg, were appointed by Republican presidents.[70] The ruling cast a shadow over many of the convictions decided by military commissions in Guantánamo.

A Refocus in 2013

Conditions at Guantánamo deteriorated in April 2013 when detainees began a hunger strike to protest being held indefinitely with no hope of trial or release, even though eighty-six detainees had already been cleared for release. Of 166 detainees, two-thirds participated in the strike. More than forty were force-fed with tubes inserted into their noses. Medical associations objected that any doctor who participated in thus forcing a prisoner to eat against his will violated "core ethical values of the medical profession" and that the procedure constitutes torture.[71] Detainees brought their legal issues to court. In some cases, a federal judge would conclude that he or she had no power to order the military to refrain from force-feeding but appealed to President Obama to address issues raised by the hunger strike.[72]

In a May 23, 2013, address at the National Defense University, President Obama responded to this problem and others in the continuing war against terrorism. Toward the end of his talk, he turned to Guantánamo. He said the base had "become a symbol around the world for an America that flouts the rule of law. Our allies won't cooperate with us if they think a terrorist will end up at GTMO."[73] He estimated the yearly cost of imprisoning detainees at the naval base at "almost $1 million per prisoner." In mid-June, the House Armed Services Committee put the cost at $1.6 million per detainee, compared to $34,046 for an inmate at a high-security federal prison.[74] Other estimates exceed $2 million per detainee. Also, as President Obama noted, the Pentagon wanted to spend another $200 million for various improvements at the naval base.

As mentioned, early in his administration Obama appointed Daniel Fried to persuade countries to resettle some of the detainees approved for release.

Ironically, instead of closing Guantánamo, the administration closed Fried's office, on January 27, 2013. This underscored the lack of commitment—or capacity—to convert a presidential goal into an accomplishment. In his address at the National Defense University, Obama announced he was appointing a new senior envoy at the State Department and another at the Defense Department to work on transfers of detainees to third countries. It would have been more effective to select these officials before making the address. On June 17, the administration picked Clifford Sloan to be the envoy at the State Department. It was not until October 9 that Defense Secretary Chuck Hagel named someone to be special envoy for Guantánamo closure.[75]

By September 2013, the six-month hunger strike at Guantánamo was largely over. At its peak, 106 of 166 prisoners participated. By September 11, only eleven detainees were participating. David Remes, a lawyer for several of the detainees, explained that the detainees had largely achieved their goals. He said that Korans were no longer being searched, one of the issues that had triggered the hunger strike. However, a colonel at the base insisted that the policy and practice of searching Korans had not changed. In May President Obama reversed the moratorium he had placed on repatriating low-level detainees to Yemen, the home of fifty-six of the approximately eighty-six who had been recommended for transfer if security conditions could be satisfied.

In July the administration announced plans for transferring two detainees to Algeria. This would be the first transfer in nearly a year. Under statutory authority, Congress had to receive a thirty-day notification before any transfer. The Algerian government stated it wanted the two detainees back and would be "willing and able as a political and security matter to accept them."[76] Defense Secretary Hagel certified that various security conditions, established by statute, had been met.[77] They were released in late August, reducing the prison population to 164.[78]

The Pentagon's plans to spend several hundred million dollars to overhaul Guantánamo were finally shut down by the Defense Department in late September 2013. The request included $49 million to replace a semisecret prison that held a small number of "high value" detainees, including KSM. The military also wanted $99 million to build two new barracks for guards, $12 million to build a new mess hall, and $49 million to replace Camp Seven, where high-value detainees are housed. The spending initiative fell for a number of reasons, including "sequestration" budget cuts that forced expenditure reductions in a number of Pentagon programs.[79]

Although in March 2011 President Obama signed an executive order directing the establishment of PRBs to determine whether it was necessary to detain an individual at the naval base, there were no reviews over the next two years, and Obama made no mention of them in his May 23 address. Finally, on October 9, 2013, the Defense Department issued a news release that the PRB process was under way. As the news release explained, detainees have the constitutional privilege of the writ of habeas corpus to challenge the legality of their detention. The PRB will consider the threat posed by each detainee, his mental and physical health, and will not rely on information that has been obtained as a result of torture or other cruel and degrading treatment. In order to support informed decision making, detainees will have an opportunity to participate in the process as appropriate. They may request the testimony of witnesses who are reasonably available and willing to offer relevant and material information. In addition to a personal representative made available by the government, detainees would have the ability to obtain private counsel, at no expense to the government. Full reviews of each detainee would be conducted every three years.[80]

In early November 2013, David Hicks, an Australian who trained with al-Qaeda in Afghanistan and pleaded guilty in March 2007 to providing material support for terrorism, which led to his release from Guantánamo, recanted his guilty plea. He did so on the basis of a ruling by the DC Circuit in the Salim Ahmed Hamdan case that material support for terrorism did not meet the criteria of a war crime that could be prosecuted by the military commission under the laws of war. Moreover, his attorneys argued that his guilty plea was an involuntary act of desperation after being held five years in custody.[81]

On December 5, 2013, the Obama administration announced it had repatriated two longtime Guantánamo detainees to Algeria, Djamel Saiid Ali Ameziane and Belkecem Bensayah. Both had expressed opposition to being returned to their homeland because of fears they might face persecution and further imprisonment, the men having fled Algeria during the country's civil war in the 1990s. Their attorneys had urged the administration to send them to other countries. J. Wells Dixon, an attorney for Ameziane, objected that the administration's action showed a "callous disregard for his human rights" and that it was "particularly outrageous" that the United States would return him to "a risk of harm in Algeria."[82]

Ian Moss, a spokesperson at the State Department for Guantánamo transfer issues, said that the decision to repatriate the two men against their will was justified because the United States was "satisfied that the Algerian government would continue to abide by lawful procedures and uphold its obligations under domestic and international law in managing the return of former Guantánamo detainees."[83] Ameziane and Bensayah had been held at the naval base without charge since early 2002. In late 2008, the Bush administration concluded there were no longer any "military rationales" to detain Ameziane and cleared him for transfer. Ameziane, a member of the Berber minority, feared persecution if returned home. According to his lawyer, he is held in secret detention in Algeria and faces a possible criminal trial for unspecified charges.[84] In the past, most Guantánamo detainees returned to North African countries were questioned by a judge and set free.[85] On December 16, the Algerian government announced that Ameziane and Bensayah had been released after an evaluation period.[86]

The political accommodation reached by the Obama administration and Congress, including the requirement that the secretary of defense notify lawmakers thirty days in advance before releasing a detainee, was placed in jeopardy on May 31, 2014. President Obama agreed to release five Taliban from the naval base in exchange for Sgt. Bowe Bergdahl, who had been held by the Taliban for five years. The administration did not give lawmakers thirty days' notice. The decision appeared to revive the legal claims of the George W. Bush administration, which asserted a host of plenary, exclusive, and inherent presidential powers that could not be restricted by Congress.[87]

Conclusion

A law review article analyzing Obama's failure to close the detention facility at Guantánamo is titled "Why Executive Orders Can't Bring About Systemic Change."[88] It could be equally asked, why couldn't the Obama administration, particularly the White House, figure that out in advance? The article correctly concludes that Obama would have been more successful had he enlisted Congress to draft and pass legislation: "His greatest misstep was assuming Congress would rubberstamp his budget request without providing Congress a comprehensive plan and consulting with the members at the outset."[89] In an op-ed, Maureen Dowd remarked that Obama "still thinks he'll do his thing from the balcony and everyone else will follow along below. That's not how it works."[90] Quite true. She noted that Congress had granted the secretary of defense authority to waive statutory restrictions on detainee release on a case-by-case basis but the administration "hasn't made use of that power once. So it's a little stale to blame Congress at this point."

Notes

1. Petition for Writ of Certiorari, *Hamdi v. Rumsfeld*, No. 03-7338, U.S. Supreme Court, 9n8.
2. John White and Julie Tate, "In Guantanamo Bay Documents, Prisoners Plead for Release," *Washington Post*, March 5, 2006, A6.
3. Moazzam Begg, *Enemy Combatant: My Imprisonment at Guantánamo, Bagram, and Kandahar* (New York: New Press, 2006).
4. Richard Wolffe, *Revival: The Struggle for Survival inside the Obama White House* (New York: Broadway Books / Crown, 2010), 217.

5. Ibid., 26, 110, 215.
6. 74 *Federal Register* 4897, 4898, sec. 3 (2009).
7. Karen DeYoung, "Obama Will Try to Quell Concern on Detainees," *Washington Post*, May 21, 2009, A1.
8. Carrie Johnson and Walter Pincus, "Supermax Prisons in U.S. Already Hold Terrorists," *Washington Post*, May 22, 2009, A6.
9. Ibid.
10. "Remarks by the President on National Security," National Archives, May 21, 2009, transcript, 4.
11. US Department of Justice, "Special Task Force on Interrogations and Transfer Policies Issued Its Recommendations to the President," August 24, 2009.
12. Wolffe, *Revival*, 219.
13. H. Rept. No. 111-105, 111th Cong., 1st Sess. 15 (2009).
14. Ibid.
15. Ibid., 111.
16. Ibid., 68.
17. Ibid., 114.
18. 155 *Congressional Record* H5595 (daily ed., May 14, 2009).
19. Ibid.
20. Ibid., H5596.
21. Ibid., H5598.
22. Ibid.
23. Ibid., H5599.
24. Peter Finn and Anne E. Kornblut, "How the White House Lost on Guantanamo," *Washington Post*, April 24, 2011, A12.
25. See Representative Wolf's floor statement, 155 *Congressional Record* H5603 (daily ed., May 14, 2009).
26. 155 *Congressional Record* S5663 (daily ed., May 20, 2009).
27. Pub. L. 111-32, sec. 14103(b), 123 Stat. 1920 (2009).
28. Ibid., sec. 14103(d).
29. Statement by President Obama in signing the supplemental appropriations bill, www.white house.gov/the_press_office/Statement-from-the-President-upon -signing-HR-2346.
30. 153 *Congressional Record* 19718 (2007).
31. Ibid., 19719.
32. Pub. L. 111-83, 123 Stat. 2177, sec. 552 (2009).
33. Pub. L. 111-84, 123 Stat. 2455, secs. (b) and (c) (2009).
34. Ibid., sec. (d).
35. Pub. L. 111-88, 123 Stat. 2962, sec. 428 (2009); Pub. L. 111-117, 123 Stat. 3156, sec. 532 (2009); Pub. L. 111-118, 123 Stat. 3466, sec. 9011.
36. William Shawcross, *Justice and the Enemy: Nuremberg, 9/11, and the Trial of Khalid Sheikh Mohammed* (New York: PublicAffairs, 2011), 112–13.
37. Jack Goldsmith, *Power and Constraint: The Accountable Presidency after 9/11* (New York: Norton, 2012), 10.
38. Jane Mayer, "The Trial: Eric Holder and the Battle over Khalid Sheikh Mohammed," *New Yorker*, February 15, 2010.
39. Daniel Klaidman, *Kill or Capture: The War on Terror and the Soul of the Obama Presidency* (Boston: Houghton Mifflin Harcourt, 2012), 1–9, 145–53, 161–72, 182–83.
40. Sari Horwitz, "Holder: 'I Was Right' on 9/11 trial," *Washington Post*, November 5, 2013, A3.

41. Nicolas L. Martinez, "Pinching the President's Prosecutorial Prerogative: Can Congress Use Its Purse Power to Block Khalid Sheikh Mohammed's Transfer to the United States?," *Stanford Law Review* 64 (2012): 1469.

42. Charlie Savage, "House Panel Rejects a Plan to Shift Detainees to Illinois," *New York Times*, May 21, 2010, A18.

43. Peter Finn, "U.S. Will Repatriate Detainee to Yemen," *Washington Post*, June 26, 2010, A8. See also Editorial, "The Gitmo Myth," *Washington Post*, June 16, 2010, A16.

44. Benjamin Weiser, "Ruling in Terror Case Leads to Mixed Views of Suspect's Fate If He Is Acquitted," *New York Times*, October 8, 2010, A20.

45. Benjamin Weiser, "U.S. Jury Acquits Former Detainee of Most Charges," *New York Times*, November 18, 2010, A1.

46. Jane Sutton, "U.S., Canadian Lawyers Working on Detainee Deal," *Washington Post*, October 15, 2010, A2.

47. Peter Finn, "Detainee Khadr Pleads Guilty," *Washington Post*, October 26, 2010, A6.

48. 156 *Congressional Record* S10937 (daily ed., December 22, 2010) (statement by Senator Leahy).

49. Charlie Savage, "Obama May Bypass Guantánamo Rules, Aides Say," *New York Times*, January 4, 2011, A15; Peter Finn and Anne E. Kornblut, "White House May Challenge Bill's Guantanamo Provisions," *Washington Post*, January 4, 2011, A8.

50. Pub. L. 111-383, 124 Stat. 4351, secs. 1031 and 1032 (2011).

51. Statement by President Obama on H.R. 6523, January 7, 2011, www.whitehouse.gov /the-press-office/2011/01/07/statement-president-hr-6523.

52. 124 Stat. 4351-52, sec. 1033 (2011).

53. Yochi J. Reazen, "The Prisoners' Dilemma," *National Journal*, March 5, 2011, 22.

54. Executive Order 13567, 76 *Federal Register* 13277 (2011).

55. Pub. L. 112-10, 125 Stat. 104, sec. 1112 (2011).

56. Ibid., 125 Stat. 105, sec. 1113.

57. Ibid., sec. 1113(c) (2).

58. Ibid., 125 Stat. 106, sec. 1114.

59. Finn and Kornblut, "How the White House," A1.

60. Ibid., A12.

61. Ibid.

62. Steven T. Dennis, "Playing Defense on Gitmo," *Roll Call*, November 9, 2011, 14.

63. Ibid.

64. Charlie Savage and Matthew Rosenberg, "Republican Report Criticizes Transfers from Guantánamo," *New York Times*, February 9, 2012, A10.

65. Pub. L. 112-239, 126 Stat. 1911, sec. 1022 (2013).

66. Ibid. at 1914-15, sec. 1028 (2013).

67. Charlie Savage, "Guantánamo Prisoner Is Sent Back to Sudan," *New York Times*, July 12, 2012, A9.

68. Ernesto Londoño, "Youngest Detainee Leaves Guantanamo," *Washington Post*, September 30, 2012, A3.

69. Del Quentin Wilber and Ernesto Londoño, "Court Overturns Conviction of bin Laden's Driver," *Washington Post*, October 17, 2012, A2.

70. Charlie Savage, "In Setback for Military Tribunals, Bin Laden Driver's Conviction Is Reversed," *New York Times*, October 17, 2012, A20.

71. Charlie Savage, "Obama Renews Effort to Close Prison in Cuba," *New York Times*, May 1, 2013, A1, A15.

72. Charlie Savage, "Judge Urges President to Address Prison Strike," *New York Times*, July 9, 2013, A12.

73. "Remarks by the President at the National Defense University," Washington, DC, May 23, 2013, www.whitehouse.gov/the-press-office/2013/05/23/remarks-president-national -defense-university, at 6.

74. Louis Fisher, "Closing Guantánamo: President Obama Must Do It Right This Time," *National Law Journal*, July 1, 2013, 42.

75. Craig Whitlock, "Hagel Appoints Envoy to Bolster Efforts to Close Guantanamo," *Washington Post*, October 9, 2013, A11.

76. David Nakamura and Billy Kenber, "Two Detainees Held at Guantanamo Will Be Transferred to Algeria," *Washington Post*, July 17, 2013, A9.

77. Charlie Savage, "U.S. to Send 2 at Guantánamo Back to Algeria, Saying Security Concerns Are Met," *New York Times*, July 27, 2013, A10.

78. Craig Whitlock, "Algerians Leave Guantanamo Bay Prison," *Washington Post*, August 30, 2013, A2; Charlie Savage, "Guantánamo Hunger Strike Is Largely Over, U.S. Says," *New York Times*, September 24, 2013, A3.

79. Charlie Savage, "Pentagon Denies Money for Guantánamo Overhaul, Including a New Semi-Secret Prison," *New York Times*, September 25, 2013, A22.

80. US Department of Defense, News Release, "Periodic Review Board Process Underway," October 9, 2013.

81. "Australian Recants Guantanamo Plea," *Washington Post*, November 6, 2013, A3.

82. "2 Guantanamo Inmates Sent Home to Algeria against Will," *Washington Post*, December 6, 2013, A9.

83. Charlie Savage, "Two Detainees at Guantánamo Are Involuntarily Repatriated to Algeria," *New York Times*, December 6, 2013, A20.

84. Editorial, "A Bad Decision at Guantánamo," *New York Times*, December 7, 2013, A18.

85. "2 Guantanamo Inmates Sent Home."

86. Charlie Savage, "Two Saudi Prisoners Sent Home from Guantánamo," *New York Times*, December 17, 2013, A18.

87. Louis Fisher, "Obama Flips Position with Prisoner Exchange," *National Law Journal*, June 23, 2014, 26.

88. Erin B. Corcoran, "Obama's Failed Attempt to Close Gitmo: Why Executive Orders Can't Bring About Systemic Change," *University of New Hampshire Law Review* 9 (2011): 207. See also Tung Yin, "'Anything but Bush?' The Obama Administration and Guantanamo Bay," *Harvard Journal of Law and Public Policy* 34 (2011): 453.

89. Ibid., 228.

90. Maureen Dowd, "Bottoms Up, Lame Duck," *New York Times*, May 1, 2013, A23.

10

Congress and Civil-Military Relations in Latin America and the Caribbean

Human Rights as a Vehicle

FRANK O. MORA AND MICHELLE MUNROE

Since the early 1970s, Congress has shown a consistent yet relatively low level of engagement on US foreign policy making regarding security and civil-military relations in Latin America and the Caribbean. Between the end of World War II and the early 1970s, congressional-executive interaction on US military programs was nonconflictive: Congress largely deferred to the president on most matters related to security relations and the military in Latin America and the Caribbean as the national security preoccupation with containing communism took precedence over concerns regarding militarism and threats to civilian governments and human rights. In fact, prior to 1973 Congress infrequently discussed human rights violations. As Lars Schoultz notes, in the period before congressional attention, the executive branch, explaining support for militaries and their regimes, "lamented the violations of human rights to recipient governments, [but] other foreign policy considerations required that the repressiveness of certain governments be overlooked."[1]

Since the mid-1970s, congressional action has been driven by a small but very engaged group of lawmakers and their staffs concerned with the alarming rise in human rights violations and the often perceived indifference on the part of the executive to adequately monitor or take action against Latin America and the Caribbean governments or institutions engaged in or concealing gross violations. Subsequently foreign policy attention focused on monitoring and responding (i.e., shaping US policy), through congressional hearings, legislation, and appropriations, to human rights violations committed by security forces in the region. Congress had multiple hearings on the challenges of civil-military relations in the region, particularly during the period of democratic transition in the 1980s. However, Congress did not legislate or seek to shape US policy or military institutions and their role in society other than through the issue of human rights—a topic of great concern to a growing number of legislators and interest or advocacy groups. Regardless of the strategic context in which the United States engaged Latin America and the Caribbean militaries—the Cold War, counternarcotics in the 1990s, or post-9/11 counterterrorism—Congress, or at least some key members and their staffs, attempted to restrain the executive's preference to work with military/police forces (and indirectly the role of Latin America and the Caribbean militaries and police forces in their societies), often at the expense of democratic practices and respect for human rights. Congress did so by legislating on behalf of protecting the political and civil rights of Latin American and Caribbean citizens perceived to be endangered by US partnerships with security forces combating communism, drug traffickers, or terrorists in the region.

Background

In the early phase of the Cold War, Congress refused requests from President Harry Truman, on two occasions in 1946 and 1947, to institute a program of inter-American military cooperation.[2] Critics in Congress argued that "military aid was wasteful, would bolster authoritarian regimes, and would trigger a hemispheric arms race."[3] However, in the context of the Marshall Plan and later the Korean War, Congress set aside its concerns about encouraging authoritarian regimes and acted, nearly without reservation or conditions, to provide the executive with the tools needed to combat international communism. As a result, the executive enjoyed, until the early 1970s, great flexibility in shaping US–Latin American military policy.[4] The Mutual Defense Act of 1949 allowed Latin American governments to purchase arms without conditions, and in 1951, with the passage of the Mutual Security Act, they gained access to US military assistance and direct grants of equipment with the goal of "standardiz[ing] the equipment, organization, and methods of the Latin American armed forces." Once again, no conditions were applied in the legislation other than ensuring that recipients of assistance participate in "missions important to the defense of the Western Hemisphere" and that their equipment and doctrine be "oriented toward the United States and mutual security."[5] Some skeptical legislators, such as senators Hubert Humphrey (D-MN) and Albert Gore Sr. (D-TN), raised questions about the benefits and dangers of providing heavy, conventional equipment to poor, weak governments, while a handful of other legislators, such as Rep. Charles Porter (D-OR), insisted that the Dwight D. Eisenhower administration "stop all economic and military aid to the despotisms in Latin America."[6] In the end, all of their demands went unheeded.

In the succeeding decade, US-military relations intensified under the provisions of the Mutual Security Act. Sixteen bilateral defense agreements, known as mutual defense assistance pacts, were signed with no approval or much oversight from Congress. These agreements institutionalized the transfer of US equipment and some training to Latin American militaries.[7] During this period, a number of coups led to military governments throughout the region, bringing an end to an important era in democratic rule and civil liberties. All throughout this period of authoritarian military regimes, Washington intensified its ties with the region's militaries. Meanwhile, Congress remained largely silent on the issue of democracy and civil-military relations. In fact, against the backdrop of the Korean War, McCarthyism, and the growing fear of communism spreading beyond Europe, many in Congress encouraged militarism as they believed it was best suited to defend against Soviet penetration, helping to "strike a balance between stability and change embodying a combination of authority and reform-mindedness."[8] In the end, as illustrated in a number of congressional hearings, the executive and Congress viewed the military as defenders of the status quo and partners of the US policy of anticommunism.[9]

By the end of the 1950s, the United States began to reassess its relationship with Latin American armed forces and military regimes. Ten military dictators fell from power while internal ferment and radicalism seemed to be on the rise. It no longer made sense to keep providing equipment and training for hemispheric defense because Latin American militaries could contribute little to it, particularly since the threat emanated more from within than outside. With the John F. Kennedy administration's emphasis on social and economic development, US security policy in the Americas shifted toward combating internal subversion through counterinsurgency training. The Cuban Revolution and fear that other Latin American governments would succumb to guerrilla insurgencies intensified Washington's efforts to enhance the counterinsurgency capacity (e.g., intelligence and urban warfare) and the role of the military in civic action programs, such as building dams and roads and other public works projects. Congress answered the new president's call for a new Latin American policy—which became known as the Alliance for Progress—with the passage of the landmark Foreign Assistance Act (FAA) of 1961, which included language governing US military policy toward the region:

> It is the purpose of this part to authorize measures in the common defense against internal and external aggression, including the furnishing of military assistance, upon request, to friendly countries. . . . The peace of the world and security of the United States is endangered . . . by internal subversion. . . . In enacting this

legislation, it is therefore the intention of the Congress to promote the peace of the world and the foreign policy, security, and general welfare of the United States by . . . improving the ability of friendly countries . . . to deter or, if necessary, defeat aggression, . . . assisting friendly countries to maintain internal security, and creating an environment of security and stability in developing friendly countries essential to their more rapid social, economic and political progress.[10]

With the FAA, Congress, without much restriction (other than ensuring the "universal regulation and reduction of armaments") deferred to the executive, providing near carte blanche for the funding and implementation of President Kennedy's (and subsequent administrations') policy of "enhancing the capability of indigenous forces to conduct counter-insurgency, anti-subversion and psychological warfare operations."[11] In 1968, with the Foreign Military Sales Act, there was one specific reference to denying sales to governments that "deny progress to their own people" (amended three years later to say "denying growth of fundamental rights or social progress"), but the executive largely ignored the congressional policy statement.[12]

The Alliance for Progress political objectives of stability and democracy were quickly dashed as eight democratically elected governments were overthrown in the first three years of the program. The Kennedy administration refused to recognize some of the new governments, suspending economic and military assistance, but fear that sanctions and isolation could weaken these regimes making them vulnerable to internal subversion led to Washington backing off quietly. In the Lyndon B. Johnson and Richard M. Nixon administrations, the United States abandoned all pretense of democracy promotion under the alliance and shifted policy, "under which the United States would no longer seek to punish military juntas for overthrowing democratic regimes." Meanwhile, as military regimes, demonstrating increasing levels of brutality against their citizens, continued to dominate the political landscape of Latin America in the 1960s and early 1970s, members of Congress (with some notable exceptions) refrained from highlighting growing human rights violations, opting in favor of "stability over democratic change."[13]

Convergence of Interests and Objectives between Congress and the White House

In the early 1970s, political scandals weakening the authority of the executive coupled with the rise of particularly brutal military dictatorships in the region led Congress to articulate a clear position in favor of changing US policy toward Latin America that contravened the position of the White House. The civil rights movement, the Vietnam War, and the Pentagon

Papers, followed by Watergate, not only fueled distrust of government but made the American public and congressional representatives feel compelled "to speak on behalf of international human rights standards," contributing to greater calls for accountability and demands that Congress act to rein in the executive's illegal activities or abuse of power.[14] Similarly some members of Congress were outraged by the support of the executive or its indifference to the emergence of more brutal forms of military rule (e.g., that of Augusto Pinochet in Chile) and a spike in human rights violations. Congress and the executive continued to share the view that military assistance was an effective tool for maintaining influence in the region, but the emergence of highly repressive regimes, coupled with demands from nongovernmental organizations (NGOs) and private citizens lobbying Washington to do more to stop abuses in the region, led Congress to take action by holding numerous hearings and passing key legislation. The executive's disregard of blatant human rights violations in Latin America and the Caribbean reached politically intolerable levels that could not be ignored by Congress.

Through the congressional budget process, Congress began to make decisions quite independently of the executive, actively limiting the scope of the executive, particularly in economic and fiscal matters directly impacting US foreign assistance.[15] Responding to the call for action, in 1973 Congress took legislative action, against the objections of a significantly weakened Nixon administration, to condition, for the first time, military and economic assistance on the preservation of human rights. Congress addressed the issue of human rights and military assistance by amending the 1961 FAA; it requires the president to deny military and economic assistance to any foreign government that practices the arrest and imprisonment of its citizens for political purposes.[16] Meanwhile, the House Subcommittee on International Organizations, chaired by Rep. Donald Fraser (DFL-MN), conducted a series of hearings on the subject of human rights and foreign policy. The hearings culminated in a 1974 report, also referred to as the Fraser Report, that dismissed the false choice between having to choose between political and economic interests and human rights. The Fraser report made a series of recommendations that called for placing human rights at the top of the US foreign policy agenda.[17]

In 1974 Congress enacted legislation amending the 1961 FAA, highlighting the commitment of Congress to supporting human rights in Latin America and the Caribbean and other developing countries by suspending military assistance to countries that, at the time, were widely recognized as violators of human rights. Against continued opposition from the executive, Congress firmly established a foothold in both the funding and implementation of foreign policy when it approved the addition of section 502B to the 1961 FAA

Senate Armed Services Committee members Claiborne Pell (D-RI, at far left) and Jacob Javits (R-NY, at far right) meet with Cuban leader Fidel Castro in Havana about the possibility of normalizing US-Cuban relations, 1974. *US Senate Historical Office*

section 502B (a), which now stated: "It is the sense of Congress that, except in extraordinary circumstances, the President shall substantially reduce or terminate security assistance to any government which engages in a consistent pattern of gross violations of internationally recognized human rights, including torture or cruel, inhuman or degrading treatment or punishment; prolonged detention without charges; or other flagrant denials of the right to life, liberty, and the security of the person."[18]

With this new congressional action, the 1961 FAA became an integral component of US foreign policy. It is the first piece of legislation that concretely linked military and economic assistance to the issue of human rights and democracy.[19] Section 502B clearly included the categories of torture, prolonged detention, and inhuman or degrading treatment or punishment of individuals as part of the definition of human rights. The amended section also required that the president specifically reduce or terminate its "security assistance" to any government that engaged in human rights abuses, thereby prohibiting all military aid and sales. More important, the legislation highlighted the resolve of Congress to hold the executive accountable for its foreign policy decisions, specifically on the issue of human rights.[20] Section 502B (b) (c) dictated a set standard by which governments can receive military assistance contingent upon their willingness to allow investigations of human rights violations: "In determining whether or not a government falls within the provisions of subsection (a), consideration shall be given to the extent of cooperation by such government in permitting an unimpeded investigation of alleged violations of internationally recognized human rights by appropriate international organizations, including the International Committee of the Red Cross and anybody acting under the authority of the United Nations or of the Organization of American States."[21]

In addition to legislative action, investigations into the activities of US intelligence agencies further strengthened the position of Congress. In 1975 the Senate established a committee to study government operations and intelligence activities, known as the Church Committee (named for its chair, Democratic senator Frank Church of Idaho), which issued fourteen reports documenting the illegal activities and operations of US intelligence agencies related to foreign and military intelligence. As a result, the push for congressional oversight intensified, creating a widening divide between the executive and Congress. Both the Nixon and the Gerald Ford administrations remained resolute in protecting executive prerogative, making every effort to carry out foreign policy decision making unimpeded from congressional restraint. However, there was no denying, especially after passage of the War Powers Resolution in 1973, that Congress was asserting its authority on key foreign policy issues.

Nevertheless, the executive continued to push back. During hearings the White House staunchly defended its human rights record in Latin America and the Caribbean, but in practice it felt it could overlook human rights requirements by taking advantage of the ambiguities found in the vague and weak language of the legislation.[22] Roberta Cohen attributes the failure of human rights policy during the Nixon/Ford years to the "executive sabotage of human rights initiatives."[23] Stephen Cohen further points out that "the absence of discernible impact resulted not only from the executive's opposition to conditioning military aid and arms sales on human rights factors, but also from the fact that for this entire period the legislation was in a form that made it advisory."[24] As 1976 came to a close, congressional attention focused on strengthening the language of the FAA, as well as ensuring that human rights legislation was binding and enforceable. Congress managed to restrain the executive's predisposition to continue providing security assistance to the Latin American and Caribbean institutions and governments involved in human rights violations, through a critical amendment in section 301 of the 1976 Arms Export Control Act, which "instructed the president to formulate military assistance programs to promote human rights and avoid identification with repressive regimes . . . reiterating the termination and restriction of security assistance to governments that consistently violate the human rights of their citizens."[25]

When President Jimmy Carter entered office in 1977, his foreign policy resonated among an American public desperate for a leader capable of restoring the ethical and moral shortfalls of previous administrations. His commitment to human rights and democratic practice promised not only a new approach to US-Latin American relations, but also one fully aligned with recent congressional attention or emphasis on making morality a centerpiece of US foreign policy. Richard Fagen goes further, adding that the policy initiatives of the Carter administration were not only aligned with those of Congress, but that they were also "deeply conditioned by the congressional action already taken place."[26] The convergence of executive and congressional foreign policy interests and objectives in pressuring military regimes in favor of democracy and human rights greatly advanced the common agenda of placing human rights at the top of the foreign policy agenda.

Concerned with the direction that Latin American militarism had taken and its threats to civilian governments, Congress, with the support of the Carter administration, sought to professionalize the training and doctrine of Latin American and Caribbean military institutions. For instance, in 1976 Congress passed the International Security Assistance and Arms Export Control Act, which established the International Military Education and Training (IMET) program. The IMET program shifted the focus of US–Latin American and US-Caribbean military relations solely from the sales of equipment and weapons to the training of military personal in order to enhance effective military leadership and management of resources. Most important, the program addressed the issue of human rights by educating military personnel on internationally recognized human rights standards, while helping to deepen relationships with this important institution in the region. During the Carter administration, congressional oversight hearings focused on the effectiveness of the IMET program as it related to the promotion of democratic rule and human rights.

Working alongside Congress, the Carter administration quickly took action by reducing foreign aid to countries guilty of committing human rights abuses. After the Argentine military ousted President Isabel Perón from power in 1976 and proceeded to engage in the systematic abuse of human rights against "enemies of the state" and after Amnesty International revealed the vast number of Argentine citizens tortured, killed, or considered to be among the disappeared, the administration had by early 1978 applied sanctions against the regime, including terminating nearly all security assistance and training with Argentina. In response to conditioning security assistance on investigations of human rights violations, military governments in Brazil, El Salvador, Guatemala, and Uruguay resisted pressures, insisting the United States had no right to impinge on their sovereignty. In protests, many of these governments, anticipating further cuts in military assistance, rejected offers of credit for foreign military sales and other forms of military assistance.

As the Carter administration entered the second half of its term, it experienced a problem converting its commitment to human rights and democratic practice into a sustainable and functioning policy. Despite pronouncements that its commitment to human rights was absolute, in practice, as members of Congress began to point out, the administration exercised a double standard.[27] Human rights sanctions were not applied based on whether an aid recipient had committed human rights violation but rather on "whether the strategic and economic interests of the US were negligible—enforcing sanctions when strategic interests were insignificant and remaining silent when strategic interests were high."[28] Congress conducted hearings and passed legislation barring multilateral aid from international financial and development institutions from providing aid to the most egregious human rights violators. In the end, however, Congress refrained from pushing the issue of implementation for fear of embarrassing a Democratic president increasingly under fire from conservatives for not taking a strong stand against regimes of the Left engaged in violating the rights of their citizens.

As criticism intensified from Republicans in Congress as well as from defense contractors and the US military concerned the United States was losing business and influence in the region, the Carter administration gradually began to either soften its criticism or lift security assistance sanctions on some countries. Also, the strategic imperative of the Cold War could not be easily set aside, as concerns with Soviet and Cuban expansionism in Latin America and the Caribbean and in other parts of the world came to the fore, shifting the focus increasingly away from human rights and democratization toward containment. Unable to balance domestic pressures and tensions (e.g., opposition from Republicans and conflicts within the executive and the bureaucracy) with the regional context, the Carter administration failed to enforce human rights legislation in a consistent and fair manner.

Despite foreign policy convergence between the executive and legislative branches, Congress expressed frustration with what it perceived as the administration's vacillating commitment to taking punitive action against military regimes in Latin America and the Caribbean. It seemed that strategic imperatives trumped the strong moral tenets that undergirded the administration's foreign policy when it arrived in office. In 1978 and 1979, members of Congress, particularly on the House International Relations Committee, expressed great unease over how the Carter White House, as with previous administrations, was not committed to fully implementing 502B. Some complained about the exceptions made under subsection (a) (2) for spare parts and other military equipment. Others felt there had been excessive use of the exception for "extraordinary circumstances."[29] As a result, the 1978 International Security Assistance Act amended section 502B by stating that not only was the president obligated by the law to maintain human rights standards when making security assistance decisions, but also that any extraordinary circumstances warranting the continuation of aid despite human rights violations must now be certified in writing by the president.

Throughout the 1970s, congressional attention and commitment to protecting the rights of citizens against abuses by military regimes in Latin America and the Caribbean reached unprecedented levels. It took on the executive (particularly through hearings) and its unwillingness to condition aid on respect for human rights. Rather than seeking to professionalize the military (other than IMET) or reform civil-military relations in the region, Congress took a more punitive approach, passing legislation that cut off military and economic aid to any government deemed to be guilty of rampant human rights violations. Heading into the 1980s, Congress, with the help of the executive, managed to enact a solid set of human rights legislation that arguably helped build the foundations for the process of democratization that was about to ensue in Latin America and the Caribbean.[30] By the end of the Carter administration, however, stability and US interests in Central America began to unravel, and Congress turned its attention to a new president committed to renewing US support for anticommunist allies, regardless of their human rights performance.

The Geopolitical Imperative and Human Rights in the Reagan Era

When Ronald Reagan entered the presidency in 1981, he arrived at a time when it seemed to many Americans that communism was on the march in several key strategic regions of the world, and conservatives strongly believed that America needed to reaffirm its influence and power in the face of a resurgent communist threat. The new US foreign policy emphasized geostrategic factors, the ideological struggle between the United States and the Soviet Union, and an explicit desire to "roll back" communism. Human rights and the north-south emphasis of the Carter administration were replaced by the geopolitical exigencies of the Cold War. In this context, Latin America and the Caribbean was considered a key strategic area in which to test a new policy of containment.[31] With respect to authoritarian regimes in the region, Reagan insisted during and after the presidential campaign that "friends be treated as friends and enemies as enemies." He suggested that his administration would once again privilege its relations with dictatorships that identified themselves as US allies.[32] Reagan pointed the finger at the Soviet Union and its allies as the real cause of human rights violations in Third World countries because of their support for communist insurgencies. Reagan believed that by focusing on containing communism, the issue of human rights would be resolved. David Carleton and Michael Stohl explain: "By identifying international terrorism as the most significant threat to human rights, and by further identifying the Soviet Union as the chief source of international terrorism, it was possible to bundle human rights, national security, and international terrorism into a single package that fit neatly (and subtly) into the broader United States fight against global communism."[33]

Jeane Kirkpatrick, a Georgetown University professor and subsequent US ambassador to the United Nations, made the analytical distinction between authoritarian regimes (friends) and totalitarian ones (enemies), indicating that the former were strategic allies more susceptible to US influence and, unlike totalitarian regimes, less repressive and on a clearer path to democratization.[34] For the administration, this approach justified deemphasizing human rights as the governing principle of US foreign policy in favor of working with allies that Washington could, at the appropriate moment, nudge toward democratic rule. Reagan had not yet arrived at the White House, but it was clear the battle lines had been drawn between a Congress that was not about to surrender its human rights record and agenda and an executive that warned against pushing human rights at the expense of US strategic interests. For many in Congress and the increasingly vocal supporters of human rights in the NGO community, Reagan was committed to dismantling Carter's policy on the issue. Suspicion seemed to be confirmed when the Reagan White House nominated Ernest Lefever, a staunch anticommunist and critic of Carter's human rights policy, as head of the State Department's Bureau of Human Rights and Humanitarian Affairs.

Congress sought to maintain its foreign policy gains, but its position weakened as the White House was able to take advantage both of President Reagan's popularity and public support for many of his programs and the division in Congress resulting from Republican control of the Senate. According to Clair Apodaca, Congress continued to use its "powerful tools: holding congressional hearings, placing restrictions on foreign aid allocations, constraining the president's budget priorities, and invoking the War Powers Act. But the Reagan administration, for the most part, simply ignored Congress's efforts to rein in Reagan's foreign policy adventures" though he did often negotiate on some key foreign assistance priorities such as aid to El Salvador.[35]

In the first term, the administration fought hard to have Congress reinstate security assistance to Latin American authoritarian governments—Argentina, Chile, Guatemala, and Uruguay—previously denied aid under the Carter administration because of their human rights record. The Reagan administration further ignored the intent and purpose of section 502B, urging Congress to increase security assistance to these countries without condition or restrictions on the executive. Refusing to bend, Congress attempted to remain firm in support of human rights legislation but, as in the case of El Salvador, "confronted with the atrocities of the Salvadoran military, and yet concerned with losing El Salvador [and the rest of Central America] to a communist takeover, Congress compromised by setting conditions for military aid"—and military assistance increased significantly from 1982 to 1988. Other than passing legislation requiring the administration to regularly certify that governments were making progress toward ending human rights abuses, in the end Congress lacked "the political will to exercise its constitutional prerogatives to direct the executive branch's foreign policy initiatives."[36] Numerous congressional hearings and legislative votes did not lead to substantive changes or shifts in US policy, but with the help of strong supporters from advocacy groups, Congress did keep human rights at the forefront of the debate on US foreign policy, preventing the White House from ignoring it as an important issue.

By the Reagan administration's second term, as democratization began in some of the more brutal military regimes, such as Argentina, Brazil, and Uruguay, the commitment or ability of the White House to keep human rights off the foreign policy agenda weakened.[37] The unwillingness of Congress to abandon its legislative work on human rights, as well as increasing pressure from public opinion and human rights interests that the legislative branch stand firm against the executive, began to have an impact. Moreover, internal wrangling and scandals, particularly the Iran-Contra affair, limited the executive's wherewithal to push back. As a result, in order to avoid losing influence and prerogative, the administration moved toward incorporating human rights into its foreign policy by applying a definition of human rights that focused very narrowly on the concept of democracy building and political rights. By narrowly identifying human rights as support for democratization, the Reagan administration was able to resume security assistance programs with less repressive authoritarian regimes on the path to democracy.[38] Human rights advocates argued that a focus on democratic institutions and political rights only embraced a partial understanding of human rights; it was nevertheless strategically employed by an administration intent on getting its own way.

In the end, however, human rights had become too institutionalized as a tenet of foreign policy for the Reagan administration to simply dismiss. The executive's slow and wavering shift toward paying more than just lip service to human rights showed that despite Congress's inability to pass substantive legislation limiting the administration's freedom of action in support of military regimes, the "human rights infrastructure" created by congressional mandate and the strong domestic constituency in favor of the United States supporting democratic rule and human rights in the region were too much for the White House to resist.[39] Human rights had become the vehicle through which Congress was to shape not only US foreign policy, but also the process of democratization and civil-military relations in Latin America and the Caribbean for years to come.

Democratization and Counternarcotics in the 1990s

By the early 1990s, the global and regional context had changed dramatically with the end of the Cold War with transition to democratic rule and market reform in full bloom in Latin America and the Caribbean. The threat from communism dissipated, but Washington took on a new security challenge that both the George H. W. Bush and Bill Clinton administrations defined as national security threats. In the context of escalating domestic concern regarding drug abuse and addiction, the American public called on Washington to prioritize and commit national resources to confronting narco-trafficking, mostly from the Andean region. Prior to the election of 1988 and well into the early 1990s, polls indicated the American public believed the United States was being overwhelmed by crime and drugs. Although the so-called war on drugs began well before the arrival of George H. W. Bush to the White House, the pressure to do more intensified once the USSR disappeared and drug traffickers came onto the scene as the new threat to US society and interests in Latin America and the Caribbean. Moreover, the vast resources at the disposal of

Colombian kingpins threatened to derail an important foreign policy priority in the region: promoting democracy and free-market capitalism.

With its new emphasis on combating the drug trade in Latin America and the Caribbean, the Bush administration sought to enhance the role of US and Latin American militaries in the fight against organized crime, particularly in Bolivia, Colombia, and Peru. The administration was committed to reducing the flow of drugs by training and supplying weapons to military units, even to those alleged to be involved in human rights violations. Despite budgetary constraints and a democratically controlled Congress, the executive branch worked with Congress to expand the scope of the US military and law enforcement, allowing them to train and operate with partner-nation security forces.[40] Congress was willing to support the executive; however, Congress and several key NGOs concerned with militarizing US counternarcotics policy raised concerns about the consequences for civil-military relations, human rights, and the consolidation of democracy. Based on previous experience with civil-military relations in the region, Congress acknowledged that the training of Latin American and Caribbean security forces had to be balanced carefully with a firm commitment to maintaining human rights standards.

Unlike his predecessor, President Bush maintained a conciliatory relationship with Congress, often consulting with members of Congress on key foreign policy priorities such as the Andean Drug Initiative, which appropriated over $2 billion in economic and military aid over a three-year period for drug-producing countries to eradicate coca plants and encourage crop substitution. However, on the issue of human rights and congressional attempts to insert language into legislation that placed limits on military-to-military engagement, the Bush administration resisted and, in fact, argued that placing human rights restrictions threatened US counternarcotics objectives in the region. Bush was generally agnostic on the issue of human rights. As Clair Apodoca notes, "if the costs of supporting a human rights agenda were small, Bush could be an active proponent. But if there were possible political costs for supporting human rights or if it competed with other interests, the Bush administration would then simply ignore the violations."[41]

During the Bush administration, the first major and most important piece of legislation tying drug trafficking to the issue of human rights was the 1989 International Narcotics Control Act. It stipulated that in order to receive any US drug-control security assistance, the Latin American and Caribbean nations requesting it must be ruled by democratic regimes and their security forces must not be engaged in gross human rights violations.[42] The act also detailed the specific purpose and nature of military and law enforcement assistance, so as to avoid the use of aid being used for unauthorized activities. The Bush administration was not opposed to the human rights limitations imposed on drug-control legislation because, as previously mentioned, while the Bush administration did not actively promote human rights in its foreign policy, it had no problem including human rights when it proved advantageous.

On the day that the International Narcotics Control Act was signed, President Bush expressed concern at the restrictive language in its section 3(g), which required the executive to submit a human rights report on the aid recipient country *before* foreign assistance could be authorized by Congress.[43] This signified a significant change in the dynamic between the executive and Congress, as section 3(g) removed the president's discretionary power to provide aid outside the scope of the legislation, placing it firmly in the hands of Congress.[44] This became particularly problematic in the case of Colombia, the central battlefield in the war on drugs, where the administration struggled between supporting the government in its bloody fight against the Medellín and Cali drug syndicates, while at least recognizing and taking some kind of punitive action for human rights violations committed by the state or self-defense militias tied to the military.[45] It is important to note, however, that despite legislation limiting some of the president's discretionary powers, Congress supported the administration's efforts to militarize the war on drugs in Colombia by authorizing the Department of Defense (DOD) as the lead agency. Nevertheless, some members led by Sen. Patrick Leahy (D-VT), along with very vocal human rights groups, argued that such a policy strengthened the one institution threatening democratic rule and human rights: the armed forces.

As Bill Clinton prepared to enter the presidency, expectations were high in Congress, particularly among Democrats, and the NGO community that his government would restore human rights to the forefront as part of the administration's larger policy of "enlarging and deepening democracies and market economies." Expectations were quickly dashed as Clinton continued many of his predecessor's policies regarding counternarcotics and human rights.[46]

Similar to the supply-side approach taken by both the Reagan and Bush administrations, President Clinton's approach focused its drug strategy on supply-side eradication programs but with a special attention given to interdiction, crop substitution, and dismantling of drug syndicates in drug-producing countries. The Democrats, who controlled Congress in 1994, began to have doubts about the effectiveness of the drug-control policies of the administration amid reports of increasing violence, corruption, and human rights violations in Bolivia, Colombia, and Peru. Prior to handing control of the House of Representatives to the Republicans, Democrats passed legislation requiring the executive to present Congress with a more effective drug-control strategy, while congressional appropriators steadily cut back funding or banned direct military assistance to the armed forces of Colombia and Peru because of their human rights records.[47]

As soon as the Republicans took control of Congress in 1995, attacks on the White House for being soft in the fight against drugs intensified. Rep. Dan Burton (R-IN), chair of the Western Hemisphere Subcommittee of the Foreign Relations Committee, took a particularly aggressive approach criticizing the administration for its lack of commitment to the antidrug campaign, while suggesting that US troops and naval vessels should be sent to take down Colombian drug traffickers. In 1995 the Clinton White House immediately responded to Republican charges of weakness by "decertifying" a number of countries in the region (including Colombia), certification being the process by which the administration verifies to Congress that a recipient of aid is cooperating with the US counternarcotics efforts.[48] After 1995 executive-congressional relations on the issue of drugs and human rights were characterized more by constant political grandstanding between a defensive Democratic president and an aggressive Republican legislature bent on using the drug issue to embarrass the president than by any serious consideration of the policy's effectiveness.[49]

Trying to avoid being politically outflanked on the issue of drugs, the Clinton administration went on the offensive by deepening the militarization of US antinarcotics policy and requesting significant increases in military equipment and training, including a $169 million package of armed Black Hawk helicopters for Colombia.[50] The escalation in military assistance to Colombia sparked a debate led by Democrats and human rights groups concerned about the implications on Colombia's already dismal human rights record. While Sen. Jesse Helms (R-NC), the powerful head of the Senate Foreign Relations Committee, struggled with the Clinton administration on whether to take punitive actions against the Colombian government for President Ernesto Samper's lack of cooperation and his alleged ties to drug traffickers, Senator Leahy worked to pass legislation that "would bar US assistance to any elements within the Colombian Armed Forces suspected of committing human rights abuses, a move revealing that Congress was not in complete harmony regarding Colombia policy."[51] Senator Leahy's amendment to the 1997 Foreign Operations Act went as far as to ban assistance to tactical security forces believed to be involved in human rights violations.[52] The Leahy amendment, therefore, prohibited the executive from providing military units or security forces accused of human rights violations with counternarcotic assistance—whether financial or tactical—unless the administration took the necessary steps to hold them accountable. The international narcotics control section of the 1997 Foreign Operations Act states: "None of the funds made available under this heading may be provided to any unit of the security forces of a foreign country if the Secretary of State has credible evidence to believe such unit has committed gross violations of human rights unless the Secretary determines and reports to the Committees on appropriations that the government of such country is taking steps to bring the responsible members of the security forces unit to justice."[53] The Leahy amendment is central to current human rights legislation as it is the first piece of legislation since section 502B of the FAA that provided the executive and Congress with a new set of requirements for the disbursing of foreign assistance. Distinct from the annual Department of State Country Reports on Human Rights, the Leahy amendment introduced a vetting and monitoring process that requires the Department of State to run background checks for human rights violations on each security official, whether he or she is operating as part of security unit or not.

An important development emerged not long after the Republican majority came to office under the leadership of Speaker of the House Newt Gingrich (R-GA): the expansion in the number and influence of interest groups and human rights NGOs shaping key foreign policy debates of the time.[54] Speaker Gingrich implemented a series of cuts in congressional resources, particularly in the number of committees and staff members, limiting the capacity of members to do all the necessary oversight and congressional information gathering and analysis previously required of the legislative process. As a result, interest groups such as Amnesty International and the Washington Office on Latin America filled the void, providing invaluable advice and analysis in preparation for hearings and legislative proposals. For example, the Leahy amendment came into being, in part due to pressure from Amnesty International, which was concerned about ties between the Colombian military and the paramilitaries. Carlos Salinas, a lobbyist for Amnesty International, worked with Senator Leahy's key staffer Tim Rieser to draft Leahy's amendment to the 1997 appropriations bill. Human rights advocacy groups certainly took advantage of this situation to "bring their concerns to the attention of Congress for redress in hearings, new legislation, or other action." In the end, as Clair Apodaca highlights, "when national security is not threatened, congressional members become more willing to push for legislation favored by their constituents and by interest groups in order to win reelection. The end of the Cold War . . . opened a larger political space for interest groups to lobby for their own particular concerns. When Congress is less deferential to the Executive's foreign policy prerogatives, interest groups, NGOs, and lobbyist have much greater influence in the foreign policy process."[55]

Notwithstanding the constant pressures from Republicans to do more by militarizing US antidrug assistance and Democrats warning against the threats of such a policy to human rights and democratization, Congress and the executive did work together on an important initiative to help profession-alize civil-military relations in Latin America and the Caribbean. At the first Conference of Defense Ministers of the Americas in July 1995, defense heads requested US assistance to enhance the capabilities of civilians in the conduct of military and defense activities. In 1997 Secretary of Defense William J. Perry, with the support of Congress, established the Center for Hemispheric Defense Studies (CHDS) with the mission of strengthening civilian and se-curity leadership in revitalized democracies. CHDS has since helped to insti-tutionalize democratic civil-military relations by offering graduate studies to civilian specialists and military officers on defense issues, such as defense planning and management, interagency cooperation, executive leadership, and civil-military relations. This is the first significant effort on the part of the executive and Congress to establish a program committed to strengthening civil-military relations in democratic societies.

In the last two years of the Clinton administration, Colombia came to the fore of congressional attention after a failed attempt by Colombian president Andrés Pastrana to negotiate peace with the most powerful insurgent group, the Revolutionary Armed Forces of Colombia (FARC). Bogotá, with the as-sistance from the United States, developed a new strategy, known as "Plan Colombia," in which it requested US assistance to combat the growing threat from the FARC. The US contribution would mostly come in the form of mili-tary equipment and training. Unlike in previous Colombia policy delibera-tions, Congress approved relatively quickly a total package of $1.3 billion in mostly military aid. (Roughly 30 percent of the antidrug assistance was pro-vided to Bolivia, Peru, and Ecuador.) The absence of a contentious fight over Colombia policy was due to (a) a threat perception, among Republicans and Democrats alike, that Colombia was on the brink of state failure and capture by drug traffickers and insurgents and therefore was vulnerable to becoming a narco-state and (b) the fact that "given the potential for congressional oppo-sition, driven mainly by the concern that the assistance package would lead the United States into another Vietnam, the Clinton administration wisely presented the plan as being primarily an antidrug effort."[56] Nonetheless, Sen-ator Leahy and his limited but very vocal cohorts in Congress and the NGO community were not about to discard or make exceptions for human rights violations because of security imperatives. Quite to the contrary, increased military assistance required a greater level of monitoring and accountability.

Post 9/11 and Counterterrorism

Prior to the inauguration of George W. Bush, the presidential transition team considered broadening the objectives of the nation's Colombia policy beyond counternarcotics to include assisting Bogotá with establishing law and order throughout the country. In other words, administration officials insisted that the distinction between counternarcotics and counterinsurgency was a false one, since the FARC was known to be a major drug-trafficking organization. In the aftermath of the 9/11 attacks, the "war on terrorism" became the dominant variable in nearly all considerations of US policy toward Latin America and the Caribbean, with Colombia as the centerpiece of US antiterrorist efforts in the region.[57] As a result, the Bush administration undertook a shift in policy that eliminated the distinction and pushed for security assistance to include combating the "narco-terrorists" in Colombia. By early 2002, the White House "requested US $98 million in foreign military financing to create an elite Colombian counterinsurgency battalion."[58] From then on, US military assistance to the Colombian military expanded significantly, helping to train and equip thousands of officers engaged in the fight against the guerrillas.

As previously discussed, since the 1970s Congress maintained a contentious relationship with the executive over US policy toward Latin America and the Caribbean, particularly with respect to US security assistance and its impact on human rights. However, as is typical in times of crisis, after 9/11 the legislative branch deferred to the executive and to the American public that demanded unimpeded action against terrorists. Therefore, Congress and the American public, "shocked and traumatized by the terrorist attacks, rallied around the flag and [mostly] supported without question the policies of George W. Bush."[59] Minimal congressional action was taken to restrain the executive as Washington forged new alliances and established military aid with weak and oppressive governments committed to fighting the war on terrorism. Norman J. Ornstein and Thomas E. Mann point out that from 2002 to 2006, congressional oversight of the executive, except in a few circumstances, had ceased to exist.[60] Until 2007, when the Democrats won a majority in the House of Representatives and Senate, the president received nearly full support for his security assistance policy and budgetary priorities in Colombia and throughout Latin America and the Caribbean. Some members, such as Senator Leahy and representatives Jim McGovern (D-MA) and Ike Skelton (D-MO), offered amendments to cut military assistance to Colombia, mostly on human rights grounds, but these legislative efforts failed. Congress stepped aside as the executive branch deepened its footprint and ties with the Colombian (and other countries') security forces.

In 2007 the environment in Washington became decidedly more hostile as some members of the Democratic-controlled Congress, led by Senator Leahy, questioned Colombian president Álvaro Uribe's democratic credentials as allegations surfaced that his government and the military were involved in corruption scandals and collaborative links with the brutal self-defense militias. Leahy, as chair of the Appropriations Committee's Subcommittee on State and Foreign Operations, reduced military assistance to Colombia as a result of leaked intelligence information claiming strong working ties between the paramilitaries and the head of Colombia's army. The overwhelming loss in the 2006 midterm elections coupled with the deteriorating security situation in Iraq weakened President Bush politically, allowing the Congress, for the first time since 2001, to reassert its role by placing limits on the executive's security-assistance policy in the region, particularly Colombia. Counterterrorism would no longer trump human rights and support for democratic civil-military relations in Latin America and the Caribbean.

By the time Barack Obama entered the presidency in 2009, America was still preoccupied with the threat of terrorism and wars in both Iraq and Afghanistan, while faced with the greatest economic downturn since the Great Depression. The Obama administration's foreign policy promised to end the wars in Iraq and Afghanistan and to strengthen and reconstruct relations with America's allies, old and new. In regard to Latin America and the Caribbean, one of President Obama's first foreign policy speeches as president came in April 2009 at the fifth Summit of the Americas in Trinidad and Tobago, in which the president said nothing about terrorism and drugs but rather focused on launching a new chapter of engagement based on equal partnership and a commitment to addressing transnational challenges by way of hemispheric collaboration.[61] After eight years of the Bush administration's war on terrorism rhetoric and militarization of the antidrug effort, Democrats in Congress and the NGO community believed the Obama administration would usher in a new era in US-Latin American relations.[62]

The Obama administration continued to focus on promoting economic growth and strengthening democratic institutions, with additional emphasis on energy and climate and the ominous challenge coming from crime and violence. In particular, the deteriorating security situation exacerbated by the drug trade, particularly in Mexico and Central America, could not be ignored by the administration. In Mexico the Mérida Initiative, launched by President Bush and his Mexican counterpart Felipe Calderón, was maintained and refined by the Obama administration with the support of Congress. The Mérida Initiative's declared aim is to combat drug trafficking, transnational organized crime, and money laundering. Initially the focus was on training, equipment, and intelligence, but by 2010 the Obama administration, fearing too much emphasis on the security component of the problem (and criticism of militarizing assistance to Mexico), "accelerated support [for] stronger democratic institutions, especially police, justice systems, and civil society organizations; expand[ing] the border focus beyond interdiction of contraband to include facilitation of legitimate trade and travel; and build[ing] strong and resilient communities able to withstand the pressures of crime and violence."[63]

In the Caribbean, the president announced the Caribbean Basin Security Initiative (CBSI), a multiyear, multifaceted effort by the United States and Caribbean partners to develop a joint, regional citizen-safety strategy to tackle the full range of security and criminal threats to the Caribbean Basin. CBSI being much like the Mérida Initiative, the Obama administration directed resources ($264 million in fiscal year 2011) toward combating corruption, promoting justice-sector reform, and assisting vulnerable populations, namely youth, at risk of being recruited by criminal organizations. The White House also designed a similar program for Central America, known as the Central American Regional Security Initiative (CARSI), centering on capacity- and institution-building of civilian institutions, in addition to assisting countries with interdiction and disruption or dismantling of drug trafficking in the region. Meanwhile, the administration continued its military assistance and training in Colombia but at lower levels in terms of budgetary requests. The United States would not abandon its regional partner as it continued to make progress in 2010, under the presidency of Juan Manuel Santos, against drug trafficking and the FARC.

During President Obama's first term, despite the deep political polarization and paralysis, Congress supported the executive's requests for funding of these security programs, though at lower levels. Republicans and Democrats alike did not oppose the administration's strategy, though Republicans argued that resources needed to focus on going after the transnational criminal organizations. The White House, in turn, concentrated on not upsetting the human rights coalition in Congress that, for the most part, remained quiet during the first term. In all bilateral and multilateral discussions regarding US security assistance and defense cooperation, the administration made sure that human rights were a key topic of discussion.

There were efforts, however, on the part of a few members, led by representatives McGovern, Joe Sestak (D-PA), and Sanford Bishop (D-GA), with strong support and pressure from very active grassroots organizations, such as SOA Watch, to cut funding or suspend operations at the Western Hemisphere Institute for Security Cooperation (WHINSEC, formerly known as the School of the Americas). For instance, Representative McGovern offered an amendment to the 2009 Defense Authorization Act that ordered the secretary of defense to provide personal information for all students and instructors at WHINSEC, which for all practical purposes had led to its closure because Latin American and Caribbean military officers refused to provide this information. And in 2011 Representative McGovern reintroduced (with twenty-one cosponsors) the Latin American Military Training Review under H.R.

3368, which would suspend operations at the facility in Fort Benning, Georgia. In each case, the DOD successfully pushed back, insisting that WHIN-SEC not only served an important strategic purpose of deepening military to military ties, but also that suspending operations at an institution considered to be the most transparent military educational institution with an extremely rigorous human rights training module simply did not make sense.

The Leahy amendment continued to be the main vehicle through which Congress kept tabs on the executive's security assistance policy, ensuring that US military and police training and equipping was not absolute but contingent on certifying/vetting units and individuals for human rights violations. The DOD discussed with Senator Leahy's office ways in which sanctions prohibiting assistance to countries or military units accused of human rights abuses years if not decades ago, specifically in Guatemala and Colombia, could be lifted to allow the US military to reinstate contact and training. The Pentagon argued that many years and reforms had passed and that now these units were free of any individuals involved in abuses. Talks did not go far in part because of the resistance by the State Department's Bureau of Democracy, Human Rights, and Labor (DRL) to making any changes. By refusing to make any adjustments, DRL used Guatemala and Colombia as examples of its steadfast commitment to human rights, though, as in the case of Guatemala, there had not been any allegations of abuse by the military in decades. It is also true that Senator Leahy's office continued to be pressured by grassroots human rights activists who felt any change would be a betrayal to the victims of the Guatemalan military's egregious human rights abuses nearly three decades ago. There was simply no incentive from Congress or the Department of State to make any adjustments.

In addition to keeping human rights off the table as a source of tensions with partner nations and the legislative branch, the administration worked diligently to dispel, often unsuccessfully, the perception among Democrats in Congress—and especially the NGO community in the United States, Latin America, and the Caribbean—that it was militarizing US security cooperation in the region. The Department of State and the Pentagon repeatedly went public, insisting the United States was not encouraging governments to deploy their militaries in law enforcement missions. In fact, the Mérida, CBSI, and CARSI initiatives were adjusted to reflect the focus on civilian capacity- and institution-building, while deemphasizing both in resources and priorities support for the military's role, despite regional governments' decision to use the armed forces as the principal instrument to combat, or at least mitigate, out-of-control crime and violence in Mexico, the Caribbean, and Central America. Not coming out strongly against partner nations' use of the military in nontraditional missions was interpreted as implicit support.

Conclusion

In the postwar period, Congress largely deferred to presidential prerogatives regarding issues related to US security policy and civil-military relations in Latin America and the Caribbean. Until the early 1970s, the geopolitical imperative of containing the threat from communism superseded any other considerations, including the breakdown of democratic rule at the hands of military coups and regimes. It was only in the 1970s that Congress began to assert its role in reining in the executive branch's nearly absolute decision-making space with respect to US ties to security forces in the region. However, its approach was more punitive in nature, as it focused on sanctioning governments—democratic or authoritarian—and military/police forces accused of gross human rights violations.

With few exceptions, such as IMET and CHDS, the legislative branch did not appropriate funds or legislate in favor of supporting the democratization and professionalization of civil-military relations in the region. The means by which Congress, backed by its allies in the NGO community, sought to influence Latin America and the Caribbean militaries was largely through the vehicle of protecting political and civil rights by placing restrictions and holding the executive accountable for its policy actions, regardless of the strategic context (i.e., communism, counternarcotics, or the war on terrorism), while threatening cuts in assistance as a way of influencing security forces to do more to respect human rights.

Notes

1. Lars Schoultz, *Human Rights and United States Policy toward Latin America* (Princeton, NJ: Princeton University Press, 1981), 247.
2. In 1946 the Truman administration established in the US-controlled Panama Canal Zone the Latin American Center—Ground Division, a US Army facility dedicated to training Latin American military cadets and officers. In July 1963 it acquired the name of the School of the Americas, and Spanish became its official instructional language. The institution did not receive much congressional oversight until the early 1990s.
3. Stephen Rabe, *The Most Dangerous Area in the World: John F. Kennedy Confronts Communist Revolution in Latin America* (Chapel Hill: University of North Carolina Press, 1999), 125.
4. Schoultz, *Human Rights*, 211–66.
5. For an extensive review of US-Latin American military relations during this period, see John Child, *Unequal Alliance: The Inter-American Military System, 1938–1978* (Boulder, CO: Westview, 1980).
6. Schoultz, *Human Rights*, 250–51.
7. Latin America signed, from 1946 to 1960, 135 bilateral military and security agreements, nearly 79 percent with the United States.
8. G. Pope Atkins, *Latin America and the Caribbean in the International System*, 4th ed. (Boulder, CO: Westview, 1999), 395.

9. Stephen Rabe, *Eisenhower: The Foreign Policy of Anticommunism and Latin America* (Chapel Hill: University of North Carolina Press, 1988). The Eisenhower administration provided $400 million in military assistance, largely in heavy equipment such as tanks and warships.

10. Foreign Assistance Act of 1961, Pub. L. 87-194, September 1, 1961, in *United States Statutes at Large*, vol. 75, www.gpo.gov/fdsys/pkg/STATUTE-75/pdf/STATUTE-75-Pg424-2.pdf.

11. These quotes are taken from a November 1961 Joint Chiefs of Staff report. See Rabe, *Most Dangerous Area*, 129.

12. Foreign Military Sales Act of 1968, Pub. L. 90-629, October 22, 1968, in *United States Statutes at Large*, vol. 82, http://uscode.house.gov/statutes/1968/1968-090-0629.pdf.

13. Tad Szulc, "U.S. May Abandon Efforts to Deter Latin Dictators," *New York Times*, March 19, 1964, cited in Mark Eric Williams, *Understanding US-Latin American Relations: Theory and History* (New York: Routledge, 2012), 205; 206.

14. Clair Apodaca, *Understanding U.S. Human Rights Policy: A Paradoxical Legacy* (New York: Routledge, 2006).

15. Douglas J. Bennett, "Congress in Foreign Policy: Who Needs It?" *Foreign Affairs* 57, no. 1 (1978): 40–50.

16. Foreign Assistance Act of 1973, Pub. L. 93-189, December 17, 1973, in *United States Statutes at Large*, vol. 87, www.gpo.gov/fdsys/pkg/STATUTE-87/pdf/STATUTE-87-Pg714.pdf.

17. US Congress, House Committee on Foreign Affairs, Subcommittee on International Organizations and Movements, *Human Rights in the World Community: A Call for U.S. Leadership; Report* (Washington: Government Printing Office, 1974).

18. Foreign Assistance Act of 1961, Pub. L. 87-194, September 1, 1961, in *United States Statutes at Large*, vol. 75, www.gpo.gov/fdsys/pkg/STATUTE-75/pdf/STATUTE-75-Pg424-2.pdf.

19. Schoultz, *Human Rights*, 253.

20. See the International Development and Food Assistance Act of 1975, Pub. L. 94-161, December 20, 1975, in *United States Statutes at Large*, vol. 89, www.gpo.gov/fdsys/pkg/STATUTE-89/pdf/STATUTE-89-Pg849.pdf. Using similar language to section 502B, the Harkin Amendment to the International Development and Food Assistance Act in 1975 added section 116 to the 1961 FAA, stipulating that no foreign assistance be provided to any country guilty of human rights violations, "unless such assistance will directly benefit the needy people of such country."

21. Foreign Assistance Act of 1961, Pub. L. 87-194, September 1, 1961, in *United States Statutes at Large*, vol. 75, www.gpo.gov/fdsys/pkg/STATUTE-75/pdf/STATUTE-75-Pg424-2.pdf.

22. See ibid. Some of the language, specifically phrases such as "extraordinary circumstances" in section 502B, needed to be more clearly defined, as they allowed for a wider interpretation for when assistance was deemed acceptable. Also the use of the phrase "the sense of the Congress" weakened the legislation, giving the executive the impression that this piece of legislation was more of an expressed desire of Congress and not a binding and enforceable agreement.

23. Roberta Cohen, "Human Rights Decision-Making in the Executive Branch: Some Proposals for a Coordinated Strategy," in *Human Rights and American Foreign Policy*, ed. D. Kommers and G. Loescher (Notre Dame, IN: University of Notre Dame Press, 1979), 225, cited in Clair Apodaca, "U.S. Human Rights Policy and Foreign Assistance: A Short History," *Ritsumeikan International Affairs* 3 (2005): 66–80.

24. Stephen B. Cohen, "Conditioning U.S. Security Assistance on Human Rights Practices," *American Journal of International Law* 76, no. 2 (1982): 250.

25. Apodaca, *Understanding U.S. Human Rights Policy*, 39.

26. Richard R. Fagen, "The Carter Administration and Latin America: Business as Usual," *Foreign Affairs* 57, no. 3 (1978): 658.

27. Schoultz, *Human Rights*, 265.

28. Apodaca, *Understanding U.S. Human Rights Policy*, 57.

29. Stephen B. Cohen, "Conditioning U.S. Security Assistance," 276.

30. Tony Smith, *America's Mission: The United States and the Worldwide Struggle for Democracy in the Twentieth Century* (Princeton, NJ: Princeton University Press, 1994), 270.

31. Lars Schoultz, *National Security and United States Policy toward Latin America* (Princeton, NJ: Princeton University Press, 1987).

32. Hauke Hartmann, "U.S. Human Rights Policy under Carter and Reagan, 1977–1981," *Human Rights Quarterly* 23 (2001): 402–30.

33. David Carleton and Michael Stohl, "The Foreign Policy of Human Rights: Rhetoric and Reality from Jimmy Carter to Ronald Reagan," *Human Rights Quarterly* 7 (1985): 208. Cited in Apodaca, "U.S. Human Rights Policy," 70.

34. See Jeane Kirkpatrick, "Dictatorships and Double Standards," *Commentary* 68 (1979): 34–45. The Committee of Santa Fe, a group of conservative analysts specializing in Latin America, also advised the president-elect to remove the issue of human rights from his foreign policy priorities.

35. Apodaca, *Understanding U.S. Human Rights Policy*, 81.

36. Ibid., 98, 102.

37. Thomas Carothers, *In the Name of Democracy: U.S. Policy toward Latin America in the Reagan Years* (Berkeley: University of California Press, 1991).

38. Tamar Jacoby, "The Reagan Turnaround in Human Rights," *Foreign Affairs* 64, no. 5 (1986): 1066–86.

39. Apodaca, *Understanding U.S. Human Rights Policy*, 111.

40. By 1988 Congress had passed legislation allowing the US military to assist law enforcement agencies in the war against international drugs if this assistance did not harm military readiness. It also authorized the military to take part in the search, seizure, and arrests outside of the United States provided their participation is authorized by law. See Donald Mabry, "The U.S. Military and the War on Drugs in Latin America," *Journal of Interamerican Studies and World Affairs* 30, no. 2/3 (Summer–Winter 1988), 63–64.

41. Apodaca, *Understanding U.S. Human Rights Policy*, 114.

42. International Narcotics Control Act of 1989, Pub. L. 101-231, December 13, 1989, 1956–57, in *United States Statutes at Large*, vol. 103, www.gpo.gov/fdsys/pkg/STATUTE-103/pdf/STATUTE-103-Pg1954.pdf

43. George H. W. Bush, *Statement on Signing the International Narcotics Control Act of 1989*, December 13, 1989, www.presidency.ucsb.edu/ws/?pid=17942.

44. "These provisions represent a major policy reversal of roles previously played by Congress and the president in the decision to deny assistance to certain drug-producing or drug-transiting countries. Under previous legislation, the president took the initiative in determining whether or not a country would be eligible for foreign assistance. Under the new law, Congress now takes the initiative in making the determination as to which categories of countries will not receive aid, while the role of the president has been reduced to either enforcing the terms of, or seeking exceptions to, this congressional determination." Quoted from Raphael Perle, "Congress, International Narcotics Policy, and the Anti-Drug Abuse Act of 1988," *Journal of Interamerican Studies and World Affairs* 30, no. 2/3 (Summer–Autumn 1988): 24.

45. The law did not allow for the Colombian government to use US counternarcotics funding against guerrilla insurgents.

46. David Scott Palmer, *U.S. Relations with Latin America during the Clinton Years: Opportunities Lost or Opportunities Squandered* (Gainesville: University of Florida Press, 2006), 25.

47. Coletta Youngers, "The U.S. and the War on Drugs: On the Wrong Path," *TNI Transnational Institute*, April 1, 1997, www.tni.org/article/us-war-drugs-wrong-path.

48. Although several countries had failed to receive full certifications, a few (e.g., Colombia) were granted security waivers allowing for a continuation of assistance.

49. Charles O. Jones, *Clinton and Congress: Risk, Restoration and Reelection* (Norman: University of Oklahoma Press, 1999), 34–40.

50. Youngers, "U.S. and the War on Drugs."

51. Russell Crandall, *Driven by Drugs: U.S. Policy toward Colombia* (Boulder, CO: Lynne Rienner, 2008), 88.

52. The Leahy amendment was the product of a "complex field of alliances between Washington-based human rights advocates, grassroots activists, and supportive Congressional staff." See Tate Winfred, "Human Rights Law and Military Aid Delivery: A Case Study of the Leahy Law," *POLAR: Political and Legal Anthropology Review* 34, no. 2 (2011): 339.

53. Foreign operations Act of 1997, Pub. L. 104-208, September 30, 1996, in *United States Statutes at Large*, vol. 110, www.gpo.gov/fdsys/pkg/PLAW-104publ208/pdf/PLAW-104publ208.pdf.

54. Ole Holsti, "Public Opinion and U.S. Foreign Policy after the Cold War," in *After the End: Making U.S. Foreign Policy in the Post–Cold War World*, ed. James Scott (Durham, NC: Duke University Press, 1998), 112.

55. Apodaca, *Understanding U.S. Human Rights Policy*, 159.

56. Crandall, *Driven by Drugs*, 123–24.

57. See Astrid Arraras and Grace I. Deheza, "Widening the War on Terror: U.S. Security Policy toward Latin America since 9/11," *Hemisphere* 14 (Fall 2004): 22–25, and Jorge Castaneda, "The Forgotten Relationship," *Foreign Affairs* 23 (May/June 2005): 67–81.

58. Crandall, *Driven by Drugs*, 139.

59. Apodaca, *Understanding U.S. Human Rights Policy*, 172.

60. Ornstein and Mann indicate that the number of congressional oversight hearings decreased from 135 in 1993 and 1994 to a scant thirty-seven from 2003 to 2004. Further, the nature of these hearings tended to center on budget review. See Norman J. Ornstein and Thomas E. Mann, "When Congress Checks Out," *Foreign Affairs* 85, no. 6 (2006): 71.

61. Much of this discussion comes from the experiences/participation of one of the authors, Frank O. Mora, who served in the Obama administration as deputy assistant secretary of defense for the Western Hemisphere from 2009 to 2013.

62. See, for example, Abraham Lowenthal, Theodore J. Piccone, and Laurence Whitehead, eds., *The Obama Administration and the Americas: Agenda for Change* (Washington, DC: Brookings Institution, 2009).

63. By fiscal year 2013, a total $2 billion was appropriated for the Mérida Initiative. See State Department Fact Sheet, www.state.gov/j/inl/merida/.

11

Conclusion

The Future of Congressional-Military Relations

David P. Auerswald and Colton C. Campbell

We conclude this volume with general thoughts and observations on the future congressional role in military policy drawn from the preceding chapters. This is a unique time for civil-military relations. The changing of the guard in the House over the past decade, the election of more women (especially to the Senate) and other minority groups, fewer and fewer lawmakers with direct military experience, and the election of more polarized members from both sides of the political aisle has brought to the fore new policy priorities and altered the distribution of influence on Capitol Hill. Moreover, the nation faces increasing budgetary pressures from continued deficits, which will be felt throughout the individual services.

In our introductory chapter, we argued that Congress has four main tools to affect military behavior: a check on officer selection through the confirmation process; influence over what authority is delegated to specific parts of the military or the military in general; oversight of the military through hearings, investigations, and reporting requirements; and incentives aimed at the military for what Congress deems appropriate military behavior, including changes in budgets, promotions rates, and military portfolios. These are obviously ideal types, in that any one congressional action could involve a number of these tools. For instance, changing promotion rates could qualify as affecting officer selection or incentives, depending on the context of congressional action. Or consider that transferring authority to prosecute sexual harassment cases outside the normal chain of command involves delegated authorities and incentives and that compliance with this directive could

The views expressed in this chapter are those of the authors and not necessarily those of the National Defense University, the Department of Defense, or any other entity of the US government.

involve oversight and might affect officer selection. Regardless, these four tools provide us with a useful typology with which to measure congressional influence over US civil-military relations.

The degree to which Congress uses these tools depends on a large number of factors that can be boiled down to whether lawmakers have the will and ability to act. We have argued elsewhere that Congress indeed possesses both, at least in theory.[1] The actual use of these tools, however, seems likely to depend on the context in which an issue is considered by the legislature. In the next section, we review four large contextual factors that follow from the chapters in this volume. Those factors include the growing partisan divide and intraparty disputes plaguing today's Congress, the lack of a foreign policy consensus in the United States, budgetary constraints into the foreseeable future, and local versus national concerns for individual members of Congress. We then turn to three emerging policy issues confronting Congress: the future of the defense budget, the use of the military as a testing ground and agenda setter for broader societal change, and the substantial divide between attitudes and experiences between Congress and the military. We explore how the aforementioned contextual factors might influence each policy issue in the future.

Context for Legislating Civil-Military Relations

There is a well-documented record of increasing partisan polarization within Congress.[2] But make no mistake: Congressional partisanship is by no means a new phenomenon and has long affected civil-military relations. Mitchel A. Sollenberger's discussion in chapter 2 of military appointments illustrates this point. Presidents made partisan officer appointments for the country's first 125 years to ensure that the military reflected the interests of their party and as patronage for the party faithful. More recently, the 2008 Commission on War Contracting in Iraq and Afghanistan, discussed in chapter 4, did not release its report until 2011, after the George W. Bush administration had left office, largely in deference to Republican sensibilities.

Partisan and Intraparty Disputes

The last two decades have chafed the nerves of partisans on both sides of the aisle. Some members, particularly those departing and reflecting on their congressional careers, readily comment about the steady march by both parties toward ever more partisan and personal attacks. "I find serving in the House to be obnoxious," declared Rep. John Dingell (D-MI), the dean of the House, when announcing his retirement after fifty-eight years in Congress.

"It's become very hard because of the acrimony and bitterness, both in Congress and in the streets."[3]

Political polarization is not limited to interparty disputes. It is seeping into the Republican Party caucus in both congressional chambers, principally between members of the Tea Party and more mainstream conservatives. For example, in the last few years congressional Republicans have fought with each other over the use of earmarks, the wisdom of shutting down the federal government in 2013 as a way of defunding the Affordable Care Act, a possible US intervention in Syria, and most interesting for our purposes, on broad defense policy.[4] On defense policy, Chuck Cushman's discussion in chapter 7 described how the Republican Party caucus in Congress is divided between the libertarian wing, which would not mind cutting defense spending, and the interventionist wing, which wants to increase the defense budget, to say nothing of staving off defense cuts proposed by the administration. Recent debates over the fiscal year (FY) 2015 defense budget have continued this trend.[5]

Combined, inter- and intraparty divisions make it even harder for Congress to act than would otherwise be the case. Congress is already confronted by institutional challenges in effectively supervising and holding accountable the expanded defense and intelligence establishments. Structurally Congress is still stuck in the twentieth century, particularly with a committee system that does not reflect current policy debates or government organizational schemes, witnessed by the dozens of congressional committees and subcommittees that oversee the Department of Homeland Security.[6] Heightened levels of partisan polarization on Capitol Hill make what is already a difficult job that much harder.

The effects on Congress are profound when it comes to civil-military relations. Each party or faction within each party has the potential to develop litmus tests when considering military appointments. Otherwise qualified appointees get holds placed on them due to partisan squabbles. Constructive oversight becomes that much more difficult and is instead replaced by partisan witch hunts or fact-finding investigations whose sole purpose is to embarrass the other party. Partisans become less willing to delegate authority to the military when delegation would result in policies that do not fit their party's agenda. Incentives for appropriate military behavior become confused, as partisans within and between each chamber send different signals to the military, to say nothing of the potentially disparate signals sent to the military by Congress and the president.

Lack of a Foreign Policy Consensus

A second (and perhaps related) contextual factor is the lack of a foreign policy consensus among national leaders in the current era. Cushman documents the disintegration of the congressional foreign policy consensus in chapter 7, with all the implications that disintegration had for "regular order" defense budgeting and, more broadly, congressional influence over military policy. Evidence presented by Sollenberger in chapter 2 and found elsewhere suggests that while there may have been a brief period of agreement across political factions in the immediate aftermath of the 9/11 attacks, that consensus was not of the same magnitude or duration as the Cold War consensus that held sway for the second half of the twentieth century.[7] Indeed, the evidence points to a steady decline since the end of the Cold War in American thinking about the world and the place of the United States in the world, to say nothing of specific US policies.

In addition to the abandonment of regular order, the lack of a consensus affects everything from defense budgets to intervention decisions to consideration of treaties by the Senate.[8] We saw these effects throughout the chapters in this book. Consider the relationship between the lack of consensus and the rise of post–Cold War ad hoc commissions, as discussed by Jordan Tama in chapter 4. Congressionally created commissions provide a way to continually kick the can down the road absent consensus. Commissions can spark action when one cannot get a congressional majority to legislate. The Commission on the Ballistic Missile Threat to the United States was one example of this phenomenon. By concluding that a ballistic-missile threat existed, the commission's findings undercut one of the main arguments of the Clinton administration and congressional Democrats against deploying an anti-ballistic-missile system.[9] Still another example comes from Charlie Stevenson's discussion of cyber and drone warfare in chapter 8. Debate over cyber and drones stems in large part from a lack of consensus as to new forms of warfare. An interesting corollary is the effects of the Cold War's end on congressional influence in Latin American civil-military relations, as discussed by Frank Mora and Michelle Munroe in chapter 10. Without a communist threat to the region, the only thing that Congress seems able to agree on is to condition US military assistance on the recipient's human rights record. So for at least this one region, the end of the US foreign policy consensus has actually simplified US policy.

The overall effects on civil-military relations of a disintegrating consensus are similar to those associated with increased partisanship, though with a slightly different flavor. Congress will continue to oversee the military on issues such as end strength, force readiness, base closings, acquisition issues, international security agreements, use of contractors to support the military, and crisis response. It is unclear, however, what will come of that oversight in the absence of consensus. It is likely that officer selection, trends in delegation, and incentives provided to the military will be haphazard and disjointed absent consensus. The implication is that the congressional role in civil-military relations will be less constructive than would otherwise be the case.

Budgetary Constraints

A third contextual factor is the budgetary constraints facing the United States for the foreseeable future. Mandatory spending, including entitlement spending, and net interests on the debt have consumed an increasing portion of the federal budget since the 1960s.[10] At the same time, discretionary spending, which includes both defense spending and all appropriated spending by civilian agencies, has declined as a percentage of gross domestic product (with a few exceptions) over the same time period. Despite this relative decline in discretionary spending, the United States has racked up significant national debt. Without significant changes to entitlements, most economists believe that these trends will continue to accelerate into the future.

The deficit debate has focused on cutting discretionary spending, given a lack of national will to confront entitlement spending. When one compares defense and nondefense discretionary spending, defense discretionary spending—including overseas contingency operations—has outpaced all other discretionary spending since 1981 and will continue to do so absent dramatic changes in law.[11] That said, discretionary spending of all types is on the decline, with defense discretionary spending facing significant cuts if sequestration caps are allowed to continue. These constraints, as we will discuss later in this chapter, make for zero-sum decisions that have not had to be confronted during the past twelve years of ever-expanding defense spending.

Budget concerns have been a consistent theme in the congressional debate regarding civil-military relations, from the formation of the 1940 Truman Committee discussed in chapter 3 to the future of military entitlements discussed in chapter 6. On that latter point, remember that Alexis Lasselle Ross argued that TRICARE-for-Life and other military entitlements are eating up an increasing percentage of the defense budget. The question raised is whether Congress will face the budget implications of TRICARE and related programs and, if so, how it will decide to make the program more sustainable in a constrained budget environment.

Budget constraints are likely to have the following effects on congressional civil-military-relations tools. One way to save money is to downsize the force, which translates into fewer officers. Indeed, the army and Marine Corps are already facing significant cuts in their end-strength totals, and officers in all four services have faced so-called selective early retirement boards (SERBs). Congress could use that development to impose more stringent requirements on military officers before confirming their appointments or promotions. No one expects Congress to return to the partisan litmus tests of the 1800s, but Congress could certainly impose new standards on ethics, education, and so forth. Congress is likely to impose more restricted delegation contracts on the military as budgets decrease or at best stay flat. Restrictions could take the form of more restrictions on weapon systems, which would have the effect of limiting the types of missions the military can conduct. To take two extreme examples, an army without main battle tanks is not going to be able to engage in major land combat. A force without airlift or sealift cannot engage in expeditionary warfare. Oversight in a budget-constrained environment is likely to be more intense. The legislature has every incentive to ensure that the more constrained pot of money allocated to the military is well spent. We would therefore expect more reporting requirements, more audits, and more demands for transparency in general to flow from Congress. Finally, budget constraints may change the incentives Congress provides to the military. Incentives could very well be focused on saving money, doing more with less, and being more efficient. This could translate into fewer incentives for reenlistment, cuts to military entitlements, and less reliance on expensive contractor support.

Local versus National Concerns

Fourth and finally are the ubiquitous tensions between local and national concerns. Members of Congress regularly are pulled in two directions. One of the great tensions in representative government is the relationship between the legislator and his or her constituency. Although individual legislators do not necessarily mirror their constituents in terms of demographic characteristics, the recruitment process yields many who favor local views and prejudices. Contacts with voters throughout the campaign process and while in office reinforce this convergence of views, as do representational norms adopted by most members. Indeed, members' electoral fortunes depend less upon what Congress produces as an institution than upon the support and goodwill of constituents who vote for them and contribute to their campaigns. Often these local interests conflict in ways that make compromise difficult across the legislature. Members of Congress also serve the nation and are expected to keep the national interest in mind when legislating, particularly on matters of defense policy. Yet they frequently are influenced by local attitudes even when those attitudes conflict with the national interest. Louis Fisher's review in chapter 9 of congressional opposition to closing the detention facility at Guantánamo, Cuba, and the transfer of prisoners to the United States is perhaps the ultimate example of local concerns trumping national interests. Members of Congress vehemently objected to detainees being located in their states or districts and blocked each of the administration's (often ham-fisted) attempts to do so.

John Griswold's focus on the National Guard and reserves in chapter 5 is a vivid example of the seesawing tension between local and national concerns. Supporting the Guard and reserves has been an easy decision for most members during the last twelve years of war. Guard and reserve units serve local interests in their law enforcement and disaster-response guises and serve the national interest when deployed internationally. Trade-offs between local and national were relatively rare in an era of defense largesse and largely focused on the local impact of a large number of first responders having to deploy for extended periods of time. The much harder trade-off took place when Guard advocates demanded a seat on the Joint Chiefs of Staff.

Two other chapters in this volume point to the potential for a more constructive balance being struck between local and national interests. The beauty of the Truman Committee, as described by Katherine Scott in chapter 3, was that it enfranchised local voices and local concerns in the investigative process. And, indeed, one of the main purposes of the committee was to serve the interests of Missouri small businesses as well as the national interest in developing and procuring quality war matériel. In Stevenson's discussion in chapter 8, the congressional reaction to weapon innovation and new strategic ideas partially depended on the degree to which said innovation affected local concerns.

As we ponder future congressional civil-military relations, one thing to watch for is the effect of gerrymandered congressional districts and an increasingly geographically divided state-by-state electorate in influencing local-versus-national calculations. If House members increasingly come from homogeneous districts and senators from red or blue (rather than purple) states, the local may come to trump the national more and more frequently. What does this mean for congressional tools? In terms of officer selection, there could very well be more pressure for more geographically diverse representation within the officer corps. There is already a debate to change the entrance requirements for the Coast Guard Academy from a merit-based system to a geographically based one, similar to those used by the other service academies. There could be less interest in conducting oversight by members from localities with significant defense industry or military bases, at least on programs that invest resources in those localities. Incentives could also become increasingly geared toward rewarding localities. Examples might include greater relative resources given to Guard and reserve units that are from and serve local communities, a resistance to closing bases, and a push to ensure that military assets are distributed geographically.

Three Emerging Policy Issues

In coming years Congress will continue to be involved in issues associated with end strength, force readiness, base closings, acquisition issues, international security agreements, use of contractors to support the military, and the response to international crises. Three new and emerging issues, however, deserve particular attention. The first is largely budget-driven and involves the choice between taking care of the people who serve in the military or providing the equipment they need to fight and prevail in current and future conflicts. A second issue is the use of the military to confront, and perhaps even solve, contentious social issues such as gay rights, gender equality, and sexual harassment. And last are changing civil-military beliefs stemming from forty years of reliance on an all-volunteer force.

Future of the Defense Budget

The first emerging issue associated with future congressional input into the US civil-military relations contract is the defense budget in the aftermath of the Iraq and Afghanistan wars. The defense budget has seen tremendous growth since 2001, both when one considers the so-called base budget and particularly when one considers the combined base budget and overseas contingency budget that funded the wars in Iraq and Afghanistan. That trend ended in the 2010–11 time period, when defense spending in FY 2014 dollars started to decline. A declining or at best flat defense budget is likely to become the new norm absent a foreign policy crisis of considerable magnitude.[12]

At the same time, we have seen a relatively dramatic increase in all major categories of the defense budget, including operations and maintenance, personnel, procurement, research and development, housing, and military construction.[13] Such increases were possible because of the sharp growth in the overall defense budget over the same period. Yet there will need to be significant trade-offs between these defense categories to bring defense spending within budget constraints if we assume that defense spending remains relatively flat into the future. Even assuming personnel costs stay relatively flat and that research and development costs decline, as President Obama's budget request would have them, congressional leaders will still need to come up with a way to pay for the escalating costs in procurement, operations, and maintenance, to say nothing of the long-term increase in military entitlements projected in the budget's out-years.

The overall growth in the defense budget in recent years has allowed the Department of Defense (DOD) to support increases in both personnel-related costs—such as pay, pensions, health care, and other benefits—and equipment costs without having to choose between the two.[14] However, as the fiscal situation of the federal government continues to deteriorate in the coming years, sustained growth in the defense budget is unlikely. When the defense budget ceases to grow above the rate of inflation, the department will have to make difficult choices between competing priorities, such as personnel and equipment.[15]

The implication of these figures is that debates over the defense budget will no longer be limited to the classic guns-versus-butter trade-off pitting the defense budget against nondefense discretionary programs. Certainly that will be part of the debate, yet future defense budget battles also will focus on the choice between taking care of the people who serve in the military—and prioritizing the personnel-related areas of the defense budget—or providing the equipment they need to prevail in future conflicts—which would prioritize research and development and procurement.

Who comes down on which side of these decisions is not necessarily as self-evident as it might once have been, as debates among Republicans have already proven. This issue is likely to lead to internecine fighting between fiscal conservatives and isolationists, particularly within the Republican Party. The ultimate choice could depend on how Congress decides to use the tools at its disposal to affect the civil-military relations contract.

Social Change Agenda

A second and related issue is how and to what degree Congress will use the military as a vehicle to advance social, gender, and human rights change. Notable examples include sexual assault (e.g., removing the military justice system from the chain of command), gays serving openly and receiving spousal benefits, greater diversity in the military's leadership, women in combat (e.g., the inclusion of women in submarine crews), and geographically based rather than merit-based admissions into the Coast Guard Academy.[16]

Such social issues are being pushed up the congressional docket as Congress increasingly reflects national demographic changes. In the 113th Congress (2013–15), for instance, House Democrats became the first caucus in the history of either chamber not to have a majority of white men. A record 102 women (82 in the House and 20 in the Senate) and 37 Hispanic or Latino members (33 in the House and 4 in the Senate) currently serve. And as their numbers have grown, so too has their seniority and impact on influential committees. Women senators now constitute a quarter of the Senate Armed Services Committee and, according to one student of Congress, differ from their male colleagues in the sort of policy questions they raise, the priorities they set, and the types of solutions they propose.[17] Female lawmakers of the 113th Congress were actively engaged in overhauling the military's legal system, known as the Uniform Code of Military Justice, in response to several high-profile incidents of sexual assault in the military prior to the DOD releasing its annual report on the subject.[18] Of the eighteen key measures in the 113th Congress aimed at curbing sexual assault in the military, as outlined in table 11.1, more than half were introduced by women.

Civil-Military Beliefs

A third and final issue is a possible growing rift between Congress and the military. We have already touched on the decreasing proportion of legislators who have direct military experience. As we noted in chapter 1 (also see figure 1.1), a mere 20 percent of current members of Congress are veterans, the lowest level of congressional military service since the Second World War.[19]

This reflects a wider trend among Americans at large, where the all-volunteer military is increasingly disconnected from the average American on a host of levels. Less than 1 percent of the American public currently serves in the military. A 2011 study by Pew Research on the opinions of almost 1,900 veterans of the Iraq and Afghanistan wars and 2,000 civilians found that there was a significant gap between the two groups in their understanding of the military. For instance, 84 percent of veterans and 71 percent of the public said that the public does not understand the problems faced by the military.[20] Senior members of the military have voiced their concerns about this gap. In a January 2011 speech at the National Defense University, the then chairman of the Joint Chiefs, Adm. Mike Mullen, noted that "we are less than one percent [of the population] and we are living in fewer and fewer places and we don't know the American people and the American people don't know us." He went on to say that "to the degree that we are out of touch, I believe it is a very dangerous force."[21]

Moreover, the active-duty and reserve components of the military have self-selected from a particular slice of the electorate, a slice that remains predominately conservative and believes in its own unique expertise on defense issues. In 2011 and 2012 the *Military Times* polled hundreds of active-duty, reserve, and retired military officers and enlisted from all four military services. Their surveys found that the military is more conservative than is the public at large. Almost 46 percent of active-duty respondents, more than 50 percent

Table 11.1

Key Military Sexual Assault Bills in the 113th Congress

Bill Number and Title	Date Introduced	Sponsor
H.R. 430, Protect Our Military Trainees Act	1/25/13	Rep. Jackie Speier (D-CA)
H.R. 671 / S. 294, Ruth Moore Act	2/13/13	Rep. Chellie Pingree (D-ME) Sen. Jon Tester (D-MT)
S. 548, Military Sexual Assault Prevention Act	3/13/13	Sen. Amy Klobuchar (D-MN)
H.R. 1593, Sexual Assault Training Oversight and Prevention Act	4/17/13	Rep. Jackie Speier (D-CA)
S. 871, Combating Military Sexual Assault Act	5/7/13	Sen. Patty Murray (D-WA)
H.R. 1864, Inspector general investigation of retaliations against protected communications of sexual assault	5/7/13	Rep. Jackie Walorski (R-IN)
H.R. 1867, Enforcement for Sexual Assault–Free Environments Act	5/8/13	Rep. Michael R. Turner (R-OH)
H.R. 1960, National Defense Authorization Act for Fiscal Year 2014	5/14/13	Rep. Howard McKeon (R-CA)
H.R. 2002, Combating Military Sexual Assault Act (related to S. 871)	5/15/13	Rep. Tim Ryan (D-OH)
H.R. 201 / S 967, Military Justice Improvements Act	5/16/13	Rep. Barbara Lee (D-CA) Sen. Kirsten Gillibrand (D-NY)
S. 1032/H.R. 2207, Enforcement for Sexual Assault–Free Environments Act (related to H.R. 1867)	5/23/13	Sen. Claire McCaskill (D-MO) Rep. Michael Turner (R-OH)
S. 1092, Inspector general investigation of retaliations against protected communications of sexual assault	6/4/13	Sen. Amy Klobuchar (D-MN)
H.R. 2397, Department of Defense Appropriations Act for Fiscal Year 2014	6/17/13	Rep. C. W. Bill Young (R-FL)
S. 1197, National Defense Authorization Act for Fiscal Year 2014	6/20/13	Sen. Carl Levin (D-MI)
H.R. 2777, Stop Pay for Violent Offenders Act	7/22/13	Rep. Tim Griffin (R-AR)

Source: Adapted from Barbara Salazar Torreon, *Military Sexual Assault: Chronology of Activity in Congress and Related Resources* (Washington, DC: Congressional Research Service, 2013).

of reserves, and 55 percent of veteran respondents self-identified as conservative or very conservative, compared to 36 percent of the public at large in a Pew opinion poll from the same time period. The differences between military and civilian partisan identification were equally large.[22]

The military's political ideology makes them natural allies for Republican legislators and puts them at odds with Democratic legislators on issues associated with the budget and social change. Starting in the 95th Congress (1977–78), House Republicans have grown increasingly and dramatically more conservative. House Democrats have slowly become more liberal between 1947 and today, though the change has been far smaller in magnitude than that experienced by House Republicans. The Senate has also grown more polarized, with both parties' average ideological position moving away from the middle. Here again the change in Senate Republicans is more pronounced in recent years than is the change for Senate Democrats. House Republicans are still more conservative than are their Senate brethren, while the average ideological position of House and Senate Democrats is roughly the same.[23] That puts Democrats further and further away, in an ideological sense, from members of the military. The reverse is true for congressional Republicans.

A final trend is worth mentioning, and it is perhaps the most troubling from a civil-military relations perspective. A full 55 percent of those on active duty, 59 percent of reserves, and 65 percent of veterans polled by the *Military Times* believed that the president and senior civilians should defer to senior military officers on military matters and wartime strategy.[24]

How then should Congress deal with the military when most congresspersons have not served in the military, and military personnel represent only 1 percent of the population, are significantly more conservative than the public at large, have an ideological affinity with one political party, and believe that civilians should defer to military officers on defense policy? These trends raise difficult questions as to how Congress can and should use civil-military relations tools in the future and the efficacy of that use. At the same time, our understanding of how, when, and why Congress uses these tools takes on great urgency.

Conclusion

We began this book by arguing that Congress plays a significant and underappreciated role in American civil-military relations. Indeed, discussions of US civil-military relations frequently overlook the role of Congress in guiding military behavior. We argued that the ebbs and flows in US civil-military relations depend in part on the use of four main tools. Confirmation of selected officers, delegation of authority to the military, oversight of military behavior, and incentives for appropriate behavior have been used by Congress to guide military behavior on important issues in the past, as demonstrated by the chapters in this volume. Consciously or unconsciously, legislators have used different tools in different circumstances. Congress has evolved in its thinking about officer selection and promotion. Congress has employed a variety of oversight tools, from committees to commissions, to ensure that its defense priorities are being implemented. Congress has protected and delegated uneven authorities to preferred military components. And Congress has provided significant incentives to reward particular behavior, such as re-enlistment or wartime service. Throughout, legislators are confronted with competing pressures to serve the national interest, local interests, or ideally both. Sometimes they balance local and national priorities, such as with specific military innovations. Other times, as with detainees, they prioritize local concerns. And in still other issues, as we saw with US policy toward Latin America, policy naturally coalesces around a particular national interest. We concluded in this chapter by reviewing a number of factors and contemporary issues that could alter congressional priorities when it comes to defense policy and, by extension, US civil-military relations. Regardless of how current debates unfold, however, we believe that Congress will continue to play a vital role in US civil-military relations.

NOTES

1. David P. Auerswald and Colton C. Campbell, "Congress and National Security," in *Congress and the Politics of National Security*, ed. David P. Auerswald and Colton C. Campbell (New York: Cambridge University Press, 2012), 3–17.

2. For recent examples, see C. Lawrence Evans, "Parties and Leaders: Polarization and Power in the U.S. House and Senate," in *New Directions in Congressional Politics*, ed. Jamie L. Carson (New York: Routledge, 2012); Francis E. Lee, "Individual and Partisan Activism on the Senate Floor," in *The U.S. Senate: From Deliberation to Dysfunction*, ed. Burdett A. Loomis (Washington, DC: CQ Press, 2012); and Keith T. Poole and Howard L. Rosenthal, *Ideology and Congress*, 2nd ed. (Piscataway, NJ: Transaction, 2007).

3. Quoted in Ruth Marcus, "Losing the Art of Legislating as John Dingell Retires," *Washington Post*, February 25, 2014, www.washingtonpost.com/opinions/ruth-marcus-losing -the-art-of-legislating-as-john-dingell-retires/2014/02/25/8b1f7296-9e5f-11e3-a050 -dc3322a94fa7_story.html.

4. Steve Benen, "Senate Republicans Launch Intra-Party Fight over Earmarks," *Washington Monthly*, November 10, 2010, www.washingtonmonthly.com/archives/individual /2010_11/026563.php (accessed March 3, 2014); Bryan York, "Are Republicans Too Divided to Have a Civil War?," *Washington Examiner*, July 29, 2013, http://washingtonexaminer.com /are-republicans-too-divided-to-have-a-civil-war/article/2533591 (accessed March 3, 2014); Alex Seitz-Wald, "GOP Prepares to Self-Destruct over Nonsense," *Salon*, August 20, 2013, www.salon.com/2013/08/20/gop_prepares_to_self_destruct_over_nonsense/ (accessed March 3, 2014); Matt Viser, "Shutdown Fight Reveals Deeper Splits within GOP," *Boston Globe*, September 20, 2013, www.bostonglobe.com/news/politics/2013/09/29/shutdown -fight-reveals-deeper-splits-within-republican-party-despite-calls-for-united-front/VW0z 8D8ZOIhBWeRt7ioUOM/story.html (accessed March 3, 2014); and Matthew Cooper, "Hagel's Military Budget Cuts Will Start a Fight in the Republican Party," *Newsweek*, February 25, 2014, www.newsweek.com/hagels-military-budget-cuts-will-start-fight-republi can-party-230199 (accessed March 3, 2014).

5. Jeremy Herb, "Hawk versus Hawk on Pentagon," *The Hill*, March 1, 2014.

6. Mark J. Oleszek and Walter J. Oleszek, "Institutional Challenges Confronting Congress after 9/11: Partisan Polarization and Effective Oversight," in *Congress and the Politics of National Security*, ed. David P. Auerswald and Colton C. Campbell (New York: Cambridge University Press, 2012).

7. For a representative sample of scholarly writing about Congress, the Cold War consensus, and the end of that consensus, see James L. Sundquist, *The Decline and Resurgence of Congress* (Washington, DC: Brookings Institution Press, 1981), 238–314; Thomas E. Mann, "Making Foreign Policy: The President and Congress," in *A Question of Balance: The President, the Congress, and Foreign Policy*, ed. Thomas E. Mann (Washington, DC: Brookings Institution Press, 1990), 1–34; James M. Lindsay, *Congress and the Politics of Foreign Policy* (Baltimore: Johns Hopkins University Press, 1994), 21–30; Eugene Wittkopf and James McCormick, "Congress, the President, and the End of the Cold War," *Journal of Conflict Resolution* 42, no. 4 (August 1998): 440–66; and Robert Zoellick, "Congress and the Making of U.S. Foreign Policy," *Survival* 41, no. 4 (Winter 1999–2000), 20–41.

8. For evidence on that last point, see David P. Auerswald, "Arms Control," in *Congress and the Politics of National Security*, ed. David P. Auerswald and Colton C. Campbell (New York: Cambridge University Press, 2012), 189–212.

9. For a discussion, see David P. Auerswald, "The President, the Congress, and American Missile Defense Policy," *Defence Studies* 1, no. 2 (Summer 2001), 57–82.

10. D. Andres Austin, *Trends in Discretionary Spending*, Report RL34424 (Washington, DC: Congressional Research Service, February 18, 2014), 20.

11. The exception is the 2009 stimulus package. See ibid., 22.

12. Congressional Budget Office, *Long-Term Implications of the 2014 Future Years Defense Program* (Washington, DC: Congressional Budget Office, November 2013).

13. Ibid.

14. Todd Harrison, *The New Guns versus Butter Debate* (Washington, DC: Center for Strategic and Budgetary Assessments, May, 2010).

15. Ibid.

16. See Daniel Sagalyn, "U.S. Military Leadership Lacks Diversity at Top," *PBS Newshour*, March 11, 2011, www.pbs.org/newshour/rundown/military-report/, and Military Diversity Leadership Commission, *From Representation to Inclusion: Diversity Leadership for the 21st-Century Military* (Washington, DC: Government Printing Office, 2011).

17. Michele L. Swers, *Women in the Club: Gender and Policy Making in the Senate* (Chicago: University of Chicago Press, 2013); Ed O'Keefe, "Women Are Wielding Notable Influence in Congress," *Washington Post*, January 16, 2014, www.washingtonpost.com/politics/women-are-wielding-notable-influence-in-congress/2014/01/16/d1c00d76-7e04-11e3-95c6-0a7aa80874bc_story.html; and Jill Lawrence, "Do Women Make Better Senators than Men?" *National Journal*, July 11, 2013, www.nationaljournal.com/women-of-washington/do-women-make-better-senators-than-men-20130711.

18. Niave Knell, "Leaning In: Actions Taken by Congresswomen of the 113th Congress to Address Military Sexual Assault," paper presented at the National War College, Washington, DC, February 2014.

19. See Drew Desilver, *Most Members of Congress Have Little Direct Military Experience*, September 4, 2012 (Pew Research Center: Washington, DC), www.pewresearch.org/fact-tank/2013/09/04/members-of-congress-have-little-direct-military-experience/; Ashley Southhall, "A Changing of the Guard among Veterans in Congress," *New York Times*, January 4, 2013, http://thecaucus.blogs.nytimes.com/2013/01/04/a-changing-of-the-guard-among-veterans-in-congress

/?_php=true&_type=blogs&_r=0; and Tim Hsia, "The Role of the Military and Veterans in Politics," *New York Times*, February 1, 2013, http://atwar.blogs.nytimes.com/2013/02/01/the-role-of-the-military-and-veterans-in-politics/.

20. "War and Sacrifice in the Post 9/11 Era: The Military-Civilian Gap," Pew Research Social and Demographic Trends, October 5, 2011, www.pewsocialtrends.org/2011/10/05/war-and-sacrifice-in-the-post-911-era/.

21. See, for example, Charley Keyes, "Joint Chiefs Chair Warns on Disconnect between Military and Civilians," *CNN.com*, January 20, 2011, www.cnn.com/2011/US/01/10/us.military.disconnect/.

22. For the *Military Times* poll results, see http://projects.militarytimes.com/2012/results/ (accessed February 17, 2014). The Pew poll results from June 2012 are available at www.people-press.org/2012/06/04/section-9-trends-in-party-affiliation/.

23. For a graphic portrayal of these trends, see Norman J. Ornstein, Thomas E. Mann, Michael J. Malbin, and Andrew Rugg, "Average Ideology of the House and Senate, 1947–2012," in *Vital Statistics on Congress* (Washington, DC: Brookings Institution Press, July 2013), www.brookings.edu/research/interactives/2013/house-and-senate-partisanship.

24. See http://projects.militarytimes.com/2012/results/.

Contributors

David P. Auerswald is professor of strategy and policy at the National War College and an adjunct senior research fellow at the Institute for National Strategic Studies. Before joining the National War College, he was an assistant professor of political science at George Washington University and served on the Senate Foreign Relations Committee staff, working for the then senator Joseph Biden (D-DE). He has served on the congressional reform team of the Project on National Security Reform, the US Central Command's Assessment Team, and the Alternative Futures project for the Office of the Secretary of Defense. He is the author, coauthor, or coeditor of books and articles on a variety of foreign policy topics, including the treaty advice-and-consent process in the Senate, the politics of US missile-defense policy, the War Powers Act, the evolution of the National Security Council system, domestic and intra-alliance debates during military interventions, and deterrence of terrorist attacks. His most recent books include *Congress and the Politics of National Security* (Cambridge University Press, 2012) and *NATO in Afghanistan: Fighting Together, Fighting Alone* (Princeton University Press, 2014).

Colton C. Campbell is professor of national security strategy at the National War College. Prior to joining the National War College, he was a legislative aide to Rep. Mike Thompson (D-CA), then the chair of the Intelligence Committee's Subcommittee on Terrorism, Analysis and Counterintelligence, where he handled appropriations, defense, and trade matters for the congressman. Before that, he was an analyst in American national government at the Congressional Research Service, an associate professor of political science at Florida International University, and an APSA Congressional Fellow in the office of Sen. Bob Graham (D-FL). He recently served on the Commander's Initiative Group for the commander of the International Security Assistance Force, US Forces Afghanistan. He is the author, coauthor, or coeditor of several books on Congress and the legislative process, most recently *Congress and the Politics of National Security* (Cambridge University Press, 2012).

Chuck Cushman is dean of academics at the College of International Security Affairs. Previously he was a senior fellow at Georgetown University's Government Affairs Institute, and he spent a decade at the Graduate School of Political Management at George Washington University, where he taught courses on political history, politics and public policy, national security policymaking, and Congress's roles in defense policy. Prior to that, he was the defense and foreign affairs legislative assistant to Rep. David Price (D-NC). He is a graduate of the United States Military Academy and served nine years in the US Army as an armor officer. He is the author of *An Introduction to the US Congress* (M. E. Sharpe, 2005) and a forthcoming book on Congress and national security policymaking.

Louis Fisher is scholar in residence at the Constitution Project. Previously he worked for four decades at the Library of Congress as senior specialist in separation of powers at the Congressional Research Service (CRS) and specialist in constitutional law in the law library. During his service with CRS, he was research director of the House Iran-Contra Committee in 1987, writing major sections of the final report. He has testified about fifty times before congressional committees on such issues as the war power, the state secrets privilege, National Security Agency surveillance, national security whistleblowers, and other executive-legislative conflicts. He is the author of twenty books and more than four hundred articles in law reviews, political science journals, encyclopedias, and other publications.

John Griswold is a major in the US Army and assistant professor in the American politics, policy, and strategy program at the United States Military Academy. He received his PhD from the University of Washington. His dissertation, "Providing for the Common Defense: Strategic Agency Adaptation and the Politics of the National Guard," examines how government agencies respond to new or qualitatively different demands. His current research focuses on emerging capabilities of the US military's reserve components, institutional and organizational adaptation of government agencies, and bureaucratic politics and homeland security.

Frank O. Mora is director of the Latin American and Caribbean Center and professor of politics and international relations at Florida International University. From 2009 to 2013 he served as deputy assistant secretary of defense for Western Hemisphere affairs and was professor of national security strategy and Latin American politics at the National War College from 2004 to 2009. He has worked as a consultant to the Library of Congress, the Department of the Air Force, the Central Intelligence Agency, the Institute for National Security Studies, the State Department, the Organization of American States, the Joint Staff, and US Southern Command. He is the author or editor of five books and numerous academic and policy articles and monographs on hemispheric security, most recently *Latin American and Caribbean Foreign Policy* (Rowman & Littlefield, 2003) and *Paraguay and the United States: Distant Allies* (University of Georgia Press, 2007).

Michelle Munroe is adjunct professor in the Department of Politics and International Relations at Florida International University, with a concentration in comparative politics. Her interests include the politics of development and underdevelopment, Caribbean and Latin American politics, and globalism. More specifically, her work examines the political economy and culture of transnational criminal groups and the way that state and nonstate actors perpetuate transnational criminal activities in Latin America and the Caribbean.

Alexis Lasselle Ross is a staff member on the Military Compensation and Retirement Modernization Commission where she analyzes the current military healthcare system and develops options to reform the health benefit provided to military members, retirees, and their families. Prior to the Commission, she was the principal adviser, on all congressional matters, to the deputy chief of staff of the army for logistics. From 2007 to 2009, she contributed to logistics priorities and strategies as the deputy director of the army's Logistics Initiatives Group. Prior to this, she served nearly six years on the staff of the House Armed Services Committee, where she was responsible for all committee action on army and Marine Corps readiness matters, including combat operations, training, logistics, and equipment maintenance.

Katherine Scott is assistant historian, United States Senate. She received her PhD in American history from Temple University. Her research interests include twentieth-century American political and policy history. She is the author of *Reining in the State: Civil Society and Congress in the Vietnam and Watergate Eras* (University Press of Kansas, 2013) and is currently working on a political biography of Sen. George McGovern.

Mitchel A. Sollenberger is associate professor of political science at the University of Michigan–Dearborn. Before this, he was visiting assistant professor and undergraduate director in the Department of Public and International Affairs at George Mason University, instructor of political science at Bowling Green State University, and an analyst in American national government at the Congressional Research Service. He is the author of *The President's Czars: Undermining Congress and the Constitution* (University Press of Kansas, 2012), *Judicial Appointments and Democratic Controls* (Carolina Academic Press, 2011), and *The President Shall Nominate: How Congress Trumps Executive Power* (University Press of Kansas 2008), as well as numerous articles and chapters on the confirmation process.

Charles A. Stevenson is professorial lecturer in American foreign policy at Johns Hopkins University's School of Advanced International Studies. Prior to SAIS, he was a professor of national security policy at the National War College from 1992 to 2005. From 1999 to 2000 he served as a member of the secretary of state's policy planning staff, working on use-of-force issues and long-range planning. Prior to joining the National War College faculty, he served twenty-two years as a staff member for four different US senators, working primarily on defense and foreign policy issues. His areas of academic specialization include national security policymaking, civil-military relations, the politics of national security, and technology and military innovation. He is the author of three recent works: *SecDef: The Nearly Impossible Job of Secretary of Defense* (Potomac Books, 2006), *Warriors and Politicians: U.S. Civil-Military Relations under Stress* (Routledge, 2006), and *Congress at War: The Politics of Conflict since 1789* (Potomac Books, 2007).

Jordan Tama is assistant professor at American University's School of International Service and research fellow at the Center for Congressional and Presidential Studies. He is the author of *Terrorism and National Security Reform: How Commissions Can Drive Change during Crises* (Cambridge University Press, 2011). He has also published articles in a variety of scholarly and popular publications. Dr. Tama has served as the lead Democratic staff member on the Tom Lantos Human Rights Commission in the House of Representatives, as a speechwriter for former representative Lee Hamilton (D-IN), and as an intelligence and counterterrorism policy adviser to Barack Obama's 2008 presidential campaign.

Index